# You and Your Baby's First Year

# You and Your Baby's First Year

## Sirgay Sanger, M.D., and John Kelly

**BANTAM BOOKS**
TORONTO · NEW YORK · LONDON · SYDNEY · AUCKLAND

YOU AND YOUR BABY'S FIRST YEAR

*A Bantam Book / published by arrangement with William Morrow and Company, Inc.*

*PRINTING HISTORY*
*William Morrow edition published / September 1985*
*Bantam edition / May 1987*

**Library of Congress Cataloging-in-Publication Data**

Sanger, Sirgay, 1935-
    You and your baby's first year.

    Bibliography: p. 253.
    Includes index.
    1. Infants—Development.   2. Infant psychology. 3. Parent and child.   I. Kelly,
John, 1945-      . II. Title.
RJ134.S27      1987      649'.122      86-32063
ISBN 0-553-34386-6

*Published simultaneously in the United States and Canada*

*Bantam Books are published by Bantam Books, Inc. Its trademark, consisting of the*
*words "Bantam Books" and the portrayal of a rooster, is Registered in U.S. Patent and*
*Trademark Office and in other countries. Marca Registrada. Bantam Books, Inc., 666*
*Fifth Avenue, New York, New York 10103.*

PRINTED IN THE UNITED STATES OF AMERICA

S   0   9   8   7   6   5   4   3   2   1

# Contents

# PART I
# The Magic
# Square

# ONE
# The Fit

$\boxed{\text{T}}$ his book is about many things. It is about babies and the wonderful ways they grow and change in the first twelve months of life. It is also about mothers and fathers and the part they play in shaping that growth. But most of all this is a book about a new way of visualizing the parent-infant relationship and the love that forms its foundation.

Of course mothers and fathers have always known that their love has a special radiance—that is what gives it its unique nurturing quality. But what the last decade of research has shown is that the symbols of affection you and every other parent use to express that love—your hugs, smiles, even your happy looks, sweet songs, and silly games—serve the baby in specific and concrete ways. Yes, they are the sources of emotional support you always knew them to be. But they also help an infant shape his social, learning, and stress-management skills.

Developmental experts call this new view of growth *the fit*. And what makes that an especially apt metaphor is that it sums up in a single, economical image our realization that when parental looks, gestures, and sounds are tailored to the infant's needs, they not only hasten the emergence of his*

---

* The pronouns *he* and *his* are used throughout this book solely to avoid reader confusion.

skills and talents, they also help to ensure he realizes these abilities to their fullest.

Underlying this new vision of how a baby grows and how a parent helps him grow are three recent discoveries which you and every other mother and father should know about. They are:

1) *Development is a two-sided process to which infant and parents actively contribute.*

   For nearly a generation, parents have been told that a baby is born with innate skills which unfold more or less automatically according to a preset biological clock. This view is popularly expressed in the notion of developmental stages. Powered by his own biological preprogramming, the infant—much like a little intellectual—is usually depicted as climbing autonomously from one developmental stage to the next. The picture of infancy that has emerged over the past ten years, however, shows that the baby's preprogramming represents only one side of the developmental equation, and what's more, that its nature is different than we had thought.

   While a child does indeed come into the world primed, he is primed not with skills—as is generally assumed—but with competencies. An example of a *competency* is the newborn's innate knowledge of where to look and which sounds to listen to. Almost from the moment of birth, for instance, a baby displays a preference for the human voice and face. An example of a *skill* is cooperation—the ability to work well with others. Competencies, such as a knowledge of where to look and what to listen to, are the building blocks and forerunners of true skills, such as cooperation, but they are not the same thing. Only under the guiding hand of a parent does one mature into the other.

2) *Mothers and fathers are primed with their own growth-promoting behaviors.*

   Caught with a new intimacy by the video camera, parents also have revealed themselves to be the possessors of a form of biological preprogramming. This priming is why the moment they turn to address their infants, African and New Guinean mothers, as well as French, German, and American ones, automatically slip into the same form of baby talk (they lower their voices several decibels and slow down their words), use the same type of exaggerated expressions, and play the same kinds of games. It is also why even the newest parent is able to read her baby's cues and signals with some accuracy and why a mother and father will gaze longer and more intently into a baby's eyes than into any other human being's. These examples of priming are ones which most parents already are aware of.

As we shall see in the pages that follow, there also are a number of more subtle primed responses which you and other mothers and fathers use every day without even being aware of it. These include such behaviors as *phatics, paragraphs, back channels, chorusing, turn-taking, as-if responses,* and *multimodal highlighting*. Each of these responses can help transform specific infant competencies into such skills as stress and frustration management, cooperation, role playing, and communication. Even capabilities that parents don't normally think of as skills, such as the ability to act intentionally and display empathy for others, are products of primed behaviors.

3) *A good fit enhances not only cognitive and social development, but also emotional development.*
While you will encounter the word *skill* a great deal in this book, nowhere will you find advice on how to help a six-month-old learn the alphabet or master the intricacies of problem solving. Most emphatically, this is not a manual about building superbabies. It is about *how you as a parent can help shape your infant into a caring, loving, competent, emotionally fulfilled human being*. And it is based on a system that is actually as old as man, though I have called it new because our awareness of it is recent. It is one which has evolved over millions of years and is shaped by the pressing biological need to prepare the human infant for the challenges and opportunities of his new environment in the quickest, most efficient way.

The molding of parental behavior to the baby's expectations of how he will be supported hastens not only the emergence of specific abilities in a *natural* way, but does something else at least as important. It tells the infant in a fashion he can understand—even if he is only a few days old—that he is supported and loved. And it is this parental message, more than any other, that fosters a sense of mastery, confidence, personal competence, and, above all, trust in a baby. Having learned in his earliest exchanges with other human beings that people can be relied on for support and encouragement, a child comes to trust people in a way that will not only enrich his life, but also the lives of those around him.

One of the most satisfying and reassuring things about this new picture of development as a process of mutually fitting together is that it restores mothers and fathers to their rightful and central place in the child's growth cycle. The picture of the infant as a kind of developmental Lone Ranger, which has dominated professional thinking for the past thirty years, has given way to the realization (which, I suspect, most mothers and fathers never lost sight of no matter what they were told) that for optimal growth a baby requires *the life-giving touch* of a parent. In the fit, nature and nurture have at last achieved a harmonious balance.

Another happy consequence of our new thinking is that it invalidates many of the rules and admonitions that have transformed child rearing into such a complicated and intimidating experience for millions of mothers and fathers. This is because the fitting-in process has revealed itself to be so individual that universal concepts, such as after-birth bonding, breast-feeding, and the developmental stages, and catch-all labels, such as "difficult baby" and "divorced parent," can no longer be said to have the same meaning and importance for every parent and every infant. Rules and attitudes that make a fit right for one family may apply only partially for another. As we shall see, the only thing that matters is that each family be helped to find its own right fit.

Simply put, that is the goal of this book. It is designed to allow you and other parents to slip beneath familiar generalizations, such as "nurturing environment," "responsiveness," and "attunement," and show you how to translate your love and the behaviors you use to express that love into a series of specific strategies that will place you and your baby inside the *Magic Square*. That is the term we use at my center— The Early Infant Care Center of New York—to describe what happens when a mother, father, and infant achieve a good fit. And it isn't a convenient abstraction we have invented. The Magic Square represents an example of a natural process called *ontogenetic adaptation*. This is the way biologists describe the robust burst of growth that occurs when an environment attains a perfect pitch of harmony with the needs of the organism it is supporting.

Ontogenetic adaptation of the human infant takes place within the realm of his interaction; which is why parent-infant interactions have emerged with a new importance from recent research on the fit. We now realize that parental looks, gestures, sounds, and movements form an environment as real and palpable for a baby as the environment of air, light, water, and soil are for a flower. And just as the fullness of a flower's blossoming is contingent on the richness of the environmental elements feeding it, so too is the fullness of an infant's blossoming on the richness of the environmental elements feeding him.

As the first book to bring our new knowledge of the fit to parents, *You and Your Baby's First Year* takes what I believe is an unusual approach to the developmental equation. It does not focus primarily on the infant, as most baby books do, nor primarily on the parent, as some others do, but on parent *and* infant *together* within the enchanted space of their interactions. And as this is the first book to translate our new knowledge of the fit into practical parenting advice, I also believe you will find that the strategies and techniques you will encounter in its pages are unique. Designed to show you how to shape your responses into a rich, nurturing interactive environment, the techniques were developed out of my work at the Early Infant Care Center and as director of the Parent-Child Interaction Program at St. Luke's-Roosevelt Hospital in New York City.

In the loosest sense, these strategies might be said to form a program. However, they do not involve a series of specific points or steps, as most programs do, nor are they governed by a group of rules, as most programs are. Given the large store of innate parental wisdom already possessed by you and every other mother and father, such directions would be presumptuous as well as unnecessary. You already know more about your baby than any expert could hope to tell you. Indeed, by the time you finish this book I think you will be astonished at how much you didn't know you knew about him. The purpose of the strategies you will encounter in these pages is simply to help you use that innate knowledge more effectively to support his growth.

Thus, in some cases, what we call a strategy involves only alerting you to the often surprising ways a subtle behavioral change can alter the meaning of one of your responses. For example:

- An infant finds some of your behaviors more comprehensible when performed closeup, others when performed at a distance. This is why inadvertent violation of the rules of distance can obscure or garble the meaning of a message you are trying to convey with a particular look or gesture.

- The same is true for tempo. You can inadvertently change the meaning of some gazes and movements by performing them either too fast or too slow.

- If you know how to build what we call a holding pattern out of your responses, you can *increase* your baby's ability to remain alert and attentive in exchanges.

Since at the center we find that the more our mothers and fathers know about the nature of their primed behaviors, the better they are at using them, many of the strategies in this book also have an informative purpose. They are meant to alert you to the ways new research has illuminated our understanding of your mediated behaviors and to outline the implications these findings have for you and your baby. Some examples of the findings we will examine later include:

- Why parental *quiet* is now considered at least as important as stimulation as a source of cognitive growth.

- The reason the fantasies and myths you and other parents construct about the baby are believed to be key factors in shaping an infant's personality as well as influencing when he will begin to master spoken language.

- Why the ability to read an infant's cues and signals (as we shall see, almost all of a baby's behaviors have meaning) is considered the single most important element in creating a nurturing interactive environment.

- The reason why the baby's ability to retrieve memory is now regarded as a most important index of the individual differences among infants.

- Why a parent's predictability is a key element in the evolution of the skill of cooperation.

- The reason why a recently studied phenomenon known as *contingent responsiveness* has come to be considered an even more important source of infant learning than parental modeling.

- And, finally, why parents needn't and shouldn't worry about getting all their responses "right." The baby has revealed himself to be so flexible that he is easily able to absorb an occasional—and an inevitable—parental misstep without effect. Only a *consistent* pattern of misreading or responding inappropriately poses a threat to his ability to fit in with you.

Hanging from the ceiling on a pole, twenty feet from where I write, is a Panasonic 3990 video camera. Box shaped with a snorklelike lens, it is an ungainly looking device, and one which is, by the standards of modern technology, unprepossessing in its capabilities. It has no capacity to store, compute, or process information; it simply takes pictures unobtrusively and untiringly. But in those two qualities lies the reason it has changed the way we see the human infant as profoundly as the space probes of the past decade have changed the way we see the heavens.

Penetrating beneath the child's seemingly random surface gestures and movements, the camera has revealed behavioral patterns of purpose and meaning which had eluded even the most alert and patient of human observers. From the very moment of birth onward, a baby is acting in and reacting to his new environment. Out of this realization has sprung our current image of the infant as competent, and our new picture of how this remarkable creature grows. In one respect, though, I think the introduction of the video camera has had an unfortunate—if entirely unintended—effect. The torrent of new findings on infant capabilities it has produced have left parents confused and wondering.

"What does it mean?" a mother will ask me on reading that a newborn displays a preference for looking at a human face within *nine minutes* of birth, or on learning that within a day or two, a baby has been shown to prefer looking at pictures of rectangles with dots in them to pictures of rectangles without dots. These and the other recently discovered capabilities that have led to current media celebration of the infant as "superbaby" are really examples of competencies.

What makes competencies important is that they constitute one of the two elements of a child's biological priming that new research shows to be directly related to skill development. In the simplest sense, you might say competencies are a form of biological radar. What they do is immediately focus the neonate's attention on the aspects of the environment he needs to learn about. What competencies do not, however, give the newborn is the ability to make intentional or conscious choices. While it's a lovely thought, a one-hour-old does not gaze into his parents' eyes because he can't wait to meet them, but because the sight of a human face triggers a form of preferential neural firing in his brain.

Taken together, the most striking thing about the research on competencies is the singular pattern that emerges from it. In one way or another, nearly all of a baby's abilities lead him to the environmental element he needs most to learn about: other people. You can see this preference for the human in the reactions of a group of five-day-olds who were offered two sets of nursing pads to sniff by Dr. Aidan Macfarlane. One set had been soaked in their mothers' milk; the others were new, unused pads. In every case, the babies preferred (as indicated by their head turns) to smell a pad that had been worn by their mothers.

In his innate knowledge of which sounds to imitate, the infant also shows a taste for things that have an identifiably human resonance. Computer-assisted studies at the Baudelocque Maternity Hospital in Paris show that by the fourth day of life a baby can identify specific sounds in his environment. Yet the sounds a child learns to mimic aren't the hum of the air-conditioner he hears in the background or the woosh of the family washing machine, but the sounds of other human voices.

The other element of the infant's priming involved in skill development is a form of knowledge that might be called a *biology of expectations*. Just as the baby knows where to look or what to listen to, he also is primed to expect that his listening and looking will elicit certain parental responses. You can see these expectations at work on the behavior of some four-month-olds who took part recently in a test at the Max-Planck-Institut für Psychiatrie in Munich. Like adults and children, babies are primed to expect that encounters with other humans will involve direct eye contact. They prefer, whether in photos, videotape or in person, to look at full-face presentations of people rather than at profile or half-profile shots, because full-face photos allow for direct eye contact, while profiles do not.

As long as the researchers, Hanuš and Mechthild Papoušek, fulfilled this expectation by showing their test infants videotapes of themselves in which they appeared in full-face, the Papoušeks had no trouble arousing and keeping the interest and curiosity of their young subjects. Many of the test babies even tried to establish direct eye contact with the image of themselves they saw playing on a video monitor. But when the Papoušeks then created a violation of this expectation for direct eye contact by presenting films in which the infants' heads were positioned in a way that prevented such contact, it produced a quite different reaction: The test childrens' interest in looking at themselves declined markedly.

The eight- and nine-day-olds in a Boston University study reacted even more emphatically to an expectancy violation created by researcher William Condon. As long as the babies were addressed in real speech, they were able to move their bodies in perfect rhythm to the words they heard, just as adults and older children do. Even the language they were addressed in did not matter. Dr. Condon found that as long as the words were real and the sentences they formed were coherent, the babies were able to maintain their sense of rhythm when spoken to in Chinese, Spanish, and English. But he also found that when he violated the expectancy that words would make sense by having a co-worker talk to newborns in a form of jabberwocky, the babies' rhythms grew disjointed as if to say, "Stop it, you are talking nonsense."

While competencies automatically focus an infant's attention on the aspect of the environment he needs most to learn about—people—his expectations lead him to anticipate that the environment will then respond to him in certain helpful ways. And those responses which a baby is preprogrammed to expect are also the ones that optimize his growth; which is to say they facilitate the development of the skills and talents he needs to get along with people.

A case in point is the infant's anticipation that interactions will be two-sided. If you have ever inadvertently interrupted one of your baby's behavioral or vocal outbursts in an exchange, you may have noticed that it produced an abrupt head turn. That's because you unwittingly violated his expectancy for reciprocity in interactions. This expectancy forms the basis for the learning of an important skill: how to play the speaker's and listener's roles in dialogue. Known as *turn-taking*, its mastery is essential to the ability to communicate effectively with others. (Imagine how hard it would be to tell anyone anything if you didn't know when it was your turn to speak and your turn to listen.) This is why an infant has been primed to expect his building block, reciprocity, in exchanges. And why when that reciprocity is provided, not only do the child's turn-taking skills blossom early and fully, but, as we will see later, his other, related communications skills do as well. It is also why a baby eventually turns away from a partner who can't or won't conduct interactions on a reciprocal basis.

Another example of how an awareness of expectancies promotes skill growth is *contingent responsiveness*. Infants are primed to expect that they can make the environment respond to their actions. And the reason attunement to this expectation facilitates skill development (in this case, learning skills) is that infants *learn quickest and remember longest actions that they initiate*. Recently, Dr. Papoŭsek provided a very vivid demonstration of this fact in another of his ingenious studies.

His experiment centered on a board of electrical lights which, when lit, formed several distinctive patterns. The question the study posed was: Are three- and four-month-olds capable of learning and remembering these patterns? Results from the first part of the test suggested they were not. Not only didn't the test infants learn and remember very well, they couldn't be induced to pay much attention to the lights. After a few desultory glances at the board, they would turn away bored. But then Dr. Papoŭsek created an illusion—one which accorded with his young subjects' expectations about how they would be helped to learn. He attached a lever to the board and encouraged the babies to press it while they gazed at the patterns of light. That had the desired effect. Believing that the lights were now contingent on their actions, interest and learning curves among the infants took a dramatic shift upward.

Standing even higher in the developmental hierarchy than a baby's expectations about learning and turn-taking is his expectation that he will be *understood*. In the daily round of exchanges, this finds practical expression in the infant's expectation that his cues and signals will be accurately read and appropriately responded to. And the difference that attunement to this expectation makes in an infant's growth can be seen in the results of a study by Dr. Michael Lewis and his colleagues at Rutgers University. They report that the one characteristic that distinguished the most advanced one-year-olds in their research group was that each had a parent who consistently and accurately read and responded to their distress cues.

Scientifically, there are a number of ways to explain Dr. Lewis's, Dr. Papoŭsek's and others' conclusions about expectancies. We will look at their results later. But what can't be quantified, measured, or placed into any of the other neat scientific forms we use to report data is the special richness of the tie that forms when there is an accurate fit between a baby's expectations and a parent's responses. The Magic Square comes closer than any other term I know to capturing the sense of enchantment and delight a mother, father, and infant share inside a good fit.

And in the form of your own primed behaviors you already have an important head start in knowing how to create a good fit with your child, but there are four reasons why our new knowledge of the fit can enhance what you already know:

1) *We can show parents how to tailor their behaviors more closely to their baby's needs.*

An example of such "fine-tuning" is a technique we call *infant-initiated imitation sequences*. Imitation is one primed behavior all parents use to teach a child how to use his sounds, gestures, and expressions to communiate messages. But in many cases at the center, we find this important lesson isn't learned as quickly as it could or should be, because in exchanges it's always the mother or father who initiates the smiles or sounds, leaving the infant to imitate *them*.

We call this *parent-initiated imitation,* and the reason it's a less-effective strategy is that it fails to take advantage of what studies, such as Dr. Papoŭsek's, have shown us about infant learning—that infants learn quickest (and also remember longest) the responses they produce in others. This is why a child who is allowed to be the initiator of smiles, frowns, and other facial expressions will be quicker to develop and display a sense of social mastery.

Another important way our new knowledge enhances your instinctive parenting skills is by showing you how to read your baby's signals and cues more accurately. Like most mothers and fathers, you are probably good at this already, but we can help you become better. One way is by giving you a better understanding of *pause cycles, distancing,* and the other grammatical codes that govern every child's expectations about how the interactive dialogue will be conducted. A second way is by showing you the often subtle signs an infant uses to telegraph his intentions. Frequently, for example, when his other cues are unclear, a knowledge of the baby's hand movements will help you to decipher his intentions. A partially opened hand extended upward toward you is a sign of alertness and usually indicates you are being invited into an exchange. Conversely, a hand held at the side in a fistlike clench is often a signal of distress and of a desire for comforting.

2)   *We can help families with special fitting problems.*
While every mother, father, and baby want to connect emotionally, sometimes subtle problems interfere. Hard to articulate, or even to pinpoint, they leave the parent feeling vaguely out of synch with the child, yet not quite understanding why they feel this way. Usually, such parents are quick to blame themselves for the disharmony they feel. When I talk to them at the center, they tell me that they are at fault; they blame their parenting skills and sometimes their love. Yet when I come to observe these mothers and fathers with their babies, frequently I find that what's keeping the family apart is a very subtle constitutional disability of the infant's.

A case in point is the child who is unnaturally subdued or unresponsive. While this infant is an understandable source of concern, usually his unresponsiveness is biological in origin. The sights and sounds that normally excite and attract a baby don't register with him because his nervous system is not quite mature for his age (in most cases this is a self-correcting condition). That, however, doesn't mean an unresponsive child can't be excited or drawn out, he just requires a variety of stimulations that are packaged to meet his special requirements. One way of catching his eye, for instance, is by shining a light on the parental face. The extra illumination not only makes it easier for a child to focus, it also adds a new interest to a mother's or father's face. Offering an exciting combination of sights is another way of engaging an unresponsive infant. Even dressing in bright, bold colors can help to peak his interest. For the infant who is easy to overexcite, on the other hand, lowering the level of stimulation by, for example, speaking softly in a darkened room, can enhance receptivity.

In the case of Anna, a three-month-old who arrived at the center not long ago in the arms of her worried parents, we employed all of these strategies as well as an ingenious flash-card game created by the play therapist who worked with her. The game, after initial observation, showed Anna to be unusually subdued. While she didn't actively rebuff people, she also didn't take much interest in them either.

Then, one day, while playing with Anna, our therapist noticed that the baby was fascinated by some sketches of faces which she had drawn on a yellow flash card. Out of this the two quickly developed a game. First, Anna would be shown a series of faces; then, the flash cards they were drawn on would be dropped to reveal the smiling face of the therapist. When it became evident that Anna's pleasure in the game was transferring itself to pleasure in being with the therapist, who was soon producing smiles without the help of the cards, we introduced two new players: Anna's mother and father. Within a few weeks, the game was beginning to work for them as well. For the first time, we noticed that Anna would brighten at the sound of either parent's voice. And this led to an even more dramatic change: She began reaching out toward them as if to say, "Come play with me."

As we will see later, there also are several other minor and, usually, self-correcting disorders that can make a baby "hard to fit." But he is not the only source of fitting problems; parents can cause them too. What we call the parental *hidden agenda* is one example (we will examine it later); another is a difficulty in reading an infant's cues. Some mothers and fathers are just naturally better at decoding their baby's signals in the same way that some parents are just naturally better than others at feeding and diapering. So possession of this skill shouldn't be taken—as it sometimes is—as a measure of parental love. Besides which, the subtlety of many of the infant's signals make them hard, especially for first-time parents, to interpret. Often we find, for example, that new parents will miss the meaning of the baby's blinking: When he increases his blinking rate, he is saying, "I'm approaching stimulation overload." Another frequently misinterpreted signal is a sudden increase in a child's vocalizations. Generally, this is a baby's way of saying that he feels thwarted in his attempts to initiate an action.

3) *We can help parents overcome the obstacles to parent-infant intimacy posed by modern society.*
Traveling through East Africa several years ago, I found myself thinking a great deal about these obstacles; in particular about the ones we have placed in the way of parent-infant intimacy. What prompted my thoughts were the mothers I met in the villages and hamlets I visited. Rarely did I see one who didn't have her baby securely strapped to her back and, for an American physician, the degree of maternal knowledge this physical proximity produced was instructive to observe. Typical was the young mother I met who already was so skilled at reading her five-day-old's cues that she could tell when he was about to urinate, and was thus able to avoid being soiled by swinging him off her back and holding him out over the road while he wet. Later I learned that such knowledge of an infant was considered unexceptional. Indeed, the women in this mother's village considered it something of a disgrace to be soiled by an infant after his seventh day.

The reasons such displays of attunement are rare on the streets of New York, Los Angeles, Paris, or Tokyo can be found in some figures from the World Health Organization. In the U.S., the average infant is held 33 percent of the time during the first three months and 16 percent of the time between the fourth and ninth month (the statistics for other industrialized countries are roughly the same). In developing nations, the figures are, respectively, 90 percent and 60 percent.

While the social and economic imperatives of modern life make it unlikely that we will ever entirely close the "holding gap," there is much we can do to restore a sense of intimacy to parents and infants. One strategy many parents have already adopted is backpacking or front-holding the baby.

Another strategy, which we emphasize at the center, is improving the quality of intimacy that families enjoy. A case in point is a technique we call *watchful anticipation.*

It involves nothing more complicated than simply sitting and gazing at your baby for a moment or two when you sit down next to him. There's no need to entertain or perform for him the second you greet him. Indeed, by sitting quietly beside him, you tell him in a way he can understand that you *trust your love for one another enough to feel comfortable just being with him.*

**4)**  *We can now free parents from many of the guilt-producing strictures and rules that govern our current ideas about child rearing.*

In many ways this is the most heartening aspect of our new knowledge, and it arises directly out of new research on the fitting-in process. As we've learned that the baby's development is largely a *subjective* process dependent on the ability of the individual parent and child to create a mesh between their responses and expectations, questions have arisen about several of the generalizations that currently dominate our thinking about infant care.

This is particularly true for the concept of developmental stages (as we shall see in the next chapter); it is also true for after-birth bonding. Few ideas have had more influence on parents than the notion that there exists a uniquely sensitive period after birth when being together confers special advantages on the mothers, fathers, and infants. In form these advantages are said to take the shape of enhanced parenting skills for the mother and father, and, for the child, an optimal course of development. But the fact that these benefits are supposed to occur *irrespective of other elements in the family's relationship* has appeared increasingly at odds with what we have been learning about the highly individual course of the fitting-in process. And that discrepancy, in turn, has prompted a new wave of studies on bonding. Over the last few years, of the more than twenty studies that have taken a second look at the phenomenon, virtually none reported finding a lasting bonding effect on either the parent or the child.

Or as Dr. Michael Lamb of the University of Utah put it after reviewing the new bonding literature: "Most [studies] show few if any differences between mothers who were allowed early contact and those who were denied it." Dr. Lamb's sentiments were echoed recently by University of Michigan developmental psychologist Dr. Marilyn Svejda, author of one of the most influential reassessments of bonding: "The effects of early contact, if any, are extremely subtle and short-lived and operate under selective circumstances."

This doesn't mean that bonding's critics don't appreciate the beneficial changes it has brought about. Birth is a deeply moving moment in the life of every family. And allowing mothers, fathers, and infants to be together makes for a happier, more satisfying, and more natural experience for all concerned. What's troubling about the concept of after-birth bonding is, first, that it has oversimplified what is a complex and long-term process: the creation of a mutually satisfying parent-infant relationship. And second, that it has produced rivers of needless guilt. Among many nonbonding parents there now exists a kind of syndrome of lowered expectations typified by the remark a young mother made to me recently. Asked how she was getting along with her two-year-old, she shrugged and said: "Fine, considering we didn't have a chance to bond."

Other sources of much current parental guilt are such popular abstractions as working mother, divorced father, part-time parent, and shy or cranky baby. The books and magazines that offer these categories do so as if being a working mother or divorced father were somehow a predicator of parenting skills, or, in the child's case, being shy or cranky a predicator of development. But knowing that a man is divorced or a woman works tells us nothing about how responsively those parents use their primed behaviors. Similarly, a label, such as shy or cranky, tells us nothing about how successfully an infant's environment has been shaped to his growth needs. If our new knowledge teaches us anything, it is that *the only way to tell how a baby comes to define himself, which of his skills and abilities he uses, and how effectively he uses them is to peel away the labels the world attaches to a parent and infant and examine the aspects each brings to their interactions with one another.*

From time to time I'm asked to lecture to groups of parents about my work. As I stand in front of these mothers and fathers explaining the concept of a good fit, I often witness a slow relaxation of faces that at the beginning of my lecture were taut with concern. A sense of preoccupying anxiety seems to have evaporated. I feel like a professor who, having just canceled the class's midterm exam, frees his students to listen and learn without obstructing worry.

Initially, I thought this response was due to my audience's surprise in encountering an explanation of the parent-infant connection that didn't involve either guilt or performance anxiety. But in my post-lecture conversations, I have found that there also are two other reasons why my discussions of the Magic Square strike such a responsive chord. In a period when the validity of the family—and, indeed, of parenting itself—has been challenged, mothers and fathers tell me they find it deeply reassuring to learn how new research has reaffirmed the central role they play in their babies' growth.

At the same time, they also say they are grateful for advice that goes beyond the usual admonitions to be "sensitive" and "supportive," and shows them, in specific terms, *how to help their babies to help themselves grow and how to use their own innate skills and talents to enhance that process.*

# TWO
# The Making of a Person

O n the television monitor above my head, two flickering images begin a graceful dance of hellos, while barely five feet away, on the other side of a one-way mirror, their real-life embodiments sit on a pile of pillows about to engage in that most intricate and subtle of movements: a parent-infant interaction. Though I've witnessed the scene hundreds of times before, as I watch I'm astonished yet again at the precise beauty of their dance, and at the economy with which nature uses it to begin the shaping of an individual life.

Out of this and a thousand similar encounters, Eric, the five-month-old whose beaming smile is beaming down at me now from the TV monitor, will learn how to assemble the bewildering swirl of sights and sounds that greeted him at birth into an understanding of the complex codes and rules that govern our behavior. And what makes the process all the more wondrous is that Eric will acquire this understanding of how to eat, dress, and sit with another person not through any special training, but in the course of the diaperings, feedings, playtimes, and other seemingly inconsequential activities that make up the daily round of interactions for most families.

This view of exchanges as a school for socialization has been with us since the mid-1960s, and it is one of the most important ways in which interactions serve a baby. But new video research shows that interactions also have another even more important, and more magical, dimension. They are where an infant is transformed into a member of the human community. Or as Dr. Kenneth Kaye of the University of Chicago put it more simply, interactions are where he learns to become a "person." This doesn't mean the newborn is something less than a human being, or that he is less "smart" or "competent" than he has been made to seem for the past decade. But it does mean that the popular picture of a baby as born with the knowledge of how to behave with intention and purpose and how to communicate his thoughts and feelings (in other words, already knowing how to be a person) is as misleading in some ways as the earlier view of the neonate as a tabula rasa, or blank slate.

Babies do indeed, in an instinctive sense, know a great deal at birth; within their gene structure they have the building blocks of such qualities as cooperation, intentionality, empathy, humor, love—in other words, all the characteristics of personhood. But these qualities exist not as preassembled skills waiting to step out the moment the developmental elevator reaches the appropriate level, but as *potentialities* whose emergence and growth are governed by something at once more powerful, special, and individual than a biological clock: *the tailor-made love of a parent.*

Interactions have emerged front stage center from this new picture of growth because they provide the setting for the interplay of nature and nurture, which shapes these potentialities. You can see this in the way the interactive environment determines the growth of such a quality as *empathy.* Nature has primed the newborn to be empathetic; as a member of a species that does most things in groups, whether it be constructing a castle from Bunny Builders or designing a fifth-generation computer, an ability to sympathize and care about another's feelings is important. But how this capability grows is dependent to a large extent on the richness of the environment it is planted in.

A mother who always observes the rules of reciprocity in exchanges and won't interrupt her infant's turn by answering the phone is creating one kind of environment for empathy.

The mother who keeps looking away during her baby's turn to make sure the family dog hasn't climbed up on the sofa, or who doesn't know how to support the child when he is having trouble organizing a burst of sound into a turn is creating another kind of environment.

Qualities like aggression and love grow, or don't grow, in the same way. At some level each of these is genetically mediated. But the father who smiles approvingly at his six-month-old's displays of assertiveness, but meets the child's glances of love with blank or embarrassed looks, is nurturing one quality and allowing the other to wilt away. Through his responses this father is also doing something else: He is telling his child that warmth is not an important part of our give and take with others. And, of course, that is not only a social lesson, it is a lesson in what kind of person he will be.

In a very real sense, our new knowledge of interactions and the role they play in the fit reaffirms the innate parental wisdom that mothers and fathers have always possessed. This knowledge shows that responding sensitively, encouraging self-expression, behaving predictably and supportively, providing stimulating sights and sounds—all the things you and other mothers and fathers already instinctively knew were important—do, indeed, constitute the elements of healthy growth. But, at the same time, our new knowledge also has deepened and enriched what you and other parents know by showing *why* these elements make a difference. They are the building blocks of a nurturing interactive environment, and because they have a biological resonance, we know that when these elements are fitted to a baby's needs, they do more than provide psychological reassurance. They produce an inner harmony at the deepest biological level—the one that can produce a feeling of *joy* in a baby.

During the first year you can see this joy displayed in the child's sense of affirmation, security, and confidence, in his excited eagerness to explore and engage the world, and in his ability to console himself in distress and sail smoothly over the frustrations and tensions that topple other babies into tears. You also can see it in the way he begins to care about others, in his easy, free laughter, in his sociability; in other words, you can see his joy palpable and alive in all the qualities that make for a happy, fulfilled, loving person.

A few years ago, researchers at the University of Miami found themselves facing a perplexing test result. Why did all the babies in their study group react with such puzzlement to the one thing that normally makes a baby burst with happiness—a smiling face? The investigators knew the infants were special in one important way—each was the child of a clinically depressed mother. Nonetheless, physically and emotionally, the babies themselves were in obvious good health and old enough to understand the meaning of a social smile. So why then their baffling reactions?

Confronting Dr. Tiffany Field and her colleagues when they sat down to analyze these results was a paradox which grew increasingly common in laboratories as the video camera replaced the naked eye as the primary observational tool in infant research: the incongruity between the neat, orderly picture of development in textbooks and the subjective, individual, and sometimes erratic process that was revealing itself on the video monitor. As director of an interactional research project at St. Luke's-Roosevelt Hospital in New York in the early 1970s, I can remember my own surprise at how wide the developmental range was among the six- and seven-month-olds whom I and my colleagues had filmed for study. While all our subjects were *supposed* to be at roughly the same developmental stage, some already were displaying the first signs of an ability to communicate thoughts and feelings through their gestures and signals, while others were quite obviously still months away from commanding this ability.

It was this discrepancy between textbook and TV monitor, and its eventual resolution through an important new wave of studies in the late 1970s and early 1980s, that led to the collapse of what might be called the Piagetian consensus. So named because it grew out of the work of Jean Piaget, the brilliant Swiss developmentalist, the Piagetian consensus shaped both professional and parental thinking about infancy for the past three decades. In your status as a new parent, you probably already have encountered several examples of it in the past few months, whether in the form of a wall-sized growth chart in your pediatrician's office or as a developmental chart in one of your infant-care books.

For the most part, the Piagetian view depicts a baby's growth largely as a stately march upward through a series of increasingly higher developmental stages. Piaget rarely acknowledged that the parenting environment influences the rate of a child's climb. But he thought a healthy infant's biology more or less reserved him a place on the developmental elevator. In his conception of growth, the child's innate skills and talents were depicted much like genetic time capsules; each was pretimed to open on arrival at the appropriate developmental level. So while one baby's elevator might bring him to a new stage sooner or later than another's, once there the appropriate skills would step out. If that happened to be an early stage, the skill might be a beaming social smile, or if it happened to be a later stage, it might be problem-solving skills.

However, recent work by investigators Erik Erikson and T. Berry Brazelton at Harvard, Jerome Bruner of the New School for Social Research, Kenneth Kaye of the University of Chicago, Daniel Stern of the New York Hospital-Cornell Medical Center, Michael Lewis of Rutgers, Hanŭs and Mechthild Papoŭsek of the Max-Planck-Institut, Munich, H. R. Schaffer of the University of Strathclyde, Scotland, and Louis Sander of the University of Colorado—to name a few of the fit's principal architects—shows that an infant's development differs from the Piagetian concept in two fundamental ways.

One is that not every infant stops at every developmental floor; nor do skills and aptitudes emerge according to an inner timetable. Furthermore, while some infants may tap an individual capacity fully, others may only realize it partially, and still others barely at all. You can see this relativity at work in the way a skill such as stress management is nurtured. One of the competencies involved in his growth is the baby's cyclical pausing. An infant knows that one way he can ventilate the stress (which at this point is produced by stimulation) that has built up inside him while the two of you were interacting *en face* is by periodically turning his head away.

Over time these pauses gradually increase a child's capacity to tolerate stress; which is to say, over time they foster an ability to manage it. But to what degree they succeed depends largely on the responses the head turns elicit. A baby needs the pauses to be respected (which means that during them he wants to be undisturbed), and when that wish is granted, he will start evidencing an ability to process increasingly larger amounts of stress-stimulation and show a decreasing need to keep turning away from you.

Consistent violations of the pause expectations, on the other hand, produce a situation much like the one I found myself confronting during the St. Luke's study. Very early on, I noticed that one of our mothers was continually following her baby daughter's head turns; as she turned away, the mother repositioned herself to face the daughter. In the first year, and especially in the first six months, such well-meant efforts to maintain contact are fairly common for the understandable reason that mothers and fathers are just getting to know the infant. Usually, though, the misinterpretations also are self-correcting. The parent sees the baby doesn't like what he or she is doing and stops.

Initially, this is why I wasn't too concerned about the mother's behavior. But when it continued into the study's eighth week, I did become uneasy. It wasn't just that the infant was having more, rather than less, trouble coping with stress; it appeared to me that the pause violations were making her retreat from her mother. In exchanges she spent more time in head turns, and often, when facing her mother, she had a glazed "I'm not home" look in her eyes.

Like many such stories, this one also has a happy ending. Reviewing a tape of an exchange between this mother and daughter made three months later, I had to remind myself that this was the family I had been so concerned about. As is so often the case, just a greater understanding of the meaning of the pauses (and several of her other cues and signals, which also were consistently being misread) had been enough to produce a dramatic improvement in the mother's attunement.

The second way new research has changed the Piagetian

concept of development is by showing that a baby's growth curve can only be understood in terms of the interactive universe that shapes him. A vivid illustration of this point is the reactions of Dr. Field's test babies. Seen through the prism of the Piagetian stages, their responses appear inexplicable. Since each was already old enough to understand and respond to a social smile, the only exlanation for their reactions is a physiologically based growth lag. But looked at through the prisms of their interactive universes—one in which smiles were a rarity—the infants' responses instantly make sense. From that perspective their responses can almost be called normal. As in every interactive system, the dancers had become the dance.

One result of studies like Dr. Field's is that we now realize that differences in such qualities as eagerness to explore, cooperation, and a sense of personal mastery almost always can be *explained more accurately in terms of a child's interactive system than by his age.*

Another result is a new way of seeing parent and infant. Instead of depicting them singly as individuals—the way the Piagetian system has—we now envision them together as occupants of a unified interactive *system.* Neonatologists have long known that a newborn's physical status can't really be understood without an understanding of the dietary, sleep, and exercise habits of the environment that nurtured him for nine months. And we now realize that where a one-year-old stands on his developmental curve as well as how he sees himself and the world can't be understood without an understanding of the interactive messages he has received during the past twelve months. These messages tell a baby which and how much of his potentials to tap, and which to leave dormant. Through them an infant learns whether a sympathy for others is or is not important, whether it is or is not safe to trust others, whether aggressiveness is or is not more important than warmth, whether exploration is or is not dangerous, and, most of all, whether he is or is not an effective person.

Rarely are any of these things stated as baldly or directly as I have put them, of course, but a parent's responses resonate on several levels. Thus, the baby whose bids to open an interaction are accurately read and responded to is being told something more than that his mother and father are willing to engage in an exchange. He also is being told that he is able to influence their behavior—to, in a sense, make things happen. And this is how an attitude of competence and mastery is fostered. Similarly, the infant who sees his mother immediately quiet when he turns his head away from her in the midst of an interaction is being told something more than that she acknowledges his physiological need for a pause. He also is being told that his mother respects and supports his need to be an individual, independent of her.

The imprint of interactive messages is still so clear and fresh on the personality of a two- or three-year-old that, at the center, often we can tell what kind of system one of our toddlers was shaped in even before we get to know his parents very well. There is, for example, sweet-faced, caring Henry, who, whenever I meet him in the hall or playroom, always seems to be holding his furry bunny in one fist and a half-eaten Oreo cookie in the other "for you, Dr. Sanger." The glow that lights up Henry and makes him such a special child to his playmates and to our staff, who eagerly look forward to his appearance at our door on Tuesday and Thursday could only have been shaped in a joyous interactive system.

Then there is two-and-a-half-year-old Robert who, despite his verbal precocity and touching thoughtfulness to playmates, has trouble reaching out and asking for help when a problem defeats him. If a videotape of nine-month-old Robert and his parents were available, I suspect it would show that for all their lovingness, his mother and father were unpredictable in their responses. Sometimes they would acknowledge Robert's gazes, sometimes they wouldn't; sometimes they would read his cues and signals accurately, sometimes they wouldn't. The message such a response pattern conveys is that people cannot be relied on for understanding, so the child doesn't develop the sense that other humans can help in solving problems and difficulties. I think that what we are seeing now in little Robert is a generalization of that interactive lesson to the larger world.

In the first years of life children are so malleable, with help, a toddler like Robert can be taught to reach out for others.

No infant's growth curve is rigidly and forever determined by the nature of his interactive experiences. Nonetheless, potentials that are brought to life early often grow more fully and naturally. This means that the difficulty—and even the emotional discomfort—that is often involved in changing the attitudes of a two- or three-year-old, like Robert, can be avoided if his early exchanges show him that it is safe to reach out to others for assistance.

When does a baby become aware of his interactive environment?

About fifteen years ago, Dr. Louis Sander answered that question in what is now rightly regarded as a landmark study. His subjects were a group of seven- to ten-day-olds, and what made his findings so significant was his demonstration that even at this age, which is regarded as still part of the neonate period, an infant already can judge an environment's sensitivity to him and will shape his own responses accordingly. Dr. Sander showed that even in the first two weeks of life, a baby already is measuring and responding to the quality of his interactive fit.

The way he demonstrated this was by gauging the responses of his young subjects to two different caregivers. His results indicated that by the ninth or tenth day, an infant is not only able to identify his caregiver, he will cry and experience eating disruptions if she is replaced by a surrogate.

At the center, we see the same level of awareness and responsiveness in the two-, three-, and four-week-olds who are brought to us for neonate evaluations. Some already will be palpably flourishing in their new interactive environments. Others will already be showing signs that they sense themselves in a poor fit through symptoms like excessive irritability, colick, apathy, and, most especially, through the absence of the beginnings of a regular pattern of sleeping and feeding times. (In a good fit, by contrast, the beginnings of such a pattern often will be apparent as early as the seventh to tenth day.)

Technically, this process of establishing biological regularity is known as organization, and it constitutes an important building block of the ability to *engage the world*, which is the first

## The Four Stages of the Fit in the First Year

### One to Three Months
Internal Regulation

> In this period, what is being fitted together is the baby's need to attain biological organization and the environment's ability to help him in the form of a dependable predictability and a capacity to read his moods and feelings. The better the fit between these two elements, the sooner the child will organize his sleeping and eating urges into a coherent pattern and evidence an ability to remain alert and attentive in exchanges.

### Four to Six Months
Reciprocal Regulation

> At this stage, the infant's cooperative and social instincts emerge. You can see this in the appearance of his social smile, his newly exhibited interest in turn-taking, and his ability to conduct a mutual reference (''Let's look at this block together, Mommy''). An environment that meets these emerging abilities is characterized by reciprocity in interactions, a knowledge of how to support the infant when he is trying to take his turn (through, for example, chorusing and back channels), and generally accommodating itself to his need to learn how to get along with other people.

### Seven to Nine Months
Making Things Happen

> During these months, the chief quality the environment must accommodate itself to is the baby's need to seize the initiative and make things happen. While he has been trying to do this all along, what is different now is that the drive is an expression of conscious intent, not instinct. When the eight-month-old smiles or points toward a block, he *knows* the response he wants back from the environment. On the other hand, he is now mature enough to enjoy your occasional variations on his expectations, as in seeing your normal facial expression change into a funny face.

### Ten to Twelve Months
Awareness of the Environment's Fit

> While the issues within the fit don't change markedly in this stage, the baby's expanding locomotion adds a new and important dimension. By the eleventh or twelfth month, a child has acquired enough learning to form a series of *learned* expectations about the environment's helpfulness, and his own ability to help himself. To illustrate the point, take the infant's reaction to rocking. If past experience has taught him that it calms and soothes him, he will actively seek it out when upset, but if he has learned other ways to comfort himself, he may reject your offer.

item on every baby's *developmental agenda*. This agenda is made up of the talents, skills, and capabilities that nature has targeted for special growth in the first year because they facilitate adaptation to the environment. What distinguishes the agenda from the traditional concept of developmental stages or steps is that the items on it are *not* primed to unfold automatically. Each is nurtured to life within the interactive environment, and the agency of that nurturance is a parent's primed behaviors. Biology does play a part in the sense that an agenda item such as, say, the ability to use cues and signals as true communication symbols is mediated by brain maturation. But whether this capability appears around the sixth or seventh month—when an infant usually acquires a cognitive capability for such communication—or in the ninth or eleventh month is determined by the fit between his competencies, needs, and expectations and his mother's and father's primed behaviors.

## Developmental Agenda

## ONE TO SIX MONTHS:

1) *Ability to Engage the World*
While early interactions have no focus in the sense that parents and infants don't yet use them to perform joint activities, such as looking at a block together, or to develop joint goals, such as passing a rattle back and forth, these exchanges are important because they are where the baby first engages the world. This is the term we use at the center to describe the early interactive periods, when with parental help the child starts observing and studying his new environment. And while that may not seem significant enough to qualify such periods as a developmental priority, it is in them that a baby comes to know the two central figures in his environmental landscape—mother and father—better; and where he begins to stretch his attention and alertness spans. Equally important, the ability to engage the world, in the form of another person, gives an

infant his first glimpse of human communication's mutuality and two-sidedness; thus, engagement sets the stage for a later understanding of such skills as ccoperation and turn-taking.

2)  *Mastery-Competency*
By the fourth month, these twin desires have become such a powerful driving force, often they outweigh even the baby's desire for food. And lest that sound like hyperbole, consider the results of another of the Papoušeks' imaginative studies. As its centerpiece, this one had a kind of baby video game which the researchers designed. They wondered what rewards would motivate their sixteen-week-olds to learn the game quickest. Not surprisingly, the Papoušeks expected food to be the most important motivator. In other words, they thought their young subjects' desire to learn how to manipulate blinking lights on the game board (which they could do by learning a series of head movements) would be hastened if a bottle awaited them at the end of a successful game. Much to the couple's surprise, however, the infants played the game as avidly *after* a feeding as before. The infants' chief motivation and pleasure, it turned out, was the sheer joy of making the lights twinkle on and off—that is, the sheer joy of displaying their mastery of the game. The Papoušeks call this desire for mastery "among the most powerful factors of intrinsic motivation." It is why infants spend so much of their time in exchanges trying to influence a parent (which is how the drive is expressed interactively), and it is why they pay so much attention to the responses their attempts produce.

3)  *Cooperation-Sociability*
Attainment of these abilities serves two needs—one general, the other specific. The general need is the developmental necessity of learning how to get along with others. If he is to function effectively in social encounters, a baby must have an easy, secure grasp of the rules that govern cooperation. This means he needs to know the eye codes people use in talking to one another, how they take turns in con-

versation, and the way they use empathy to enhance their work together.

The other, more specific reason why cooperation is a priority agenda item is that it facilitates the infant's grasp of *spoken language*. While traditionally this capacity has been viewed as largely a biologically mediated function, as we shall see in Chapters Six and Seven, new research shows that social—and, in particular, cooperative—learning are key factors in determining when a baby comes to the spoken word. Or, to put it more directly, this new work shows that *the growth of verbal skills is less a matter of reaching the right developmental stage than of being planted in the right interactive environment*. Therein lies a major reason why some children come to the spoken word at thirteen months and others as late as the eighteenth or nineteenth month. Very often, the difference can be explained by differences in their interactive fits.


## SEVEN TO TWELVE MONTHS:

### 4) *Intentionality*

While its importance to the infant is self-evident, intentionality's appearance on an agenda of *developmental* priorities may seem surprising. Isn't it (the understanding that if you do A, B will happen) part of the very essence of being human? Yes, but as with verbal skills, a newborn's or, indeed, a four-month-old's biological knowledge of intentionality isn't as advanced as the infant's current superbaby image would suggest. At birth he does have a *competency* for intentionality in that even within the first few days of life, a child can identify connections between things. Within ten feedings, for example, a neonate already knows from the way his mother props him up on her chest that he is about to be fed. What he doesn't yet understand, however, is that he can control these connections. In other words, that he can use *his* cries to make his mother pick him up and feed him.

### 5) *Communication*

Development of biological cues and signals into a vocabulary of true communication symbols is another important infant priority. But the three-month-old who raises his hand upward toward his mother is like the newborn who randomly cries; he doesn't yet know that a hand can be used to tell his mother he would like to play a finger game, just as he doesn't yet know that he can use his glances to tell her he would like her eyes to follow his to that block over there. In other words, he, too, doesn't yet understand that his cues and signals can be used to make something happen. That is what an understanding of acting intentionally involves. And as we will see a bit later in this chapter, the understanding which allows a child to transform his capacity to see a connection between his smile and his mother's response (a smile) into a knowledge of how to use his smiles intentionally to make her smile, is acquired in interactions.

### 6) *Attachment*

First, it is a priority for the elemental reason that for the infant, human love is a matter of physical necessity. You can see the effects of its absence in failure-to-thrive babies, who are barely able to sustain even minimal levels of growth in a period when the human organism normally enjoys unusually robust growth. At the same time, attachment also serves the more specific developmental purpose of fostering an eagerness to explore, since the closer and richer the tie parent and baby share, the more secure the child feels about leaving that parent to examine his new environment.

Attachment is the happy outcome of a good fit, and, for the infant, the starting point of a satisfying, confident and productive life.

The most remarkable thing about the developmental process that has unfolded before our eyes over the past decade is its symmetry. In one form or another, every item on the baby's developmental agenda has a counterpoint in one of his parents' primed behaviors. In the second part of the book we will take a closer look at these two sides of the developmental equation. But to illustrate how the sides are designed to fit together within exchanges, let's stop for a moment and look at three of your primed behaviors and the ways they help a baby to implement his developmental agenda.

## Paragraphs

At the center, this is the term we use to describe the combinations of four and five behaviors that parents string together in interactions. A typical paragraph might include a nod followed by a smile or a vocalization topped off by an exaggerated roll of the eyes. And while it may sound surprising to describe something as seemingly inconsequential as a wink, a sound, and a smile as part of a complex developmental plan, the fact that paragraphs are used universally—they appear in the filmed exchanges of New Guinean mothers as well as American and Italian ones—and that they have been found to serve the baby in two important ways indicates that they are a product of priming.

Paragraphs' first function is the specially developmental one of enabling the baby to fulfill the top item on his agenda—that is, to engage the world. Growth of this ability is contingent on a capacity to maintain attentiveness and alertness in exchanges. But as every new parent knows, for the first four or five months these two capacities are precariously balanced. Either a fraction too much or too little of stimulation produces disruptions. Paragraphs are intended to steer a child clear of both potential hazards by ensuring he is exposed to behaviors that are at once steadying enough to anchor his attention and alertness, while also being interesting and varied enough to keep him from growing bored.

Instinctively, you and other parents already know this, which is why paragraphs are among your most commonly used interactive behaviors. But a mother's or father's skill in paragraph construction also makes a difference in the sense that the closer the elements in a paragraph are tailored to a baby's needs, the more his ability to engage the world is enhanced. You can see the difference this individualization makes very clearly in the results of a study by Dr. T. Berry Brazelton and his colleagues at the Child Development Unit at Boston's Children's Medical Center.

Why the combination of a smile, a song, and a wave soothes and entertains one baby, while a nod and a wink have the same effect on another is still a mystery. But what Dr. Brazelton and his colleagues found is that the mothers who took the time in exchanges *to identify which of their responses had the greatest steadying and entertainment value, and built paragraphs out of those behaviors,* had babies measurably different on two test indexes. First, over the course of the study, what I'll call the paragraph infants showed the greatest growth in attentiveness and alertness—which is to say, an ability to engage the world. And second, they displayed an active sense of being supported and encouraged by the environment, as manifested in their contented coos and smiling.

Attention and alertness spans among other infants in the experiment, that is, those whose mothers hadn't tailored their paragraphs to their infants, either grew more slowly, remained the same, or in a few cases actually declined.

The other role paragraphs play in the development cycle is more general: They are a way of enhancing the baby's sociability. No, this doesn't mean an infant has to be "sold" on people; in a sense, he is primed to like them. Not part of his priming, however, is an awareness that, aside from returning looks and taking turns in interactions, people also make wonderful and stimulating companions. This important piece of intelligence has to be learned, and one agency for its learning are your paragraphs. The whimsical combinations of sight and sound that you create are the child's first introduction to the exciting, imaginative ways another human being can invent to entertain him. And when they are tailor-made to his tastes and stimulation levels—the way Dr. Brazelton's mothers tailored theirs—paragraphs also do something else. They tell the infant that other people *care* enough about him to want to entertain and support him. (Also, once paragraphs become predictable, even slight variations cause mirth in the baby.)

## Reciprocity

That mothers and fathers, like infants, should be primed to behave reciprocally is hardly surprising. Reciprocity is, after all, a centerpiece of human communication. But within the context of the fit, parental reciprocity also is meant to serve a specifically developmental function: It is one of the tools a baby uses to implement his third agenda item—*cooperation.* Its two main building blocks are turn-taking and empathy. By learning how to share the speaker's and listener's roles with a partner and how to show understanding for that partner's point of view (empathy), a baby, in the most fundamental sense, is learning how to cooperate. And, as Dr. Edward Tronick of the University of Massachusetts pointed out in a recent paper, the degree to which an infant develops these two building blocks of cooperation is a direct outgrowth and reflection of the degree of reciprocity available in his exchanges.

When the rules which govern reciprocity are observed, Dr. Tronick notes, a child is given an opportunity—his first in life—to play different roles. He is allowed to assume the parts of speaker and listener, initiator and recipient. One result of this experience is an understanding of how people *share* roles when they communicate with one another. Another, more subtle result, is that multiple role playing creates an awareness of and, ultimately, a feeling for the points of view of the other people who inhabit those roles.

Not that an eight-week-old thinks anything so direct or explicit as "Mommy's talking. I won't interrupt because I don't like to be interrupted when I talk." But by the second month, if there is a satisfying degree of reciprocity in exchanges, a baby does begin to get a sense of mutuality and shared goals with his mother. And as Dr. Tronick notes, those feelings make an excellent seedbed for the growth of empathy, and, I would add, for cooperation as well.

But don't mothers and fathers instinctively allow for turn-taking in interactions just as they instinctively allow for it in conversations with adults? Yes, except when a parent is unaware of how to structure an exchange in a way that permits a still organizing infant the time and room he needs to take his turn (this technique, called back channels, will be examined in Chapter Seven). Another exception is when a turn is interrupted because a parent wants to bring a baby's attention to the teething ring in his or her hand.

An instinctive understanding of the *full-face rule* also is a part of every parent's priming. Mothers and fathers know, without being aware of it, that in the complex code of reciprocal obligations that govern interactions, presentation of a full parental face means only one thing to a baby. He is being asked into an exchange. They also know, without being aware that they do, that if a child signals his acceptance of the invitation with a smile, he expects the parent to smile back. This little ballet of smiles goes on at the doorway to interactions all the time. But sometimes, say, in the rush to get a baby fed and themselves out the door to work in the morning, or because a phone suddenly rings, a mother or father unwittingly breaks the rule by presenting a fullface, and when the baby smiles back, not returning his smile.

Not that this violation is deliberate, but as Dr. Tronick demonstrated in a study, this particular rule of reciprocity is so deeply ingrained, even unwitting and rare violations distress a baby. Thus, while his study mothers were all normally loving and nurturing figures, when he asked them to break just briefly the full-face rule, it produced perplexity and distress in their infants.

At first, the babies were only confused. Why after offering her full face and then seeing his beaming smile of acceptance did Mother remain sober faced? After a moment of bewilderment the children decided the answer was that their mothers' missed their acceptance cues, so each flashed another smile, as if to say, "Hey, Mom, didn't you see my smile, I'm ready." When this second smile failed to produce a desired response, the infants became more confused, but they didn't give up on their mothers. Each briefly turned away, but then turned back with a bright anticipatory look, as if to say, "I'm still ready!"

Every baby repeated this dance of turning away and turning back with a bright face several times before finally abandoning all hope of producing a maternal smile. Physically and emotionally, there was a visible withdrawal from the mothers at this point. Upset, each baby resolutely turned its head away and began sucking its thumb, stroking itself, or engaging in another self-comforting behavior.

For self-evident reasons, long-term studies similar in design to Dr. Tronick's are nonexistent. But I don't think we need their results to imagine how a consistent pattern of full-face violations might affect the development of cooperative skills, or how it might influence a baby's feelings about the person who keeps violating the full-face rule.

## As-if behaviors

If we were to go frame by frame through a tape of the interaction I described briefly at the beginning of this chapter, I think that at some point in our joint analysis you would turn to me with a concerned look and say, "That mother is overinterpreting her baby." And, in one sense, you would be right. At three months, Eric, the baby on the tape, still lacks an understanding of *intentionality*. In other words, he still doesn't understand that he can use his looks, gestures, or vocalizations *in order* to deliberately produce responses in others. Yet his mother, Carol, indeed is responding as if Eric were using his looks and movements intentionally—in order to tell her or make her do something.

It might even seem that on this tape Carol is responding to *two* babies: the three-month-old strapped in the infant seat across from her, and another, slightly older, more skilled and capable child. And again, in a sense, you would be right. There is another baby present. He is invisible because he is inside Carol's mind. He is the product of the fantasies, daydreams, and myths Carol has been constructing about who Eric is since that moment in her obstetrician's office twelve months ago when she was told: "You're pregnant!"

Parents and professionals have long been aware of these fantasies. But it has only been since the introduction of the video camera that we have realized that parents, especially mothers, act them out interactively in the form of *as-if responses*. In exchanges, a mother or father behaves as if the baby is able to respond as capably and skillfully as the child they have been dreaming about. And, over time, if those fantasies are—as we shall see later—tailored to *who* the baby is, he does begin to take on aspects of that imaginary infant in his parent's mind's eye. Dreams do come true!

Dr. B. Hopkins of the University of Groningen, Netherlands,

calls this beguiling parental trait "adultomorphosizing." And we have also learned recently that it has an important developmental function. It is how a capacity for intentionality is fostered in a baby. An example is the way as-if responses—which are the practical expressions of adultomorphosizing—are employed to teach a child he can use his looks, expressions, and vocalizations *in order* to make his mother smile, frown, hand him a rattle, or bring him a bottle.

On the tape, Carol is doing this by responding to each of Eric's smiles as if it were intended to make her smile. Because even very young infants have a capacity to identify connection, on some cognitive level, Eric is noting that there is a tie between something he does (smile) and something his mother does (smile). And while it will be another three to four months before he puzzles out the full implication of this intriguing connection (that Carol's response means he can use his smile to make her smile), when he does, Eric's facial expressions, movements, and gestures will undergo a nearly miraculous transformation. No longer simply reflections of inner moods, Eric will employ his smiles, frowns, and vocalizations the way you and I employ words—as true symbols of communication which he uses to state his intentions to others: "Mommy, I want you to smile because *I'm* smiling."

Equally important is the other role as-if responses play in the growth cycle. While every infant is born with a capacity for warmth, love, tenderness, aggressiveness, laughter, musicality, and excitement, it's through as-ifing that a baby learns which of these personal qualities to tap and which to leave dormant. Think of that father I mentioned earlier—the one who rewarded his baby's aggressiveness with a smile. While the child's assertiveness was only the reflection of an inner mood, if his father continues to give it an approving smile as if the child were deliberately trying to please him, at some point the baby will identify a connection: "When I hit the dog with the rattle, Daddy smiles." And so he will begin to bang on the dog *in order* to make Daddy smile.

A trait, such as humor, is or isn't encouraged in the same way. In the most specific sense, reacting to the funny things an infant does as if they were meant intentionally to provoke laughter helps the baby to identify what is or isn't funny, as well as the wonderful ways funniness lubricates social exchanges. At the same time though, those responses also tell the child how much value is to be placed on humor. Is it to be encouraged? Discouraged? Or is humor a matter of indifference?

It is through the answers to such questions that that most miraculous, mysterious, and important of human processes occurs: the making of a person.

# THREE
# The Partnering Parent

**A**gainst the far wall of the playroom, two windows open out onto a small courtyard bathed in early spring sunlight. Against the near wall, a tunnel of brightly colored cotton snakes along the wall toward the door. There are also a wooden slide, a Cabbage Patch doll, a three-foot-high teddy bear named Albert, and Eric, who is strapped into an infant seat in the middle of the floor. Sitting directly across from him is Joan, one of our play therapists, and behind her, propped on the edge of a chair in full view of Eric, is Carol, his mother. I am standing in the doorway about to signal Joan to pick up the first of the three tiny toy animals lying in front of her.

As I nod my head she selects a furry horse and hands it to Eric, who responds with what to an experienced eye is a revealing gesture. Instead of putting the horse into his mouth—every baby's first impulse—he looks to Carol for an approving smile. Then he mouths it. Mother and baby again exchange looks when Eric is handed the second animal—a rubber zebra. He mouths that, too! This morning we are doing a reference test at the center. And in the first two trial runs, Carol and Eric have performed well. Though thus far, Carol's approving smiles have acted largely as a reinforcement. As for most infants, "mouthing" is a principal way to explore new objects, so Eric has been following a natural impulse. What will happen in the third test run when Carol gives him a disapproving look?

At first, the new reaction clearly puzzles Eric. Why has his mother suddenly changed her mind? While he ponders this question, Eric fingers the elephant Joan has given him. Then, deciding that perhaps there has been a misunderstanding, slowly he starts moving the animal toward his mouth, stopping as he is about to put it between his lips. He looks at Carol a second time. Seeing that she is still frowning, he holds the elephant motionless in front of his mouth for a moment, then drops it to the floor.

Technically, a test like this is designed to measure how eagerly and effectively a baby uses his parent as a resource in exploring the world. But whether it's the world of new people, new things, new activities, or, as in this instance, new objects, the readiness with which a mother or father is enlisted as a helpful guide and the readiness with which his or her advice is heeded is also a reflection of a family's interactive fit. Which means the test also tells us a great deal about the atunement of a parent's primed behaviors.

Analyzed another way, however, the test becomes a way of assessing a group of characteristics that both encompass and transcend those behaviors, and which we have found to be an even truer gauge of fit. Eric's willingness to heed Carol's signals, for example, indicates that their relationship has achieved a satisfying *predictability* (in other words, he has found that her advice has predictably been significant; otherwise he would have ignored her looks). And his ability to read her signals indicates that they had developed a smoothly operating *communication* system. These two characteristics are among the five shaping elements we employ in our Partnering Parent Program. The other three are *quiet, menu offering,* and *parental flexibility,* and each was developed to meet a dilemma facing all of us who work with parents and infants: how to help mothers and fathers attune their responses without also creating self-consciousness, which inhibits their spontaneity in interactions.

Above all exchanges should be enjoyable, and, for a mother or father, a large part of what makes them enjoyable is not having to be burdened by worries about the proper sequencing of behaviors or attaining just the right vocal pitch. Furthermore, the mechanical or stilted responses such forethought produces can be just as disturbing to an infant as a wrong response. The shaping elements are designed to leave you free to concentrate all your energy, attention, and love on your baby.

At the same time, your responses *correspond with your baby's innate ideas about how the world ought to work* because they are built around the infant's biology of expectations. This is why a mother or father who responds quietly, predictably, or with an enticing menu of choices doesn't have to worry about her baby talk's pitch, her paragraphs' holding power, or her smile's brightness. The right behaviors follow automatically when the environment conforms to the infant's larger needs. Being right in this case, moreover, means more than just providing the correct response in the textbook sense. As a parent learns how to use such principles as quiet, her responses become more attuned to the baby's ability to absorb information as well as taking on a new variety and interest for him. Following are examples of shaping elements, which perform on all these various levels.

### Quiet

So much has been written about stimulation's importance that, almost automatically, parents assume its opposite is harmful. Or as one young mother said to me recently, "Dr. Sanger, quiet gives my baby nothing." Professionals felt the same way until a few years ago, when some new research produced a revision in our thinking. Essentially what this work shows is that while stimulation in the form of exciting sounds, sights, and movements is important, in many instances, quiet, in the shape of either slow, rhythmic body movements and receptive facial expressions or what we call attentive stillness, is even more important because it makes the parent's behavior more comprehensible. Or to translate it into the language of fitting in, quiet attunes responses to the baby's natural rhythms.

A study we did at the center recently illustrates the point nicely. Our general goal was to determine what most aids infant attentiveness and alertness in interactions: a high, moderate, or quiet level of stimulation. As general markers, we focused on three parental facial expressions used regularly in exchanges: smiles, frowns, and looks of mock surprise (where the widening of the eyes and the O-shaped mouth seem to sing out: "Well, hello there."). These looks are primed behaviors in the sense that they are universally employed as a way of getting into synch with a baby by stirring his attention and interest.

The videotapes we made of the study confirm a common research observation about mothers and fathers: Instinctually, they do modify these looks, which are also part of their adult repertoire of signals, in interactions. During exchanges, the mothers in each of our three study groups automatically slipped into exaggerated smiles, frowns, and looks of mock surprise the moment they turned to face their babies. This was true of our *high* stimulation mothers, who for the test had been told to deliberately speed up these looks as well as their other movements and sounds. It was also true of the *moderate* mothers, who because they were told to follow their own rhythms, paced their smiles and frowns the way they would with another adult. And it was true of our *quiet* mothers, who when told to follow their babies' pace, slowed their looks and movements.

On the videotapes we made of the study, two important characteristics distinguished the expressions of the quiet mothers. First, their looks formed more slowly; and second, they held longer. Seen on film, this had an important effect—one somewhat akin to drawing attention to a word by underlining and putting quotation marks around it. At this slower pace, expressions were framed more clearly and distinctly for the babies. And because that made it easier for the babies to focus on them, the quiet mothers' expressions proved to generate the most interest (we will see why in Chapter Five). By a wide margin, their children emerged from the test with the highest scores for interactive alertness and attentiveness.

## Predictability

If quiet attunes responses by packaging them in what to the infant is a readily identifiable form, predictability furthers the shaping process by transforming those responses into landmarks that can help expand a baby's understanding of his new world and the way it operates. One example is what happens when predictability is coupled with as-if responses. During the first month, the combination produces only a simple cause and effect relationship in a child's mind (cries bring a response). By about the twelfth to thirteenth week, it's created the glimmerings of a distinction (cries bring a *particular* response, whether food or comforting). And by the twenty-fourth to twenty-eighth week, it's given rise to a network of new expectations. By this time, the baby associates the reaction to his cries not just with a single event, like feeding, but with the sound of a distinctive set of footsteps hurrying across the living-room carpet, with the squeak of an opening door, the click of a light switch (if it's a night feeding), and a reassuring, "It's all right, I'm here."

Which means that over the months, the combination of predictability and as-if responses has nudged him into a series of new insights. First and most important, it has shown him that the environment is predictably trustworthy—it *always* responds to his cries; and second, that he has the power to influence it through his actions (crying, in this instance). In addition, it has also given him an important first lesson in intentionality (causes produce effects: crying causes feeding) and has taught him another way of identifying his mother or father (by their distinctive footsteps). Furthermore, you can see—or rather hear—the results of all this learning in the baby's cries. Instead of the long, insistent, uninterrupted wail of a *demand* cry, he now adopts the more modulated, frequently interrupted *request* cry. The baby cries, then stops (Do I hear footsteps on the rug?), cries again (Hurry up, please!), pauses (There's the familiar squeak of the door.), then emits a half-cry, half-gurgle (Ah, Daddy, you're here!).

In the course of our stimulation experiment, we saw several examples of another important way predictability shapes fitting-in behaviors. This one involves communication; by consistently using frowns, smiles, or looks of mock surprise in certain contexts, several of our mothers were able to make these general signals of pleasure and displeasure carry more specific, nuanced messages. When they smiled or frowned at particular times or in particular situations, their babies knew from past experience that something more definite than general parental pleasure or displeasure was being indicated.

A young mother named Nan provided a particularly good demonstration of this "nuancing." Through consistent use, she had transformed a mild frown (actually, more a look of concern) into a kind of interactive break for her four-month-old. As we will see a little later, babies have their own natural breaks, or decelerators, which allow them to modulate and control stimulation high points, for instance, excitement. But because Heather (Nan's baby) had a susceptibility to overstimulation—not an unusual condition in infants—she needed an additional control mechanism. So we showed Nan how to use her serious face to signal Heather that she was approaching stimulation overload. Our aim was to provide Heather with a reference point that she could use to monitor and regulate herself. And over time and with consistent use, that's what Nan's serious face became—a monitor. In the tape we made of Heather and Nan for the study, you can see how Heather uses the serious face, along with her natural decelerators, to pace herself.

## Communications system

This is the single most important structural element of every family's interactive network. First, for the immediate, practical reason that it is the vehicle for conveying each partner's thoughts and feelings to the other. Second, for the more long-term reason that the better a system's fit, the sooner (as we shall see in the second part of the book) the child comes to *spoken* language. And last, and most significantly, because a well-developed system enhances an infant's feeling of being *understood and supported*.

The most important way that you, as a parent, can convey this understanding is by being able to read his cues and signals accurately. And while we will look at the often surprising meanings that lie behind them in Chapter Eight, let's stop here for a moment and examine some of the ways you can make your own signals more comprehensible to the baby:

## Distancing

Your cues gain in clarity and comprehensibility when conversations are conducted on the baby's visual plane. In practice, this usually means sitting or lying on the floor, but the extra straining and craning for the infant that it avoids allows him to devote all his energies to decoding parental messages. The distance at which certain cues and signals are sent also affects their intelligibility. Videotape analysis that we've done, for example, shows that when entering a baby's line of vision, leaning forward, adjusting his clothing, or touching him, being very close (usually within eight to ten inches) increases his comprehension of these gestures. On the other hand, the meaning of a look, a smile, a bob of the head, or a sound (particularly if it's loud and delivered rapidly) are better understood when there is some space between parent and infant.

## Tempo

The tempo at which a parental signal is made affects not only the clarity of the message it sends, *it also influences the meaning of the message itself,* A good example is arm waving. In exchanges, arms are often moved up and down in waving motions and, depending on the rate of movement, one of three messages is sent to the infant. Performed slowly, like other rhythmic movements the waving has a mildly hypnotic effect which soothes the baby. In effect, this tells him: "Let's be calm." Performed at a moderate rate (one which roughly matches the baby's pace) it turns into an "alerter," which says: "Hey there sleepy head, let's play now." And performed at a fast rate, it becomes an interactive destabilizer—the rapid movement produces too much visual information. So, like an adult who is being overwhelmed with stimulation, the infant adopts the self-protective strategy of "tuning out" on the exchange.

## Cycling

One of the most common parental misconceptions I encounter involves the infant's attention span. Often, mothers and fathers blame themselves when, inevitably, the baby turns away in an exchange. This isn't a sign of rejection or an indication that the infant finds his partner boring. The cyclical head turns are part of an important biological reality. For the first twelve months, all babies have cycles of withdrawal and attention. In practice, this means that during exchanges typically there is an alternating pattern of looking at and looking away from a parent. The head turning away, in other words, is normal. Though, as we saw in the last chapter, it can become something more ominous if an infant is repeatedly chased when pausing to digest an experience or regain a sense of self. As a principal building block of stress management and attentiveness, he expects them to be respected by his partner.

### Menu offering

In their abilities to become and remain alert, in their capacities to send, receive, and interpret signals, in their tolerances to stress, stimulation, and discomfort, all babies are inherently different. As a concept, menu offering was developed both as a reflection of these differences and as a tool for meeting the needs they create. It allows a mother and father to get to know their infant in the intimate way a parent must to produce attuned responses.

In its simplest form, menu offering is built around two procedures: always offering a range of options (which has the added advantage of extending the initiative to the baby), and translating the knowledge gained from observing the baby's choices into a program that bolsters his strengths and corrects his weaknesses. We have already seen an example of how this strategy produces paragraphs with more holding power.

It has a special relevance, moreover, because it is linked to a parental concern I hear voiced a great deal: "My baby isn't responsive." Understandably, this is a source of great worry to parents. Yet almost never is it the sign of rejection that it's often taken to be. Usually, it occurs simply because the baby's special talents and interests haven't been identified and used. Every child is born with a few special abilities. Some babies, for example, are immediately drawn to bright colors, others are attracted to sounds, still others to movement.

And while that doesn't mean your four-month-old's fascination with the red pattern in the curtains is an indication that he is about to become Picasso's successor, it does mean that a parent who knows how to identify a child's special interest in color, sound, or movement has found another way of tailoring interactions to his needs, and also another way of comforting that child when he is upset or distressed.

Scientifically speaking, knowing how to dress a baby in a way that doesn't make him fuss impatiently, or how to wipe his face without making him go "echh," aren't biologically primed behaviors, but sensitivity in these little everyday matters makes an enormous difference too. Thus, if past experience has shown that your baby's patience is limited, when the two of you are going out to the park or for a visit, get yourself ready first—meaning do your hand- and baby-bag check and put your coat and hat on before jacketing or sweatering him. Being able to wheel him out the door as soon as he's fully dressed will save the two of you needless aggravation. Similarly, when wiping his face, don't use pressure or force. I know babies squirm and squiggle endlessly. But if you put a cloth under warm water and gently stroke his cheeks with it a few times, usually he will voluntarily surrender his mouth for cleaning too.

A parting comment on menu offering—it is a precursor to democratic, as opposed to authoritarian, attitudes; the baby's wishes are solicited before decisions are made. This respect for the infant teaches self-respect and thoughtfulness.

## Parental flexibility

While most parents are aware that their baby's developmental curve is unique, and many realize that this uniqueness has important implications, some mothers and fathers, nonetheless, resist the need to fit their responses to their infants. Sometimes consciously, but usually subconsciously, they establish their own *hidden agenda,* which they place in opposition to their infant's agenda.

As we shall see in the next section, these hidden agendas develop for several reasons. One we often encounter at the center involves a process we call *emotional editing.* When a mother has trouble with anger, intimacy, or another emotion, it's not unusual for her to edit out her infant's signals that deal with those emotions. If the discomforting feeling is anger

or protest, for instance, signals involving them go unacknowl-
edged, or if it's intimacy, the baby's affection signals are ignored. This selectiveness has the effect of putting the proscribed
emotion off limits, which means the baby is never given a
lesson in how to deal with it effectively. At the very least,
this has the result of passing on the parental vulnerability to
him and at worst, it may make him prone to somatization
and emotional flatness, which is not an uncommon product
of denial. Later, the suppressed feeling can reappear in the
form of sleep or stomach disturbances.

The best way I know to demonstrate how the shaping elements instinctively produce the kind of attuned response that
is so important to the baby's development is to show the difference they make on the level of an individual interaction. So
I have asked Carol for permission to analyze one of her exchanges with Eric. In order to follow it, you will have to
use your imagination, since we can't recreate the tape on the
printed page. But I think you will find the effort worthwhile.

Before we begin, let me briefly give you some background.
The interaction was taped during the family's fifth visit to
the center, and if Carol's responses sometimes seem intimidat-
ingly "right," I should point out that like a great many of
the mothers and fathers we work with (and like a great many
parents generally), it is because her innate knowledge of her
baby and how to meet his needs was great to begin with.
With the aid of the shaping elements, we simply helped her
and her husband, Bob, who had to absent himself from this
final exchange because of an emergency at the school where
he teaches, to fine-tune what was already a very nurturing
interactive system.

The morning of the taping, Eric arrived wearing what Carol
proudly announced was his first pair of Oshkosh jeans. Though
from the way the loose folds of denim continually threatened
to swallow him up during the exchange, this appears to have
been a case of the clothes wearing the man. Eric, however,
seemed happily impervious to his sartorial problems. As the
camera moves in on him, see how content he looks sitting in
the infant seat playing with the cloth block. This is the last

time we will see him so still. Over the next ten minutes, as
he passes through the four stages of his—and every infant's—
interactive cycle, a series of highly visible physical and emotional changes will transform him.

The same is true for Carol, who is lying on her side on
the studio floor directly across from her baby. In their earlier
exchanges, I noticed that she regularly assumed this attitude
of watchful anticipation when she wanted to signal her desire
for an interaction. And it's worth pausing to examine for a
moment because her stance serves Eric in several subtle, but
important, ways. First, Carol's *predictability* in using it has
transformed it into a mutually understood cue that economi-
cally and unobtrusively tells Eric he is being invited into an
exchange. And second, she has chosen a cue that is nicely
suited to her baby's ability to process information. By getting
down on the floor, for example, she places her eyes on the
same plane as Eric's, making mutual communication that much
easier, and by maintaining a stance of *quiet* alertness, she permits him to slowly awaken to her eyes, which is a very enticing
way to be asked: "Shall we dance?"

### Warm-up
Watching Eric in this early portion of the dance, you may
find yourself mentally comparing him to a waking sleeper.
Like a newly roused sleeper, his body movements are slow,
relaxed, almost torporous, and his eyes dull and slightly glazed.
As he turns to look up at Carol (remember, he's been staring
at a cloth block), though, notice the way his face brightens.
Also, notice how he has started fidgeting in his infant seat;
he's trying to place himself squarely in Carol's line of vision.
The exchange is now at a delicate point. Both of these changes
are signs of mild alerting, but whether mother and child will
build into a vigorous dance, or Eric will return, solitarily, to
his block, depends on what happens next.

Like most infants, Eric's slowly building alertness needs a
supportive (but not too rousing) bit of stimulation to focus
it. Soft humming or funny faces work for some infants at
this stage, baby talk for others. For Eric, a smile and soft
stroking are mildly stimulating. And thanks to the knowledge

she's accumulated through menu offering, Carol is aware of this and responds accordingly. That her smile and stroking have the desired effect is evident not only from the growing brightness of Eric's eyes (notice, however, that he has still not established prolonged eye contact; his glances are still fitful), but also from the way he's begun pointing his fingers and toes in Carol's direction; this is one way a baby accepts an invitation to the dance.

## Early excitement

Some infants signal their entrance into this stage (its distinguishing characteristic is gathering alertness) with slow, pedal-like movements of the arms and legs. Others indicate their arrival by a rhythmic opening and closing of the hands and fanning of the toes, the way Eric is doing. In a moment, we will see him start moving around circularly in his infant seat, first leaning toward, then away, from Carol, as if he were alternately reaching out for her, then lying back waiting to receive her. Another common feature of stage two, the circular movement, is also an important indicator of fit since the amount of energy a child expends on reaching out and waiting to receive tends to correspond to the expectations he has for the about-to-unfold exchange. And those expectations, in turn, are a reflection of how satisfying his past interactive experiences have been.

Significantly, see how Eric tingles with anticipation. Also, see how, for the first time, he has established prolonged eye contact with Carol. This new level of attentiveness signals the arrival of an important point in Eric's cycle. Through her quiet alertness, Carol has gently shepherded him to the launching point; now he's ready to begin actively engaging the world. In order to maintain and lengthen his alertness, however, Eric requires further maternal assistance in the form of something interesting to do or look at. Some parents respond to this need with a string of paragraphs; others make a menu offering. Either response has ''holding'' power in the sense that each allows the child to anchor his attentiveness on a concrete sound, movement, or gesture. Though menu offering has the additional advantage of also allowing him to exercise initiative, Carol selects this response, deftly presenting a menu of three possibilities. Eric's interest in an eye game is tested by some exaggerated eye rolling. When this fails to rouse interest, a smile and a series of vocalizations are offered. The wide-eyed expression this combination offering produces indicates that Eric's interest has been piqued. Carol, nonetheless, decides to add a third option to her list. Unstrapping him from the infant seat, she whisks Eric up into her arms and gently swings him around.

On being returned to the seat, notice how Eric turns his head away, and also notice how *Carol has let him.* A University of Miami study indicates that head turning is one of the baby's most commonly misunderstood signals—usually being taken either as a sign of rejection or of boredom. But Carol understands why Eric has turned away: He's contemplating her menu offerings. And by resuming a stance of quiet alertness, she gives him the time he needs to digest her suggestions.

A baby may signal a menu selection in one of several ways. The most direct way would be with a facial expression. Eric's disinterest in the eye game was evident by the blank look on his face; a smile or widening of the eyes, on the other hand, would have indicated acceptance. More subtly, a child may use a physical cue. On facing Carol again, see how Eric begins to move his arms and legs in full, pedal-like motions. Such large body movements usually signal a desire for physical stimulation, which in Eric's case means he's telling his mother: "Swing me around one more time, Mommy."

That our two dancers are approaching the end of early excitement is apparent once Eric again is aloft in Carol's arms. One sign of this is the noticeable jerkiness in Eric's previously smooth body movements. See, for example, how unrhythmic his pedal motions are. Another sign is Eric's tonguing. These signs, along with the half-gurgling, half-laughing sound we hear, are outward manifestations of the barely containable excitement that is about to sweep Eric into the third peak—and most important phase—of his cycle.

### Pinnacle

As the dance we've been watching gathers momentum, we are about to see our two dancers make their most dazzling moves. And since at this, the exchange's emotional high point, each is at peak form, the level of harmony they have achieved over the months also will become visible to us in a palpable way. A case in point is Carol's response as Eric returns to the infant seat. From the increasing jerkiness of his movements, he seems about to burst with excitement. And a slow-motion running of the tape would reveal that he has, indeed, reached a new pitch of excitement. Though to the naked eye Eric appears as attentive as he was in stage two, the slowed tape would show that his looking at Carol is being increasingly interrupted by blinking, and blinking, along with jerkiness, is a key indicator of a pitch level of excitement.

Because of the threat of overstimulation, very often it is at this point in the dance that parents break step with the infant—reining him in. What makes Carol's response notable is that she not only avoids this misstep, but avoids it by the seemingly surprising strategy of *continuing to follow her baby up into his excitement.*

Given what we have learned about the importance of quiet, Carol's action may seem paradoxical, but the peak she and Eric are scaling represents a high point of parent-infant joy—one whose resonances will influence every aspect of their bond. Moreover, the experience also allows Eric an opportunity to learn how to use his own natural decelerators to modulate a peak emotion. Notice the way he has begun rubbing his hands together. Along with yawning, looking away, and thumb and tongue sucking, it is one of the half dozen ways an infant can maintain himself on a smooth plateau of excitement. Not that Carol is aware of these capabilities in a technical sense, nor need she be; she has something that serves Eric and their interactive harmony even better—the *flexibility* to follow her baby wherever he leads and the confidence to feel that whatever the ultimate destination, she not only can maintain her rhythms, but help Eric maintain his.

Why this isn't the case perhaps as often as it should be we will see when we take a closer look at the parental hidden agenda in Chapter Eleven. Suffice it to say here that the desire to "save" a baby from overexcitement by reining him in often has the contradictory effect of leaving him suspended in midair while you have returned to the ground.

Parents also possess their own interactive decelerators: looking away, looking back, and looking dull being three prominent examples. And as our dancers move into the second, or plateau, phase of pinnacle, we can see how Carol's synchronization of these parental decelerators with Eric's allow both of them to prolong their shared moment on the mountaintop.

Like Carol's earlier readiness to follow her baby, what creates the ability to sustain and regulate this plateau isn't a technical knowledge of her interactive decelerators. The leaning back we see her do is done instinctively, spontaneously, though once again her use of a natural fitting-in behavior is induced by a shaping element. In this instance it is *menu offering,* which because it has been steadily employed over the months, now has produced sufficient maternal knowledge of Eric's sensitivities and tolerances to enable Carol to harmonize her decelerations to his effortlessly.

Run at normal speed, the tape makes it difficult to see this particularly subtle step in the dance. But if I put the videocassette recorder (VCR) back on slow motion, we will see that each of Eric's decelerations, which now have changed from stroking to head turns, immediately produces a leaning-back-away-from response in Carol. While these millisecond pauses act as emotional regulators comfortably prolonging each partner's excitement, individually they also serve Eric in another, more subtle way.

If the time between each of his head turns were now being marked by a stopwatch, the watch would show that, despite his excitement, for the first time in pinnacle, Eric is increasing his uninterrupted looking at Carol. Exactly why head turns foster infant attentiveness and the ability to engage the world is still unclear. But the cause and effect relationship between the two is well documented. Furthermore, being able to synchronize with infants' pauses not only helps to keep excitement alive, it also becomes a way of teaching the baby two important lessons: (1) how to regulate a peak emotion—excitement—in a nondisruptive way by pacing oneself, and (2) how to maintain attention in the always-fluctuating flow of emotions, which occurs whenever two people of any age interact.

As Eric turns back to her, see how Carol builds from a snatch of song to a smile, segues into baby talk, touches Eric's hands and legs, then slides back into a song. For the first time in the interaction she is paragraph building, and while the deliberate, methodical way she is constructing them may suddenly make her seem out of synch with the still obviously excited Eric, in fact, by switching to a slower rhythm by adding behavior to behavior, Carol is building a series of props that will "hold" her baby on pinnacle a few seconds longer.

When Carol completes the paragraph she is building, watch the way she stops after the last behavior in the chain (in this case, a smile) and waits for Eric to respond with a smile. She's done the same thing at the end of each of her earlier paragraphs. Whether concluding with a song, a smile, or a stroke, she stops and waits for her baby to respond in kind before proceeding. To put what Carol is doing into the language of reciprocity, she is turning the end of her paragraphs into an invitation to her baby to respond. And this not only fits Eric's sense of how the rules of reciprocity ought to work, it also gives him a practical lesson in the turn-taking he must learn to become an effective social partner.

Eric is about to slide into the last, or "winddown," stage of his cycle, but before he does, let me stop the VCR on the close-up we have of him on the TV monitor. Look carefully at his expression in freeze frame. It's more than excitement, it's even more than happiness. Eric has attained the state a baby reaches when the interactive environment perfectly harmonizes itself to the infant's biology of expectations, which is why the infant peering at us through the camera now looks so *joyful.*

## Winddown

If one common interactive misstep occurs at the top of pinnacle when the infant is prevented from scaling all the way up his emotional register, another almost equally common one occurs at its bottom on the rundown to stage four. This misstep, however, is made by dancers of a different style: parents and infants who *do* follow their excitement all the way up.

Pleased by the baby's smiles, the parent ratchets the excitement level up one extra notch in the expectation that happy as the baby is now, laughter will make a still happier baby.

Often, however, the result is a destabilizing emotional tension; for most infants six months and younger, prolonged laughter is overwhelming and unsustainable. This is why, in many ways, the most notable thing about Eric's glide into winddown is what doesn't happen. Instead of tumbling into it in a wail of tears triggered by a laughing bout, Eric lets down smoothly, gently, softly, effortlessly—a perfect landing.

Physically, the most arresting sign of arrival at winddown is a sudden dulling or glazing over of a baby's eyes. Several other more subtle physical changes may also occur, however. Notice, for example, how Eric's body movements are becoming smooth again. The jerkiness is nearly gone, and instead of reaching out to his mother, now his hand and arm movements are directed inward toward his own body, almost as if he were saying: "It's time for me to be alone."

While Carol is unaware in a technical sense that a new interactive stage is being heralded, her ability to read her baby allows her to adjust her behavior appropriately. A correct series of responses is especially important now, because, emotionally, winddown is a particularly fertile period of the cycle for a baby. It is, at once, a period of rumination—a chance to savor the delicious experience he has just shared with his mother or father, while at the same time it is also an opportunity for him to begin learning how to be alone with himself comfortably. And, as we shall see in the next section, that is one of the most important skills any of us ever develops.

# PART II
# Building
# the Magic
# Square

# FOUR
# Strategies of Predictability

 $\boxed{\textbf{S}}$  haring my office with me
this afternoon is Tommy Ryan, a normally bouncy eight-
month-old with blond curls, impish blue eyes, and the beginnings of what one day will be an irresistible pug nose. Between
us on the shag rug is a small wooden truck which I have
been diligently pushing back and forth for the last minute or
so in slowly declining hopes of inspiring Tommy's interest.
Under ordinary circumstances there would be no problem;
its shiny redness already would have him riveted. But now,
despite my best efforts, Tommy barely notices the truck. His
eyes keep darting anxiously across the room to my office door,
behind which his mother, Chris, disappeared a moment ago
with a big smile and a wave; thus setting the stage for what
is known as a Strange Situation Test.

This procedure is one of our most sensitive barometers of
parental predictability* because the degree of consistency or
inconsistency a mother or father generally displays toward
the infant is mirrored back with great accuracy in the quality
of the baby's welcoming response to the parent in the test's
reunion phase. If his greeting is, like Tommy's is to Chris,
enthusiastic and joyful, it tells us that the returning parent
is viewed as a reassuring and predictable presence. But if the

---

* The test is used primarily to measure infant attachment. And parental
predictability is an important building block of attachment.

baby's greeting has undertones of ambivalence—if, for example, there is a puzzling alteration between beaming welcoming smiles and head turns—that inability of the child to make up his mind about what kind of greeting to offer usually is a reflection of the returning parent's not having behaved consistently.

Chris looked surprised to hear this. "Predictability isn't a characteristic one thinks of in connection with a baby," she said, carefully smoothing the wrinkles of her skirt. "I mean it makes sense that it would be important, especially for a child of Tommy's age, but I would have thought that a two-, three-, or four-month-old wouldn't even be capable of noticing a parent's behavior patterns." As she spoke, Chris's eyes moved continually back and forth between me and Tommy, who once again was seated on the shag rug, this time deeply entranced by the redness of the truck he had been too distracted to notice before.

In the tapes we had made earlier of mother and child, this sensitivity toward her baby was evident in Chris's every gesture and look. Reviewing them the morning of our talk, I was particularly struck by her ability to transform herself into a predictably reassuring interactive partner. Though I could have guessed at this skill, even without the help of the tapes. Evidence of it was apparent in Tommy's bold, confident personality, his almost palpable sense of mastery and personal competence, his eagerness to learn and meet new challenges, and, most significantly, in the trust he placed in his parents and in the human environment generally. From his behavior toward me and some of the other members of the staff who worked with the Ryans during their visits to the center, it was clear that Tommy sees people as sources of support and reassurance. And as I explained to Chris during our talk, this quality, as well as the others I had mentioned to her, is a direct outgrowth of and tribute to her own constancy.

## How Predictability Serves a Baby

As my colleague Dr. Daniel Stern of New York Hospital–Cornell Medical Center noted recently, a central tendency of the baby's mental life is to seek out regularities and predictabilities in the environment. And it is for the same reason that a central tendency of his hearing is to seek out human voices in the environment. Just as he is primed to prefer human sounds over the hum of an air-conditioner or the purr of a car engine, the infant is primed to have an eye for human predictability because his knowledge of it also is essential to his knowledge of the human environment and the kinds of support he can expect to receive from it.

One important way predictability services him, for example, is by providing a series of dependable anchors around which he can begin structuring his inner and outer lives. As he learns—through his parents' constancy—that each day has its own regularly recurring schedule of events, such as napping, feeding, and playing times, it becomes easier for him to begin organizing his own biological and social urges into a coherent pattern.

For a baby, this knowledge of a day's pattern creates a reassuring quality of "what's nextness." And knowing how the day flows not only makes him feel more secure (can you imagine anything more upsetting than not knowing what comes next), it also nurtures a sense of patience, since he now knows what it is he is waiting for.

The other reason nature has primed the infant to identify predictable patterns in the human environment is that knowing those patterns is one of the ways he develops and sharpens his skills. Take as an example the baby's innate knowledge of the use of direct eye contact in interactions. This capability is important because it tells even a four-day-old where to look in exchanges. He knows that you don't look at your partner's arms, or at his ears, but gaze directly into his eyes. It is also an important forerunner of the skill of cooperation, but it isn't the same thing as cooperation, nor does this innate knowledge of where to look automatically grow into an understanding of how to get along with other people. A baby has to be *taught* how to use his gazes to establish a sense of cooperation with others. To acquire this knowledge, he needs a number of specific learning experiences; and these must be repeated over and over again in a predictable way.

One such experience is *mutual gazing,* which is a central

## Principal Building Blocks of Three Key Skills

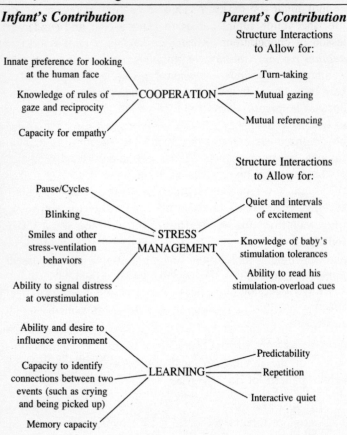

*Infant's Contribution*                    *Parent's Contribution*

Structure Interactions
to Allow for:

Innate preference for looking
at the human face
                                                          Turn-taking
Knowledge of rules of ——COOPERATION——Mutual gazing
gaze and reciprocity
                                                          Mutual referencing
Capacity for empathy

Structure Interactions
to Allow for:

Pause/Cycles
                                                Quiet and intervals
Blinking                                        of excitement
Smiles and other                STRESS
stress-ventilation            MANAGEMENT        Knowledge of baby's
behaviors                                       stimulation tolerances
                                                Ability to read his
Ability to signal distress                      stimulation-overload cues
at overstimulation

Ability and desire to
influence environment
                                                Predictability
Capacity to identify
connections between two——LEARNING——Repetition
events (such as crying
and being picked up)                            Interactive quiet
Memory capacity

leitmotiv of interactions during the first three months. This mutual pleasurable looking of mother, father, and baby isn't about anything specific. But because it is one of the first activities a child conducts with another person, it gives him a foretaste of how you work with others. While a six- or eight-week-old knows that alone he can twirl his mobile, as he observes his mother's and father's looking he begins to realize that joint activities—even simple ones like looking—are *rule bound*. Mobiles stay put; people can get up and walk away.

A person and a toy behave differently, because the next time your gaze strays and then goes back to your partner, he may not be looking at you anymore. Thus, over the first twelve weeks of life, the young infant comes to learn a first and fundamental lesson of cooperation: *In order to conduct a joint activity with another person, you have to pay attention to their behavior.*

Simple as this rule is even for a six-week-old to master, a baby who sees it sometimes applied and sometimes ignored, because a parent is distracted by a phone call or is half listening to a song playing on a stereo in the other room, is going to be confused. Is paying attention when you are with another person something you do all the time? Or is it something you do only part of the time—when you feel like it? In saying this I don't mean that mothers and fathers aren't entitled to phone calls or to listen to music or, generally, to a rich personal life away from the child. They need other interests not only for their own sakes, but for the baby's as well; the satisfactions and fulfillment those other interests bring make a parent a more engaging and interesting interactive partner.

At the same time, though, it is also important to try to separate outside distractions from time spent with the infant—that time should be as *pure* as possible. Otherwise, the interruptions caused by ringing phones, simmering vegetables on the stove, or the impulse to clean up *right now* may produce a subtle pattern of inconsistency in a parent's behavior, and though a mother or father won't be aware of it, usually the child, with his unerring eye for the consistencies, will be.

Even in the first twelve weeks, when predictability is tracked largely through biology, its presence or absence makes a difference. A two-week-old may not yet be able to say to himself: "Why isn't Mommy or Daddy more consistent?" But looks that are sometimes returned and sometimes not, or vocalizations that are sometimes pitched to his hearing range and sometimes not, feel wrong to him because his biology tells him that nearly all his gazes should be returned and that the sounds filling his ears should be soft and singsong. Just as his biology tells him something is wrong when he bumps his head against a crib post even though he can't yet put what he feels—discomfort—into a thought.

Later, in the fifth or sixth month, patterns of parental behavior do begin to produce conscious expectations in an infant, and these expectations become reflected in his interactive behavior. You can see this in Tommy's response to Chris in one of the tapes we made of them. Over the months, he and Chris have developed a little game that might loosely be called bang the drumstick. As Tommy starts it by banging his stick against a Raggedy Andy doll, his eyes light up with such anticipation you can almost hear them say: "I bet I know what you are going to do next, Mommy." And when Chris fulfills Tommy's prediction by bringing her stick down on poor Andy, Tommy's whole being seems to sing out: "See, see, I knew you were going to do that."

You can also see how disappointed a child feels when a prediction of his isn't fulfilled in an incident that happens a few moments later on this tape. Tommy smiles with the expectation that Chris will answer back with a smile of her own because that's what she always does. But at this particular moment, a hum in the overhead microphone intrudes, distracting Chris, who, instead of smiling, instinctively looks upward toward the noise. From the sudden droop in Tommy's body posture, it's clear how disappointed this makes him feel.

The innate flexibility that makes babies so adaptable, however, allows Tommy to sail over this incident without ill effect. What matters to a child are *long-term patterns* of parental behavior, and when those patterns have been as reassuringly predictable as Chris's have been, an exception like this one is quickly forgotten. *Parents should not worry about them.* (In fact, occasional inconsistencies create discrepancies which challenge the infant and, thus, help him to stretch his comprehension.)

What is a legitimate source of worry, however, is a pattern of consistent inconsistency. In the case of the shaping of such a skill as cooperation, for example, you can see its consequences very plainly in the two- or three-year-old who doesn't yet know how to share. Very often at the center, we find that a principal root of this kind of uncooperativeness is an unpredictable experience with *mutual referencing,* which, like mutual gazing, is another important early interactive building block of cooperation.

Mutual referencing emerges between the fourth and sixth month as the baby develops the ability to point at and bring a parent's eye to a toy or other object and, through his excited vocalizations and gestures, even to have a kind of conversation with mother or father about that object. When a parent is predictable in following a child's eye and consistent in understanding his comments (which means consistent in reading his cues and signals accurately), the baby learns a second important lesson about cooperation: Joint activities that are centered on a specific thing, such as looking at a block or having a conversation, require *empathy*. You have to be sympathetic to your partner's point of view or he won't cooperate with you. The infants who never learn this lesson firmly frequently become the toddlers who try to snatch a toy away from another child rather than share it, or who push other youngsters out of line because they want to be first.

Another trait we often find in these uncooperative two- and three-year-olds is excessive anger. It is a characteristic, generally, of babies nurtured in unpredictable environments. And it arises because uncertainty places a child in a kind of emotional limbo. The baby who is consistently ignored will eventually begin to try to figure out on his own the developmental steps needed to master a skill or group of skills. And because infants are competent creatures, he will have some success at this. But what I'll call the unpredictable child is placed in a more ambiguous dilemma. Because some of his parents' responses are right, he thinks: "Maybe I will get the help I need after all," but because some of those responses also aren't right or aren't there when he needs them, he thinks: "Then again, maybe I won't get that help." The upshot is that he is left uncertain about what to do, and it is this uncertainty that lies at the heart of his anger.

The way this ambiguity and the parental uncertainty that inspires it erodes an infant's sense of self-esteem emerges clearly in a new study by Dr. Michael Lamb of the University of Utah. Dr. Lamb found that in the long run, an inconsistent environment is even more damaging to a baby's sense of his personal self-worth and competency than a consistent pattern of parental avoidance. Talking about his results, Dr. Lamb says that eventually the ignored baby's attempts at self-development give him some notion of his personal effectiveness, but the child raised in an unpredictable environment lacks even this basic perception of himself as personally effective.

The brighter side of the coin is the baby who is nurtured in a predictable environment, like Tommy. Chris's consistency in mutual gazing and referencing can be seen in Tommy's already evident ability to get along with others. But it's also apparent in other qualities as well. Having learned that his mother and, it's important to add, his father, Tim, are always there to support him, Tommy has developed an implicit *trust* in them. And if he follows the pattern of other infants raised in similarly happy interactive environments, eventually that trust will spread to people generally. Chris and Tim have taught Tommy that people can be relied on to support him, so later, if Tommy finds himself having difficulty with a playmate or in school, he will instinctively reach out to those around him for help. Because his parent's consistency also has made it easier for him to master not just cooperation, but the other skills he needs, Tommy also has begun to make a prediction about himself: "I am a competent human being and I can master any challenge I set my mind to." The evidence of this can be seen in his eagerness to explore the environment and the readiness with which he greets the new learning challenges that Chris and Tim create for him.

Predictability's importance to the baby also has been documented in a number of new reports. The relationship between it and trust, for example, emerges very clearly in that study by Dr. Lamb. By studying the ways a care giver nurtures the sense that people can be dependably relied on to be consistent or appropriate, he concluded that above all, the growth of this attitude is inspired by the infant's feeling that there is "a predictable association between his behaviors and his parents'." In other words, like Tommy's expectation that Chris would echo the banging of his drumstick, the more predictable a baby finds his bids and expectations met, the more he comes to see his mother and father as trustworthy figures.

In the case of competence and mastery, the relationship emerges in a recent study which found that the distinguishing characteristic of infants with the most pronounced sense of personal competency was that each baby had a mother who predictably responded to his vocalizations and looks. Equally significant was the reports' other major finding: The high-competency babies also mastered new learning tasks rapidly and easily.

It was this sense of mastery that was so important in inspiring Tommy's eagerness to learn. In a recent study, Dr. M. J. Riksen-Walraven threw some light on how a parent encourages this self-motivation. He also identified a correlation between the degree of a mother's or father's predictable responsiveness and the infant's ability to learn, along with his sense of self-esteem. But Dr. M. J. Riksen-Walraven took the correlation one step further and found that an environment's consistency also indirectly influences a child's *motivation to learn*. In infants, our best yardstick of such motivation is an inclination to explore the environment, and Dr. Riksen-Walraven reports that his study infants with the highest scores on competence and mastery were also the ones most eager to transform themselves into little Columbuses.

## Establishing Parental Predictability

Sometimes a baby will make the most significant revelation with the simplest gesture. I saw Tommy do this the afternoon of his final visit to us. Earlier, his dad, Tim, had dropped by to join Chris and me for a conference. Later, when I came out of my office to say good-bye, I found Tim in our foyer putting on his overcoat. Tommy, who was sitting nearby in his stroller, watched with great curiosity as his father slipped into his mackintosh, but the infant gave no indication that this episode held any special significance for him. He continued playing with the Raggedy Andy doll he had formed such a strong attachment to during his visits (and which was my good-bye present to him). Then Chris, who had been delayed talking to my secretary Jane, appeared and reached for *her* coat. Suddenly, Tommy's entire body lit up with anticipation. Seeing his mother take her coat from the rack, Tommy now knew that *he* was leaving too.

What he said in this gesture, of course, is that his expectations have been largely shaped by his *mother's predictability.* When Tim puts his coat on, to Tommy it may mean that Daddy is either leaving alone or he is coming along, but when Chris puts her coat on, to Tommy it almost always means *we're* going out. Most infants think the same way—even ones reared in two-career families, like Tommy. Not for any biological reason; it's simply that, despite the social advances of the past twenty-five years, mothers, on the whole, still spend much more time with a baby during his first year than do fathers. And so infants gear their expectations accordingly. This is why it's especially important for a mother to be aware of the three ways a child assesses the environment's predictability in the first year.

In his initial twelve weeks, the baby's primary measuring tool is what is known as the *distress-relief sequence.* This is the technical term for the cycle of infant cries and parental responses so familiar to every mother and father. And there are several reasons why it is uniquely important to the infant's sense of the environment's reliability. One is that unlike other important early experiences, such as mutual gazing, the distress-relief sequence has an all-encompassing quality about it. A baby being picked up doesn't just look at his parent, he feels that parent's touch and body against his, he smells her and moves with her. And all of these different ways a mother— or father—enters a baby's senses as he's being held and comforted makes it easier for the child to identify that parent later.

Second, from a physiological point of view, the distress-relief sequence is perfectly matched to a young baby's cognitive powers. Which is to say it is the aspect of parental behavior he finds easiest to get an intellectual fix on during his first three months. It requires only the ability to identify and remember a particular parental response and which of his behaviors produced it (that is, to notice that his crying leads to his mother or father picking him up). Then the next time he cries he can note whether his crying elicited a similar response (being picked up again), a different one (being gently shushed), or no response at all.

The other factor that makes the distress-relief sequence so

important to the baby's assessment of parental predictability is that it also is his first time experiencing how a negative state (crying) can be transformed into a positive one (being picked up, rocked, and hugged). It is also his first time experiencing how reliable his caregiver is in helping him make this transition. In other words, the distress-relief sequence is a primal event and, like all primal events, it leaves an imprint that is a little deeper and a little sharper than those left by later experiences. This is why when a parent uses the sequence to establish her reliability as a comforter, the baby's memory of being gently picked up and soothed shines with a special luminosity whose glow is still evident many months later.

Reflections of it can be seen in a study by Dr. Mary Ainsworth of Johns Hopkins University. Dr. Ainsworth found that children whose distress cries were responded to promptly and predictably had by the last quarter of their first year developed two significant characteristics. First, they were quicker than the other study infants to switch from crying to more mature forms of communication, such as vocalizations. And second, they displayed a greater confidence in their mothers' emotional accessibility. Having learned that mother was dependably there in the past to offer help and comfort, these infants had now come to believe that she would be just as accessible to them in the future. And I can't think of a better foundation upon which to build a good fit.

Somewhere between the end of the third and the beginning of the fourth month, the types of environmental predictability on which a baby focuses begins changing. While he still is careful to note how promptly and consistently his cries lead to being picked up, his growing awareness and cognitive sophistication prompt him to notice the consistency of other kinds of parental behavior. From around the thirteenth week, for example, the predictability with which a mother or father try turn-taking in exchanges begins to be noticed. Also, he now notices how consistently they respond to his smiles and respect his need to pause in exchanges. Another new characteristic the baby notes in this period is how reliably and accurately his cues and signals are read.

The last major change in his perception of the environment's consistency occurs between the sixth and seventh month. Though he's been trying to elicit parental responses almost from the moment of birth, it's only between the twenty-fourth and twenty-eighth week that this innate drive begins to be directed by what we would call conscious awareness. What's different about an eight-month-old's smile is that behind it is a rudimentary idea of the kind of response he would like back— another smile. This change makes a marked difference in social behavior. Beginning in the seventh month, for example, the infant starts to pay close attention to how consistently his bids to open an exchange are acknowledged and encouraged, how predictably his requests for a toy are satisfied, how much success he has in bringing his interactive partner's attention to a block or other object, and how dependably are heeded his "statements" that the environment is going too fast for him, is overstimulating or is boring.

Each of these, of course, is an example of a *contingent response*. And as we saw in the first section, these responses not only motivate a baby to learn, they also are a key ingredient in his self-esteem. By making you smile to his smiles, or by you acknowledging his bids for an exchange, he demonstrates to himself *and* to you that he can make something happen. And the more predictable you are in echoing him back, the more firmly the baby comes to believe in his ability to be a mover and sharer of events.

A recent study by Dr. Stern, however, shows that as important as predictability in nurturing this feeling of personal competency is *timing* of responses. In order for the child to see a connection between his behavior and your echo of it, your responses have to be made within several seconds of his bids; otherwise your behavior appears random. Most emphatically, this does not mean you should keep a stopwatch nearby when you and the baby are together. *Always respond at your own natural pace.* But if he seems to have trouble following the thread of the exchange, it probably means you are falling outside of Dr. Stern's three-second limit and should try to speed up your responses just a bit.

Here are some of the other strategies we have devised to help parents construct a predictable interactive environment. There are seven of them.

## FIRST STRATEGY

### Be predictable: always start from the baby's starting point

The point of this strategy is to help the baby develop an ability to make smooth transitions. This skill is an important first step in organization, because a child who is helped to move comfortably from, say, sleep to wakefulness, then to a diapering and feeding, is better able to note and remember the events which make up that sequence. And hence, he is that much closer to an understanding of how the day flows for him and his mother. The reason a child sometimes has trouble internalizing this pattern is that its sequences are not repeated in order often enough or he is moved too quickly from one event to another. Not given time to adjust to the fairly sharp physical and emotional changes involved in such transitions, he dissolves into tears of fussiness which leave him too distracted to notice what he and mother are doing or have just done. This is why when moving the baby from inside to outside or from the floor to the changing table, you should always take the infant's mood as your starting point.

This will have the effect of making transitions slower, but that slowness gives the baby the time he needs to adjust to the changes in heart rate, vision, and position produced by your lifting him up from the floor and placing him on the changing table, or by your bundling him up in a snowsuit and taking him from the warmth and controlled light of the house and into the cold and sharp sunlight of the street. Another way of easing the pang of transitions for a baby is by incorporating what he *was* doing into what he *is* doing *now*. For instance, the child on the changing table will feel more comfortable if the doll he was playing with on the floor is brought along. The same is true if the block he's been playing with is brought up on the high chair with him while he eats.

This strategy also has some important implications for approaching an infant. If he's just waking up, watchful quiet will put you in emotional tandem with him. Similarly, if he's hurt himself, don't immediately try to brighten him out of his discomfort with a smile. Place yourself next to him with a look of concern and an attitude of quiet sympathy. As the baby watches you apply this strategy, he learns an important lesson about you: "I can count on my parents to always be sensitive to my needs."

## SECOND STRATEGY

### Use your predictability to enhance the baby's cognitive powers

Once you have established a clear pattern of how the day flows in the baby's mind, you can use that knowledge to help him build his stress- and frustration-coping skills. One way of doing this is by creating minor delays that force him to begin drawing on his own inner resources. Thus, instead of rushing in the very moment he cries after waking from a nap, delay your response five to ten seconds and see how he reacts. Often, after a week of such minor delays, a baby won't cry the instant he wakes because he's made a wonderful self-discovery: Sometimes it is nice to be by yourself. And it's through such little epiphanies that a child learns he has the resources to master stresses and frustrations. Scheduled feedings and playtimes also are good times to enjoy a delay strategy.

Let me also add one word of caution. Wait until the fourth month *after* the distress-relief sequence has established you as a predictable presence in the baby's mind before using this technique. Also, only a well-organized infant should be nudged by delays. Their knowledge of what's next makes waiting tolerable in a way that it won't be for a child who still has no coherent idea of how his feeding, sleeping, and playing patterns are organized.

## THIRD STRATEGY

### Be consistent in setting aside pure time for you and the baby

Shut off the TV and radio, unplug the phone—short-circuiting all the potential interruptions before they have a chance to happen is the best way to ensure that outside distractions won't

**S**obering face
(indicating
early
surprise)

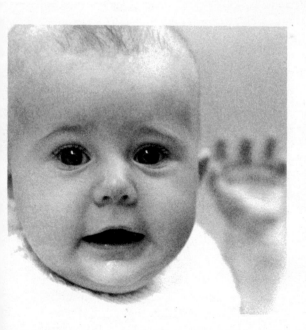

**A**pprehensive
(indicating
early fear)

Brightening
(indicating
happiness)

Early laughing

**J**oyful self-
satisfaction

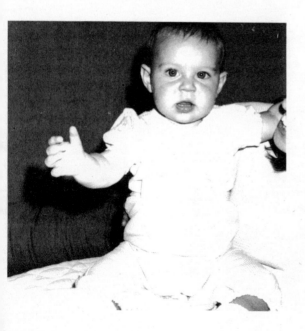

**W**ariness

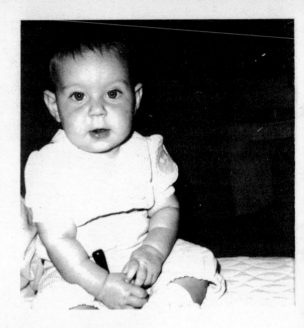

**I**n-between state (positive/ negative alertness)

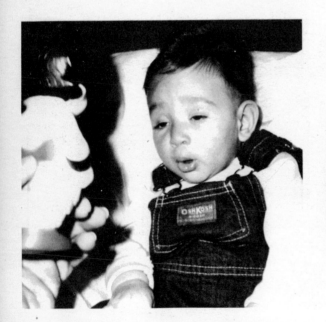

**A**bout to cry

Early interest/
negative
direction

Early interest/
positive
direction

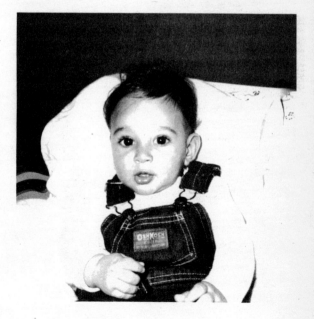

Apprehension

Quiet alertness

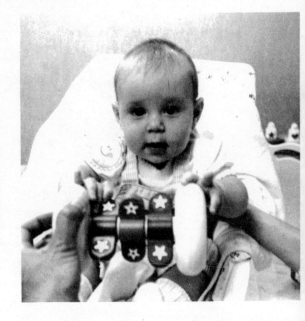

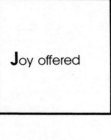

Joy offered

Joy
reciprocated

**J**oy digested

**E**ye-hand
exploration

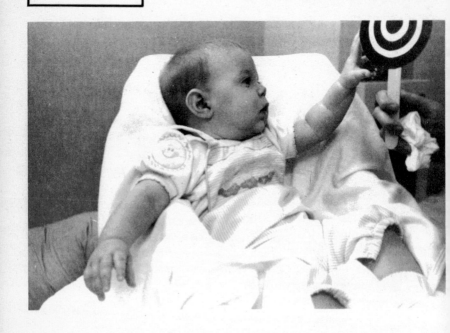

create a subtle pattern of unpredictability in your behaviors. And though there are always going to be times when it isn't possible to shut the door on the world completely, there should always be one special time set aside each day when it is possible. Whether it is after a nap or a feeding, or in the evening before bedtime, this special interval (of at least twenty minutes) should belong only to you and your child. You will find that this interval so delights him that he quickly comes to recognize this as your special time together. Your quieting of the house will become a cue to him; as he sees you walking around shutting off radios and TVs, his face will light with anticipation.

## FOURTH STRATEGY

### Always move from the familiar to the unfamiliar

There are two important variations on this theme: With a baby always go from slow to fast and from simple to complicated. These simple rules, along with the general principle of going from the familiar to the unfamiliar, are designed to help nurture an attitude that is not only important to the infant now, but will remain important to him later. Namely, the conviction that from the unpredictable (that is, from the new and unknown), predictably good things will come (understanding and mastery). At the center, we've found that the children who evidence this attitude share one similarity: Each has a parent who consistently puts presentations of the new into a form the baby finds easy to digest. The way mothers and fathers do this is by combining the new thing with something old and familiar. And the reason the combination facilitates the infant's comprehension of the new—whether it be a new toy, game, or even a new person—is that the presence of the known acts as a landmark, which makes it easier both intellectually and emotionally for a baby to orient himself to the new.

A case in point is the way the combination of new and old gently nudge a child toward cognitive insights. In form, a baby's mental breakthroughs are no different than ours. They occur when he finds an unexpected connection between two seemingly diverse things—usually one of them new, the other old. This is how Einstein arrived at the theory of relativity, how Newton came upon the laws of gravity, and how, one day, the infant realizes that this new ball and the old block in his toy box belong to the same larger class of objects called toys. This represents an important cognitive leap because it means the child is now doing what adults do: thinking in abstract categories. And one way to facilitate this intellectual expansion is by taking care to ensure that the new ball you offer him is the same bright yellow as his old friend, the block. Or to take another example, a baby will see the link sooner between the dog he met this afternoon on a stroll and the toy dog in his room if on arriving home the toy version is presented to him, along with appropriate bowwows, as a fresh reminder of his earlier encounter.

Emotionally, this gradualism of the baby's can also be used to assuage his normal anxiety in the presence of the unfamiliar, particularly unfamiliar faces. One of the things that often baffles parents is the infant's seemingly whimsical responses to strangers. If he seems almost arbitrarily to like some of the new faces he meets and dislike others, it's because his gradualism applies to people as well as things. In this case, the familiar is represented by his parents. The closer a new visitor comes to sharing their general gestalt—that is, their general physical and emotional demeanor—the quicker the infant will feel comfortable with him or her. Conversely, the more dissimilar the new visitor is from the parent, the more anxiety an infant is likely to feel in his or her presence.

This has important implications for the way a baby should be introduced to strangers. If a friend or relative shares your— or your spouse's—general physical and emotional set, usually the baby won't require an elaborate introduction. As long as you remain nearby, he won't even mind being picked up and cuddled by the new person. If, however, this new visitor is notably shorter or taller, younger or older, darker or lighter, or if he is bearded and Daddy isn't, then you should make the introduction with great care. One technique that helps is giving the new face a familiar object, such as a favorite toy, to make as an offering to the baby; also, throughout their meeting you should remain close-by in the child's visual field. Another way to put the infant at ease is to let him see you chatting warmly with the new face.

## FIFTH STRATEGY

### Know when the environment is behaving unpredictably
Two examples:

- A mother walks into the baby's room expecting to get her usual "Good morning, Mommy" smile. But as she approaches the crib, she sees that something is wrong. The baby is behaving very fussy and cranky. Thinking a bottle will soothe him, she offers him one only to find that her offering produces a wail of seemingly inconsolable tears. Why?

- Getting the baby's blocks out, she finds herself thinking about his latest triumph: For the first time, yesterday afternoon he managed to pile one block on top of another. Yet later, when the two of them are seated on the living-room floor (she is happily anticipating a repeat of yesterday's success), baby looks at the blocks piled up neatly between the two of them as if he were utterly dumbfounded by them. Again, why?

In both cases, the answer is unpredictability. Within the confines of these familiar and otherwise reassuring scenes, something unpredictable has happened. And while it has escaped the parent's notice, the baby in each instance spotted it. The telltale sign is their regression (and, in their different ways, both infants in these examples regressed). This is the baby's most common reaction to an unpredictable event, and it occurs because the startlingly unexpected disturbs his still tenuous sense of emotional equilibrium. Not surprisingly, this vulnerability gives a child a much sharper eye for unpredictable elements in his environment. This is why instances of inexplicable regression should be a cue to you to examine your own behavior and immediate environment for sources of the unpredictability. Often, they can be quite subtle.

A case in point is the first example I described. The reason the mother didn't receive her usual bright "Good morning" was that she hadn't been wearing her own good-morning smile. Feeling a bit rushed she had walked into the baby's room looking preoccupied, which had the unhappy effect of disproving the infant's first prediction of the day: that his mother would greet him with a smile as she did every other morning. His crankiness and fussiness were attempts to reproduce the reassuring and comforting figure he was used to waking up to.

In the second case (the infant with the blocks), the source of unpredictability was not the parent, but the general environment: the siren of a passing police car which unsettled the baby. And while it is among the disruptions you can't control, there are—as we've seen—many other disturbing environmental noises you can do something about.

## SIXTH STRATEGY

### Always make the baby a winner

Since no one can win all the time, some parents worry that this principle may foster an unrealistic prediction. They're afraid the baby will expect to succeed no matter what he attempts. And as one concerned mother objected to me: "Isn't that going to make my child's disappointment all the sharper when he does fail at something?" Paradoxical as it may seem, no; winning has just the opposite effect. Early success produces positive predictions in the infant, which is why a baby who is helped to win will, as a child and perhaps even as an adult, not only be more likely to display a more robust sense of self, but will also show a greater resiliency in rebounding from defeats and disappointments.

Nurturing a winning attitude, moreover, doesn't mean resorting to artifice; you can do it naturally. Say you and your four-month-old are about to play a game of Retrieve the Block. At its start, make sure you place the block within easy arm's reach (once he's crawling he will enjoy the challenge of scampering after an object placed beyond his reach). Since for a sixteen-week-old, hand-eye coordination still isn't an altogether reliable skill, this isn't quite the giveaway it may sound. In fact, in his first few passes at the block, the child will probably fail. If he does, don't criticize him. Not that you would deliberately, of course, but while watching a baby struggle with what to us is a simple task, it's easy to unthinkingly blurt out: "No, no, honey, not that way." Meanings may elude him, but an infant can tell from a delighted "Hey, great, you almost got it" that he is halfway toward mastering a task; just as he can tell from an exasperated "No, you did it wrong" that he has a long, long way to go.

With a little imagination, other, more subtle forms of winning also can be made into a predictable part of the baby's day. I say "more subtle" because an infant doesn't have our narrow adult view of winning as only a task successfully completed. For him, a win is anything with a happy outcome. Even the removal of soap from his eyes or the retrieval of a dropped toy can be made to seem like a win, given the right strategy.

In the case of soap in the eyes, for example, a win involves avoiding the immediate impulse to whisk the baby out of the tub and begin toweling him. A better strategy is to towel him in the tub, restore his calm, and then put some more soap on the cloth (let him see you do this) and gently wash his face again, taking care not to get any more soap in his eyes and letting him help with the washing. The happy outcome this produces adds up to two important kinds of winning: (1) It leads the baby to make a happy prediction about people: With a responsive partner, even extreme circumstances can be made to have a satisfying outcome; and (2) it forestalls the possibility that a painful encounter with soap will become the basis of a future aversion to bathing.

The goal of retrieving a toy has the same general aim: It shows that when things disappear, they can be made to reappear; and in an infant's terms that represents a very happy outcome, indeed. At the same time, it also provides an answer to an important question. Since deliberately dropping an object is one of the ways an infant asks "Is my caretaker predictable?," picking it up again is a way of answering that question positively.

## SEVENTH STRATEGY

### Always (at least temporarily) go where the baby goes

One question I'm often asked is: "What do I do when my infant suddenly decides to play peekaboo in the middle of a meal?'' Or what do you do when he engages in one of the alterations of this ploy, like turning his bedtime hour into a game of Catch Me If You Can? Is it better to go with him even if that risks stimulating him to the point where the task itself becomes a distraction, or should you impose your will? Involved in this dilemma are some very real practical issues bearing on elements like discipline and scheduling. But even more important are the psychological issues the dilemma raises, since by interrupting a meal, crawling away, or otherwise punctuating a planned event with an unplanned diversion, the baby also is asking questions of his own—that have great bearing on the environment's perceived trustworthiness: ''How far are you willing to go with me? Can I vary my routines, or am I rigidly bound by them? If I have an idea for something to do, can I demonstrate it to you?''

Not that this query is posed so directly or formally. Nor are the child's diversions themselves necessarily deliberate attempts to probe his surrounding reliability. But, intended or not, that is the effect they have, since one of the ways the environment establishes its reliability (or lack thereof) is by demonstrating its willingness to predictably go where the baby goes. Before you throw your hands up in exasperation at the thought of all those missed meals and nap times, let me quickly add that this doesn't mean that in order to demonstrate your bona fides as a trustworthy figure you should abandon a meal or appointed bedtime hour at the child's merest whim. But what it does mean is that you should join the baby in his diversion for four or five minutes, and then gently begin redirecting his attention back to the meal, bedtime, or other matter at hand. If this happens to be going to bed, stroking of his arms and legs will soothe him; if it's a meal, then pick up the spoon to suggest what you have in mind.

I think you will find that over and above its psychological benefits, this strategy also has some immediate practical advantages in the form of better preparing the baby to sleep or eat. Most of his interruptions aren't gratuitous. If he disrupts a meal, it's usually because his hunger isn't great enough yet to focus his attention on eating. Playing an eye or hand game is not only a much better way of passing the time than scolding until his appetite sharpens, it will also contribute to that sharpening.

"All that is well and good, Dr. Sanger, but life would still be a lot easier if Jennifer didn't use my good-night kisses as an excuse for a round of fun and games." I suspect the father who made this complaint was voicing the majority view on infant disruptions. Life would indeed be a lot simpler without them, but, of course, it also would be a lot duller. You can reduce their incidence to a manageable level, though, by being aware of which of your behaviors have unwittingly become cues for the baby. This happens when your constant repetition of a thing or activity produces an expectation in an infant's mind. For example, the reason this father's presence at cribside had a rousing rather than soothing effect is that over the months he had transformed himself into a play cue for his daughter. Even being in her darkened room bending over to give her a gentle good-night kiss immediately made Jennifer think: "Oh good, Daddy's here, it's playtime."

One way to soften such cues is to alter the association the baby has developed. In this case, for instance, I recommended that the father become more involved in nurturing tasks, such as bathing, feeding, and changing, so Jennifer would also come to see him as a nurturing figure as well as a "play pal." Other parental behaviors, which through their predictable repetition often become cues for a baby, are facial expressions (they, too, frequently become play signals) and carrying of his clothing ("Oh, no, she's got the snowsuit, we must be going out again").

# FIVE
# The Uses of Quiet

nother videotape we will
ask you to watch with your imagination:

## Two scenes of Michelle

*Scene One:*
As the first scene opens you will be able to see why Michelle
Caine's precocious good looks have caused such a stir even
among our staff. Already in her bold, dark eyes and well-
formed features you can catch a glimpse of the beauty that
one day will shine through in a child's, and then an adult's,
face. When the camera moves back a bit, you also will be
able to see that sitting directly across from her is a young
woman. Her name is Ann; she is one of my graduate students.
I have asked her to serve as Michelle's partner today as part
of an experiment designed to demonstrate the different ways
parental quiet—in the form of a quiet face—and parental stimulation influence a baby's ability to open an interaction.

Ann has been designated our stimulating parent. Beforehand
she was told to try to encourage Michelle to make a bid in
any way that feels natural to her. And so for the next four
minutes Ann sings, gently prods Michelle with questions, and
offers her one of the dolls lying nearby. She rocks her own

body back and forth. On several occasions, these sights and sounds bring Michelle's eyes to Ann's face, but never does Ann succeed in producing the firm eye lock which infants use to signal their interest in opening an exchange. Nor can this reticence to lock gazes be attributed to Michelle's stranger anxiety; at fifteen weeks she is still too young to experience this fear.

*Scene Two:*

This scene was made a few minutes later, and as it opens I can be seen stepping over Benny, one of our Cabbage Patch dolls, to replace Ann as Michelle's partner. The sudden sneeze Michelle emits as her eyes follow Ann to the door indicates the change has upset her. (Sneezing can be a sign of minor stress in infants.) So when Michelle's eyes move back to me, as part of my role as the quiet parent I offer her a soft hello, but deliberately do nothing else with my voice or face, which is formed into a warm, inviting, but quiet expression. At first this stillness of mine makes no impression on Michelle. But within less than a minute you can feel the atmosphere between us begin to change, even through the tape.

At this point, Michelle starts to hide her face from me by turning away, as the camera tracking her from a wall position shows, but there is nothing negative in the gesture. The visible widening of her eyes in the turn indicates that she is carefully tracking my quiet and is becoming increasing intrigued by it. The momentary averting of her head is simply intended to give her a few seconds to ponder its meaning. And, indeed, as she turns back to me, a new crispness and alertness is visible in her posture, and her eyes, now twinkling brightly, lock firmly with mine.

"You can almost hear her ask, 'What would you like to do next, Dr. Sanger?'" said Michelle's father, Peter, as he watched his daughter's image flicker across the TV monitor. Sitting next to him, her mother, Diane (the source of Michelle's good looks), signaled her agreement with a laugh. No other issue so concerns our parents, and parents generally, as that of stimulation and its role in the baby's growth. I had made this tape for Peter and Diane because I wanted to illustrate one of the several new ways research has taught us to think about how interactive sight, sound, and movement levels influence an infant.

Taken together, this work represents a major revision of the current, popular view of stimulation. No, this doesn't mean that what mothers and fathers have been told about stimulation's importance for the past twenty years is wrong. An exciting and imaginative use of parental sight and sound is a key element in cognitive growth. But new studies show that *as* important to that growth is parental *quiet*. A case in point is how a quiet face, like the one I used with Michelle, enhances a baby's willingness *and* desire to open an exchange.

In selecting this situation as the subject of our demonstration to the Caines of why less is often more in the case of stimulation, I had two points in mind. First, I wanted to illustrate how, by creating the right interactive atmosphere, quiet enhances a baby's ability to seize the initiative—to make things happen with all the important consequences that has. And second, I wanted to dramatize for them the results of a recent study by Dr. Kenneth Kaye of the University of Chicago. Using an experimental situation somewhat similar to the one Ann and I employed with Michelle, Dr. Kaye produced a similar result, except that his findings were even more dramatic. He reports that his test mothers were much more likely to catch their babies' attention with a still, quite face than with a smile or other form of facial stimulation. As I explained to Peter and Diane, one of the reasons the quiet mothers received so much flattering attention is that the appearance of momentary quiet on a usually mobile parental face has a dramatic eye-catching quality for an infant. Examining my expression on the tape, you can almost hear Michelle thinking, "Hmmmmm, how intriguing." The other even more important reason why quiet proved to be such an eye-catcher in Dr. Kaye's study is that while sound and movement often wall off a parent, quiet makes them accessible to the infant. A quiet, receptive face is like leaving a light in the window, which tells the baby, "I'm home."

Another important index of an interaction's nurturing quality is the amount of time a baby spends looking at a parent.

When an exchange's atmosphere fits—that is, when it allows a child to maintain his equilibrium comfortably and to follow the drift of things—he will spend a great deal of time looking at his partner. Michelle's failure to engage in this kind of sustained gazing was one of the concerns that had brought Peter and Diane to the center. So during our talks I also told them about a recent study by Dr. Tiffany Field, which examined how interactive sound levels influenced this kind of infant looking.

Dr. Field came up with two major findings. The first is that even slight increases in parental stimulation create a ripple effect much like that created by a stone tossed in the water. Thus, when her test mothers increased their normal interactive stimulation by *less than 10 percent,* the amount of time their babies spent looking at them dropped by *nearly 30 percent.* The test's next phase—a *drop* in normal interactive stimulations by *nearly 30 percent*—also produced a dramatic shift, but in a much more positive direction. Suddenly, Dr. Field's test mothers found themselves the subjects of *much more sustained looking* by their infants. While this result may seem paradoxical, there are two simple reasons for it. The first is that lower levels of sight, sound, and movement add spaciousness to an interaction. Against such a backdrop, the sights and sounds a parent makes stand out in sharper relief, the way a picture does against an uncluttered wall. The second reason is that the interactive atmosphere created by quiet fosters the baby's ability to concentrate. In many ways, the effect is the same as running a videotape in slow motion. Just as that slowing down allows a researcher to focus more easily on the individual movements he wants to study, your quiet makes it easier for the baby to focus on what you are doing.

At the center, we call the technique Dr. Field used in her test—lowering the stimulation level—*interactive quiet.* And, along with a number of other investigators, we have found an association between it and an enhancement of a baby's sense of personal competence, and also an increase in his parental gazing time. And as we shall see later in this chapter, along with other researchers, we have also found that parental quiet in another form—one we call *open spaces*—plays at least an equally important role in the developmental cycle. It is a key element in nurturing to life an infant's sense of self.

## How to Create Interactive Quiet

One of the most exciting aspects of the new work on stimulation is that, while illuminating the importance of interactive quiet, it also has alerted us to the more subtle patterns of overstimulation, which can interfere with quiet. Often, these patterns can disrupt a baby's behavior in the small but significant ways parents find hard to define—even to themselves. Thus, beyond the feeling that Michelle didn't seem as focused as some of their friends' three-month-olds, at our first meeting Peter and Diane confessed they weren't quite sure why they had asked their pediatrician to arrange an appointment with me.

Reviewing the exchange we taped after this meeting, I could see that while Peter and Diane were the thoughtful, sensitive parents they had seemed to be during our talk, I could also see that their concern about Michelle was not unfounded. In the interaction her behavior did appear to be unfocused, though not in a way that would suggest a physiological problem. Naturally bright and quick, she was fully capable of maintaining her alertness and interest. If she didn't give much sign of either quality in this interaction, it was because, unwittingly, Peter and Diane were setting the stimulation level several decibels too high. And this was interfering so much with Michelle's ability to focus, that in three different ways she was asking them: "Please, Mommy and Daddy, I need more quiet."

One way was by her *pattern of head turns.* Though these are (as we've seen) a normal part of an infant's behavior, when their incidence *increases,* as Michelle's did, over the course of an exchange, the baby is saying that she is beginning to find the sight and sound levels overwhelming. A second way he expresses his discomfort and displeasure at the stimulation level is through his *coughing, sneezing, and hiccuping.* Each can be a sign of minor stress in a young infant, and on the tape, Michelle could be seen and heard doing all three. Even *her body posture and tone* suggested discomfort, her third signal to her parents. Only at three or four points did her body assume the firm, taut posture that suggests an alert, interested baby. For most of the exchange, whether sitting in the infant seat or propped on Peter's lap, her head remained limply slouched on her chest and her arms and legs moved in a lethargic, uncoordinated fashion.

The most significant thing about Peter and Diane's behavior on the tape is that nothing they did could be called overtly stimulating. We find this pattern common. Recent research has made parents acutely conscious of the baby's limited tolerance to sights, sounds, and movements. So they are aware of the need not to raise their voices too high or move too quickly in exchanges. At the same time, the current emphasis on stimulation and the amount of parental anxiety it has created has led to a new, more subtle form of overstimulation. Often, mothers and fathers will get out in front of the infant to try to push and pull him faster and further than he is able or willing to go. This is what Peter and Diane were doing.

One example of *how* they did this was the *amount and kind of language* Diane used. Her long, complex sentences, while always spoken in a low, gentle voice, had none of the musicality or rhythmicity which makes the human voice so alluring to a baby. These, of course, are characteristics of baby talk, and though Diane's intention in eschewing it for more "adult conversation" was to try to stretch Michelle a bit, as the tape shows, her complex language had the opposite effect. It only succeeded in confusing her daughter; this is one of the reasons why Michelle's eyes kept sliding away from her mother's face.

Like most fathers, Peter served as the major source of zestiness and excitement in the exchange. But Michelle wasn't as responsive to his enthusiasm as he or she would like her to have been because Peter almost never used her emotional level as a starting point for any of the interchanges. An example is the way Peter presented her with a teething ring. The great flourish of excitement he displayed in introducing it is akin to a sudden, strong gust of wind. This is why Michelle turned away. Instinctively she knew that if she tried to meet this burst of enthusiasm head on, it would topple her. She could, however, have responded as Peter wanted if he had presented the teething ring in a low, soft voice, then slowly increased his enthusiasm as he talked about it. This would have had the effect of placing him at Michelle's—and every baby's—natural starting point of quiet. Together, father and daughter then could have built up to a zesty interchange about the ring. But without the opportunity to process her father's enthusiasm, Michelle had to turn away in self-protection.

At this point in the exchange, Diane displayed what my analysis may obscure, but what would be apparent the moment you met her: her deep and very palpable regard for her daughter. Earlier, Michelle had spilled baby food on Diane's dress, and just as Michelle began exploring the teething ring, Ann entered the studio from a side door with a box of tissues for the soil mark on the dress. Afraid that the intrusion would break her daughter's concentration on the ring, however, Diane silently shook her head "no," and Ann quietly retreated back through the studio door.

Like every mother, Diane loves and wants to help her baby. It is just that sometimes she isn't sure of how. A third example of this is the way she and Peter don't allow Michelle to take full advantage of her innate stress-coping mechanisms, which babies use to deflect the impact of environmental stimulation. These regulators include not only head turns and blinking, but also *smiles*. A child's heart-stopping grins are one of the early ways he ventilates tension. And while Peter's and Diane's impulse to build each of Michelle's smiles into laughter is understandable, it also has the effect of depriving her of an important tension release. So Michelle falls back on two more familiar ones—fussiness and crankiness.

Large and bearded, Peter looked very much the way I imagine a worried bear might look as he listened to my analysis of the interaction. Next to him, Diane's face was knotted into an expression of concern. "And we have tried so hard with Michelle," she said softly as I finished speaking. I told her that I understood and shared her and Peter's concern, but I added that they had to keep what I'd just said in perspective. "Getting to know your baby's tastes and tolerances—really, getting to know who she is as a person—takes time," I declared.

"The tape simply shows that you, Michelle, and Peter, are still in the normal period of adjustment which every new family goes through.

"Even without our help, eventually I'm sure the three of you would arrive at the right tone for your interactions. Given the way both of you feel about Michelle, that would have to happen. Our goal is just to make that happen sooner. And more important, it will eliminate the stumbling blocks that are interfering with the desire all three of you have to be closer to one another."

Over the next month, I had several other opportunities to talk to the Caines, since they and Michelle returned to the center a half dozen times for taping sessions. And while the program of interactive quiet that arose out of their visits was tailored to Michelle's individual needs and tolerances, the three general principles that underlie the program are ones that can be used by every family to improve the pacing and increase the amount of nurturing quiet in their exchanges. The three principles are:

1) *Echo the baby.*

Of all the natural growth-promoting behaviors a parent possesses, none is more important or versatile than echoing. One example of how it benefits a child can be seen in the emotional and learning changes that occur when you begin to echo his interactive pace. This is what Dr. Field had her study mothers do, and it also is what we had ours do in the study of quiet I mentioned in the first section of the book. In both cases, participants were told to mimic their infants' noise, movement levels, and visual patterns; and, in both cases, the mimicking produced the same result: The mothers spontaneously shed unnecessary interactive behaviors.

Also, in both cases this reduction enhanced the quality of subsequent exchanges. One way was by making their babies feel more emotionally comfortable. With fewer sights and sounds filling up the interactive space, the children had more time to process the stimulation that was presented. Another way was by increasing the children's ability to learn. This is because the elimination of unnecessary stimulation enhances the effect of a second kind of echoing: contingent responsiveness. Seeing you echo his smiles, frowns, and vocalizations is how a baby learns that each of these behaviors has a symbolic meaning that can be used to convey messages to others. And with unnecessary distractions eliminated, he is quicker to see the connection between his behavioral initiatives and your echoes.

I think you can see why if you put yourself in the baby's position for a moment. Imagine trying to identify the behavior intended to echo you when your gurgle produces a stream of five or six fast-moving parental responses. Which is meant to be echoed: the rapid flash of eyebrows you see first, the arm wave you see immediately following it, the wiggling of fingers, the rolling of eyes, or, finally, the gurgle you see following those responses? You would probably have trouble deciding, especially if you were four months old and this string of parental behaviors flashed before your eyes in something under two seconds. But if the only response your gurgle produces is a parental gurgle, framed, perhaps, by some eye-rolling to add a touch of zip, the surrounding interactive quiet would make that parental gurgle stand out boldly, making it easy for you to identify it as your mother's or father's echo of you.

2) *Use quiet to frame excitement.*
It often strikes parents as paradoxical that quiet also can enhance the exciting zesty high points, which need to be a part of every family's interactions. But it does and there is a simple reason why. It has to do with the baby's homeostatic function. That is the term we've adopted from the physical sciences, and in its simplest sense, homeostasis means being in balance. This is the state the infant is in when he starts to engage the world alertly. From then on, each sight, sound, movement, and gesture coming to him from the environment temporarily disrupts this balance. In themselves, these momentary upsets can be beneficial. Since as the child discovers he has the ability to regain

his equilibrium after each upset, it becomes easier for him to maintain his balance in the face of an even larger upset next time.

The reason quiet facilitates this process and enhances the baby's excitement at the same time is that it gives him a chance to adjust after each upward ratchet in stimulation. Thus, having momentarily been startled by your soft hello, your starting quiet still gives him a chance to regain his equilibrium before the appearance of your smile, and that, in turn, is already processed by the time you blink to test his interest in an eye game. One result of interactive quiet, then, is that it permits an infant to follow comfortably if later in the exchange you should increase the stimulation level (provided you do it gradually). Over time, however, this approach also has the longer-term effect of building stress-stimulation coping skills, since the more stress a baby *has* successfully handled, the more he *can* handle. And aside from its practical value, this competency is one way a child can demonstrate his mastery to himself.

**3)**  *Eliminate distracting background noises.*
If there were ever a question about quiet being the natural state of the human infant, research has forever laid it to rest. In the first year, quiet is as much the baby's natural home as the womb was in the preceding nine months. What effect the recent invasion of radios, televisions, video recorders, and stereos are having on this home can now only be guessed at; their introduction into our lives is still too recent to allow for any sweeping or definitive statements. But I strongly suspect that this tidal wave of distractions is having a disruptive effect on the baby and the parent and on the system nature created to serve them. That system evolved and was meant to function in an environment where quiet defined the shape and rhythm of everyday life. And in parts of the third world, where this kind of life-enhancing quiet still prevails, parents and infants achieve a degree of attunement, which is beginning to seem increasingly unattainable to families in industrialized societies.

In saying this, I realize there is a danger of contributing to what I sometimes think is the overromanticization of family life in third-world countries. For infants as well as for their parents, life in the parts of rural Africa and Central America I have visited is hard, sometimes brutally so. Nonetheless, the memories of those trips that linger in my mind's eye—of the young Kenyan mother who was already so in synch with her seven-day-old that she could anticipate his urinations, and of the Honduran mother so alive to her baby's needs that in the week I visited with her and her husband (I was staying at a nearby guest-house), I never heard the infant cry—make me feel that modern technology has put families in advanced societies at risk of losing a precious natural resource: the almost telepathic sense of communication that an attuned parent and infant can achieve.

This is why at the center, a key part of our interactive-quiet program revolves around the elimination of disruptive and intrusive background noises. While I realize there is only so much a parent can do about the roar of a plane overhead or the startling clang of a passing fire engine, there is a great deal they can do in the home to create an environment that encourages and nurtures attuned communication. One example is the elimination of artificial noises, such as radios and TVs, when the baby is awake. I know that for some parents a limit on the use of these represents a real hardship, but the richness and satisfaction the resulting quiet adds to exchanges is out of all proportion to the sacrifice involved.

## Supportive Quiet

One of the most surprising uses of quiet that the Caines learned about during their visits to the center was how *supportive quiet* can be used to help a baby maintain an *open space*. "What is an open space?" asked Diane. I repeated the words for her and explained that these intervals were first identified several years ago by Dr. Louis Sander of the University of Colorado.

More recent work, I added, indicates that these spaces are where the baby experiences his first moments of what we would call alert aloneness.

Typically, they begin appearing sometime between the third and sixth week, as the infant's growing homeostatic control allows him to turn his gaze inward on himself. Now, for the first time, he notices things he was too distracted or preoccupied to notice before. And out of these moments of self-scrutiny arise a series of epiphanies that are rich in implications for the shaping and growth of the child's future personality.

As he looks around, for example, for the first time the infant becomes aware that he has preferences—that he likes looking at the red block more than the pale-yellow teething ring, and that he prefers being propped up in his infant seat to being propped up in the crib. And in such realizations lie the origins of what we would call personal tastes.

The discovery that feelings can be generated from *inside* as well as from *outside* also is made in these intervals of quiet. Up until now, the baby has functioned largely as a reactor whose emotions are produced by outside events, such as Mother's picking him up and rocking him and Daddy's stroking him. Now, with the world placed safely at a distance, he starts to notice that such sensations as comfort or discomfort can also arise from within him. Thus, the baby takes his first step toward realizing the Platonic admonition "Know thyself."

Dr. Sander calls the self-scrutiny that goes on in open spaces the beginning of a baby's interior life. I would agree, but I would add one important corollary. In order to use these intervals as the starting point of a rich and complex interior life, a baby has to learn how to be alone with himself comfortably. And that is the purpose of supportive quiet. It involves nothing more complicated than hovering protectively in the background while the baby is in an open space, and by making sure that intrusions, such as background noises, aren't allowed to disrupt his contemplation.

While some parents find it hard to understand why you wouldn't want to talk to or play with or otherwise try to engage a visibly alert child, as he slips into an open space a baby is in the paradoxical position of wanting, yet not wanting, to be alone. He wants to have a trusted figure nearby for reassurance, but he also wants to be left undisturbed. And the advantage of supportive quiet is that it allows a parent to fulfill both roles unobtrusively.

How do you recognize the signs of an impending open space? One indication is the baby's gaze. As he enters a space, generally the infant's eyes have an alert, distant look. Another important indicator is time. Usually, a child is most anxious to have a quiet moment alone with himself after feedings and particularly energetic interactions.

When it is encouraged and supported, you will find that the skill for comfortable aloneness shaped in these intervals begins to make a palpable difference in the baby's behavior. A case in point is the relationship between being alone and an infant's ability to sleep through the night. In a recent study, Dr. Isabel Paret of Stanford University found that the most important difference between a group of nine-month-olds labeled sound sleepers and another group labeled frequent wakers wasn't so much their incidence of waking during the night, but rather that the sound sleepers were able to be alone with themselves comfortably. Content with their own company on waking, they didn't need to call for someone (a sleepy mother or father) to amuse them, keep them company, or help them fall back to sleep; they could do all this by themselves. Lacking this skill, the frequent wakers did need parental support and help, which is why each of their night wakings roused the entire household.

A skill for aloneness nurtured in open spaces may influence long-term development. Dr. D. W. Winnicott of the University of London has suggested that the ability to enjoy a rich and satisfying interior life protects a child later against what he calls "a false life built on a reaction to external stimulation."

"We've already seen so many positive changes in Michelle," I told the Caines, "I think the two of you have every reason to be optimistic about her future." One of those changes, which had been proudly announced to me one morning three weeks earlier by Peter, was an alteration in Michelle's sleeping habits.

Just after entering her seventh month (and six weeks after her parents had been shown how to use supporting quiet), Michelle's incidence of wakings had dropped from an average of three or four to one or two episodes per night.

The tapes we had been using to monitor her interactive behaviors also contained gratifying evidence of change. With Peter's and Diane's stimulation levels lower, Michelle was taking the initiative more often in opening exchanges. The amount of time she spent gazing at them also increased, as did her number of vocalizations. The most important evidence of improvement contained on the tapes, however, was the near-perfect match that interactive quiet had produced in Michelle's and Diane's *pause times.*

In a system full of unexpected elegances of symmetry, these pause times easily qualify as the most surprising. Quite spontaneously, in an attuned exchange, a baby and parent automatically pause nearly the exact length of time before a vocalization, movement, or gesture. Neither partner is aware of this synchrony; it just happens naturally—a reflection of the emotional attunement they share. For that reason, pause times make a very accurate barometer of the extent of an exchange's nurturing quality. And while there was very little evidence of such symmetry in the first exchange we had taped of the Caines, in the last, made four months later, Diane and Michelle moved across our monitor like two exquisitely tuned dancers who had so internalized one another's moves and pacing that, at times, watching them was like watching two extensions of the same spirit.

Some of the other uses of quiet that Peter, Diane, and Michelle were introduced to during their visits to us are listed below.

## Quiet is a way of changing the tone and direction of an interaction

One of quiet's most valuable uses is as a throttle or regulator that can subtly change the course of an interaction that is moving in the wrong direction. This happens occasionally because exchanges have a way of generating their own momentum. A case in point is the satisfying playtime that suddenly has escalated the baby's excitement to a flashpoint of overstimulation, or the shared smile that has built into semi-hysterical laughter. Or, alternately, the interaction that has achieved a perfect pitch, but a feeding time lies immediately ahead and you don't know how to break for it.

In each of these, and other, cases, where you want to move the exchange in a new direction, your best strategy is to quiet your behavior slowly by lowering your voice and reducing your body and facial movements. In most cases, the baby will happily follow suit, and the island of interactive quiet the two of you thereby create gives each of you an opportunity to regroup emotionally, and to draw up a plan for the next phase of your encounter. If, for example, the peekaboo game you were playing was too arousing, you might want to restart the action with a soothing, simpler game, like blinking. Or you might let the infant suggest a new activity. As a regular aspect of exchanges, these intervals can become like the neutral position on a car's gear shift—a place where you and your baby automatically return to when you want to change directions.

### Quiet is a way of saying to the baby: "I'm sorry"

Why would a parent want to say such a thing? Because we are all fallible and that fallibility means that sometimes, however unintentionally, we do or say things that upset an infant. It may be by using too much language, or by moving a favorite toy out of reach (and since a baby can't tell you directly about his likes and dislikes, this is easy to do), or by putting his seat in the wrong place (like you, he has places in the room where he prefers to sit), or by one of many inadvertent missteps which may leave the baby feeling in need of an extra-special reassurance.

A sharp, emphatic, and long head turn is his way of expressing deep distress at a parental behavior. And while on these occasions your natural inclination would be to rush into the turn and try to reassure him, the best response you can offer is to respect your child's need to ventilate his distress and anger (yes, babies do get angry) by remaining outside the turn—that is, by not intruding—and by quieting your behavior. Some videotapes we made of families in this situation illustrate quiet's healing power. In the tapes, when a parent is still, you can almost feel a regenerative atmosphere emerging. The babies respond to the quiet (and the parents were told to do nothing until the child signaled he was willing to resume the exchange by turning back and facing them) almost as if their mothers or fathers had just whispered: "I'm not sure what happened, but I'm sorry it upset you. I'll wait until you are ready for us to try again."

## Quiet is a way of expanding your vocabulary of activities with the baby

One of the most precious resources a parent can possess is a knowledge of the games and activities that have a special soothing or calming effect on the baby. With it, a mother or father has a palpable way of demonstrating their love (they show the infant *they know* him by knowing what pleases him) as well as an effective but subtle means of keeping tears and crankiness in check. The role interactive quiet plays in this process is that it enhances his confidence in others while also creating an atmosphere conducive to infant decision making, by allowing him to exit from quiet on his own initiative.

No, the baby doesn't consciously decide his likes the way you or I do. Until about the sixth month, his preferences are shaped more by physiological factors, and these factors continue to have a significant influence on his likes and dislikes throughout the first year. The gentle pressure of your fingers on the infant, for example, produces a pleasant sensation, so he develops a fondness for finger games. Where the baby does resemble us, though, is in his need for some quiet to identify his feelings about the games and activities he is offered. If an adult has trouble forming impressions about new data when there are a half dozen distractions present, imagine the effect distractions have on an infant's decision-making powers.

Interactive quiet also gives a parent time to notice the baby's responses to the sights, sounds, games, and activities he's offered. It's through such observation that a mother or father is able to compile a list of the special activities that can soothe, comfort, and entertain the child when he is in need of special comforting or wants a special kind of excitement.

## Quiet can be used to stretch an open space

While a mother's or father's role in the open-space phenomenon is largely supportive, they can help stretch some of these
intervals. I say "some" because of the four points in the day
when spaces most often occur, three—after playtimes, during
feedings, and before naps—don't lend themselves to active intervention, though the fourth, waking—either in the morning
or after a nap—does. On these occasions, if the baby is wearing
a preoccupied look when you enter the room, just whisper a
gentle "hello" and sit down near the crib (make sure you
remain in his visual field). If this produces immediate crying,
you might pick him up and cuddle him. But if the baby seems
content just knowing you are there, wait until he summons
you, which he will at the space's conclusion. Not every child
wants or can tolerate these parental pauses, but we find that
those who can will, within a week or so, acquire the ability
to inhabit an open space for an extra few minutes.

## Your quiet can be a way of (gently) telling others how you want them to behave with the baby

This particular point has a very personal meaning to me since
one of the most trying aspects of my own experience as a
young parent was the greetings I saw offered to my infant
son, Terry. Twenty years ago, of course, quiet and its role in
the baby's growth cycle remained unexplored, but I didn't
need a developmental text to tell me how upset little Terry
was by the big, loud hellos and How are yous he received.
All I had to do was look at him. His eyes would go blank
and his body tighten, as if in self-defense. Nor was Terry's
response due to a hypersensitivity. For the first six months,
big, booming greetings upset all babies because their nervous
systems aren't mature enough to comfortably process the large
chunks of audio and visual stimulation such a greeting represents.

What should you do, then, when a favorite uncle, aunt, or
close friend offers an all-stops-pulled-out hello to the baby?
It presents a rather ticklish social problem because you don't
want to risk offending the friend or relative, but at the same

time you also don't want your baby exposed to the stimulation overload such behavior represents. One solution, of course, is simply to tell the person to use a quieter greeting. But you may be able to avoid the awkwardness and hurt feeling that can accompany that admonition by doing what I did with Terry's visitors, which was to use my own behavior as an example of how I wanted them to greet him.

When I brought a friend or relative into his room to say hello, I would quiet my own behavior just an extra bit by lowering my voice a decibel more and slowing the speed of my gestures. Much to my surprise—and delight—I discovered that this technique was infectious. Without my having to say a word, often Terry's new guest would begin mimicking me. If you try it, I think you will find that this strategy will produce the same happy results for you and your baby.

# SIX
# Language Learning and
# Life Learning
## (Communication—
## Part One)

**T**hough it's still well before nine A.M., the humidity is so thick on this steamy July morning that from my office window I can see a thin layer of mist beginning to rise on the street. "I'll need a minute to freshen us both up," Amy announces brightly at my doorway, looking as if she and the slightly wilted four-month-old under her arm had just stepped out of a sauna rather than having just crossed Central Park on a morning in high summer. The four-month-old's name is Herschel, and already there is something distinctly scholarly about him. In part it is due to his large eyes, which seem to radiate with wisdom, and in part to what Amy and her husband, Steve, jokingly refer to as his Talmudic *gravitas*—a thoughtful, serious quality which recently earned Herschel the family nickname of "the little rabbi."

The reason I've asked mother and son to come to the center this morning is to take part in a taping session—the focal point of which is to be a game called Give and Take. As its name implies, the game involves the passing of an object back and forth. For Amy and Herschel, that object will be a bright yellow rattle. By comparing Herschel's performance of Give and Take on the tape we make today with his performance of it on two later tapes we plan to make—one when Herschel is in his eighth month, the other at the end of his twelfth month—we can quite literally chart his emergence as a social person. Therein lies the reason why, better than any other procedure I know, this simple game symbolizes how profoundly our ideas about language development in infancy have been altered by the introduction of the videotape camera.

After a decade of watching families closeup, laughing, playing, looking, listening, and sometimes even crying, we've come to realize that the baby's language learning is inextricably connected to his social learning. This isn't to say that the traditional view, which holds that acquisition of the spoken word is primarily a biological process that comes largely from *inside* the infant, is wrong, but rather incomplete. Babies do, indeed, as that view holds, possess a great many innate language capabilities. But recent video studies show that in order to shape those capabilities into true skills, a child *first* has *to understand the social rules and conventions* that govern human communication.

A case in point is the infant's ability to track, identify, and mimic the sounds people use. This capability is self-evidently important to language acquisition, since it's how a child creates a vocabulary. But a baby can't begin to bring it or any of his other language-related talents into play until he first has mastered the basics of human dialogue. These include how to play the speaker's and listener's roles in conversation, how to focus his mind on an object with another person for a conversation, and, most important of all, how to use his facial expressions, gestures, and movements to state his intentions to his partner. And since these are primarily *social* lessons, and because they are taught in exchanges during his first year, one effect of the new interactive research is that it has made us realize that the starting point for language acquisition isn't the moment when the baby utters his first identifiable word in the twelfth or thirteenth month, as we used to think, but the moment when he and his mother and father first lay eyes on one another in the hours after birth. (In Chapter Seven we will explore the implications of this discovery.)

Another important result of the new video research is that it shows that the smiles, frowns, gestures, movements, and looks that parents and babies exchange with one another form part of the complex interactive communication system that serves as the child's introduction to the concept of communication and the crucial role it plays in human life. Our new awareness of these elements and the important role mothers and fathers play in shaping them not only challenges the traditional biological view, which holds that parents play a largely passive role in language acquisition, it also means that by creating a "well-fitted" communication system a parent can help to hasten her baby's mastery of spoken language.

One way is by showing him how to shape his vocalizations and behaviors into turn-taking forms so that he can participate in two-sided dialogues. Another way is by illustrating how gazes, gestures, and signals can be used to focus his mind with another person's on a single topic, which is what we do in conversations. A third way is by introducing and showing the infant how to play with an object in a fashion that helps him remember the name of that object later, which is one of the ways a parent builds vocabulary in a preverbal child. A mother's or father's skill at melding and varying their own and their baby's vocalizations also is important since the magic a parent creates with sounds is a way of demonstrating to the baby the special grace the human voice lends to social companionship.

Of all the lessons about communication that mothers and fathers teach in the first twelve months, however, none is more important than *intentionality*. And the way they teach it is one of the sweetest discoveries to emerge from all the recent work on the parent-infant system. Above all, what breathes life, meaning, and purpose into an infant's behaviors are the fantasies and myths his parents create about him from pregnancy onward. We are learning that, like the wand waved over Cinderella, these paternal, but especially maternal, myths and dreams have a transforming power. Over time, the baby actively begins to try to match the image of himself he sees reflected in his mother's eye. It's this picture of his better self that inspires him to transform his random interactive behaviors gradually into something like purposeful dialogue behavior. By about the fifth or sixth month, his random gestures, movements, facial expressions, and, finally, his sounds come to be used to express his thoughts and feelings so that he can declare his unique vision to the world.

A recent Stanford University study illustrates the power of these myths dramatically. It found that the pregnant women who had the most positive fantasies about their unborn children were also the mothers who, a year later, had children who scored highest on indexes of intellectual achievement and emotional adjustment. You can see why these myths are such a life-giving force on the baby if we stop now and look at the first tape of Amy and Herschel playing Give and Take.

What makes the game itself such a good example of why a baby's social learning influences his language learning is that each player needs the same kinds of social skills to play Give and Take that he or she needs for a conversation. Give and Take requires, for example, a knowledge of turn-taking—you have to know when to give and when to take the rattle. It also necessitates an understanding of how to focus your mind on a single topic—the rattle—with another person. You also have to have an elemental grasp of empathy; otherwise you would take the rattle but not give it back. And, finally, it requires an ability to act intentionally. Each partner has to know how to tell the other he wishes to give or take the rattle.

As parents of young infants know, these skills are well beyond a sixteen-week-old. But so strong is the power of the myth Amy has constructed about her baby that she behaves on this tape as if Herschel were already an accomplished Give and Take player. One effect of this is that without thinking about it, Amy ends up playing both the giver and taker roles in the game. Mothers do this all the time in exchanges with young infants and, aside from keeping the action moving, this dual-role playing also serves the practical purpose of showing the baby the different parts people play in conversations. Another even more important effect of Amy's myth making is that, also without thinking about it, she treats *all* of Herschel's behaviors *as if* they had meaning. And despite his age, this fact registers in Herschel's mind.

Later, he won't remember the specifics of this exchange, such as the way Amy treats his randomly outstretched hand as if it were a request for the rattle, or the way she responds to his gurglings about the bright yellow object he is holding so precariously in his hand as if each contained an important piece of intelligence about the rattle. But what will stay with

Herschel long after the memories of this interaction have faded
is the image of himself as the effective, competent, intentional-
acting human being his mother is presenting to him. And because that is the person Herschel is preadapted to be, and
also because he loves Amy and wants to please her, Herschel
will gradually start to stretch himself into that image of his
better self which his mother is inspiring him with.

Amy's skill as a myth maker also is evident in the *lightness*
with which she holds her fantasies. The picture of the competent game player she reflects in this exchange is close enough
to the baby Herschel will be in a month or two so that her
image has the effect of stimulating and challenging him, rather
than overwhelming or daunting him. Which is how Herschel
would feel if the image he saw reflected in his mother's behavior
were that of an Olympic-class Give and Take player, or if
she were trying to force-feed him vocabulary lessons from a
flash card, or expecting him to master the workings of a Busy
Box.

Just as other parents who are accomplished myth makers,
Amy also is an unusually sensitive and patient teacher of such
individual communication-social skills as turn-taking. What
gives Herschel's behavior a semblance of a speaker's and listener's quality in this exchange isn't his innate understanding
of the form—he's too young to be able to translate this knowledge into action—but the delicate way Amy gathers up her
baby's behaviors and gently organizes them. Her tool is a
technique we call *back channels*. Completing the vocalization
during her turn, Amy sees that Herschel is still looking a bit
dreamy. So she emits a series of uhhuhs and yeahs. These
sounds have the effect of small talk in adult conversation. They
keep the action flowing until the other person—in this case,
Herschel—organizes himself sufficiently to take his turn with a
burst of activity. And indeed, as soon as Herschel starts to
babble, Amy immediately quiets.

At the beginning of the game, however, Amy does make
one small misstep. Instead of letting Herschel discover the
rattle in her hand on his own, she thrusts it toward him. In
other words, in a sense she makes the discovery for him. This
is an example of what's called *leading,* and it is best to avoid
it because the discoveries an infant makes himself are the ones

that contribute most to his sense of competence. "I can do things for myself," he thinks, and that not only makes him grateful to the person who has subtly shepherded him to this realization, but the discovery that he can do these things also encourages him to try to do other things for himself.

Amy, however, is very inventive and imaginative in the way she uses the rattle to give Herschel an opportunity to practice an important social-communication skill. She does this by talking about it in a melodic, ear-catching voice (and, significantly, Amy always refers to the rattle as "rattle" and never "it"), by waving it gently back and forth between her and Herschel, by rubbing it on Herschel's arms and tummy, and even by letting him lick it. Amy firmly, but gently, fastens her baby's attention on the rattle; which is to say, she gives Herschel a foretaste of what it is like to focus your mind on an object— or topic—with another person. And this is a skill that is essential not only to conversing with other people, but to getting along with them. Herschel will need it at three if he is to help a playmate build a sand castle and at thirty if he is to help his wife make dinner.

The other effect of the multimedia show Amy has put on with the rattle is that it gives Herschel several different kinds of knowledge of the rattle. He now knows not only how it looks, but also how it feels, sounds, and tastes, and those added bits of intelligence will help hasten the day when he can look at the rattle and *say* to Amy, "Rattle, Mommy."

Of all the inventive ways Amy has opened the world of communication to her baby in the exchange, none is more striking than her use of sound. By infusing her vocalizations with excitement, color, and energy, and by creating imaginative variations on Herschel's sounds (significantly, she *never* babbles when she initiates a line of dialogue, only when she is echoing Herschel's babbling), she demonstrates how the human voice can be used to illuminate and enrich social intercourse. At the same time, by focusing her talk on Herschel's *feelings* about the rattle and not on the rattle itself, Amy keeps the topic of conversation focused where a three-month-old wants it focused: on himself and his emotions, not on aspects of the environment he is still only dimly aware of. (In the next chapter we will examine the ways in which the content of baby talk must shift to keep up with the infant's cognitive growth.)

Looking unexpectedly rakish in an Irish fisherman's sweater and a pair of alarmingly red workman's boots, Herschel appears to be an altogether different baby on our second tape. It was made on a bitingly cold December day just a week after Herschel passed into his eighth month, which is one of the reasons why he appears so much more alert and interested on it. The other reason for the dramatic change is that Herschel has now come to resemble the competent, purposeful baby Amy was interacting with in her mind's eye on that steamy July morning. It is immediately apparent now, for example, that what Herschel is doing with his mother is playing a two-sided game. And it is also clear why Herschel's recently acquired social-communication skills, which make him a more skilled Give and Take player on this tape, are also laying the groundwork for his eventual mastery of the spoken word.

A key element in that mastery is an awareness that people communicate through *symbols*. That's what the words we speak to one another are. And though Herschel isn't yet aware of them, this tape shows he has grasped the more important general principle that symbols are the tools people use to express their thoughts and feelings. This means that when he does discover words, he will simply see them as a logical and natural extension of the communication symbols he already is using. On this tape those symbols are Herschel's smiles, frowns, and hand and leg movements. After months of watching Amy respond to each as if it had meaning, Herschel now has begun to use them *in order* to convey meaning. Also new on this tape is the comprehension he shows of his mother's gestures and movements.

As a result, the rattle doesn't have to be thrust into his hand the way it did on the first tape. Amy just has to present it in front of her. Herschel now recognizes that simple gesture as a signal that it is his turn to take the rattle. Indeed, on this tape Herschel is so alive to the notion that in this game he gets to take a turn that he hollers furiously when Amy pretends to deprive him of it, violating the game's rules by briefly holding the rattle out of reach.

Another sign that Herschel's interactive learning is preparing him for a smooth transition to spoken language is the ease with which Amy is able to get him to align his mind with hers. No longer does she have to work to bring his eye to the rattle or the Busy Box lying nearby. When, absentmindedly, her eye wanders toward the box, Herschel's immediately follows as if to say: "Hey, Mom, what's that?" Herschel's gurgling—or protolanguage—also indicates growth in his capacity to focus his mind with another person's. This is apparent from the look of bright anticipation on his face when he babbles about the rattle; now he expects his mother to reply with a vocalization of her own. You also may have noticed that there's been a subtle but important change in Amy's baby talk. On this tape, very little of her conversation is focused on Herschel's emotions, and a great deal on the rattle itself. As we shall see in the next chapter, this change reflects an important change in Herschel's thinking.

However, Amy does, in this interaction—as she had in the last one—make one small misstep. This time it occurs in the form of her response to the mirror I had just handed to Herschel. The sight of the dashing looking baby in it naturally makes him bubble. As he examines the image, Herschel coos and smiles delightedly as if to say: "So nice to meet you, what a splendid fellow you are!" Instead of letting him relish this encounter with himself, however, Amy intrudes. Peering over the top, then around the sides of the mirror, she announces several times in a loud voice, "Peekaboo," disrupting Herschel's concentration.

Overall, though, the exchange indicates that mother and son have between them created a very compatible fit—one which is advancing Herschel closer and closer to a grasp of the social rules that govern human communication. Indeed, the only conversation rule he *hasn't* entirely grasped yet is that two-way activities—whether they be games like Give and Take or conversations—require empathy; in order to get the rattle you have to give it away first. The evidence of this is Herschel's response when Amy signals she would like the rattle back by holding out her hand. Though Herschel clearly understands what she wants, from the way he clutches the rattle fiercely to his chest, it's equally clear that he doesn't have much empathy with his mother's desire. Watching from the observation booth, I could see that this reaction upset Amy, and after the taping she pulled me aside to ask me about it. While I told her Herschel's response was common for eight-month-olds, there was also another reason why I wasn't concerned about his behavior. Having become acquainted with the shimmering vision of Herschel in Amy's mind over the months, I had no doubt that one day very soon the empathy of this imaginary Herschel would begin to be reflected in the behavior of the child in our foyer who was now being bundled up in a snowsuit against the December cold.

The expanse of white that fills the screen for the first eight seconds of the third tape isn't a snowfield; it's the back of my white coat. When the technician gets the lens into focus, the back of my head also will be visible, as will the fact that I'm sitting on a rug in the studio. Sitting on my right is Amy, and on my left, now able to hold himself erect unaided, is Herschel, who will be thirteen months old in two days. No special expertise is needed to analyze this tape. Even a casual observer can tell that Amy and I are passing a yellow rattle back and forth between us while our avid audience of one— Herschel—watches raptly. What might escape that casual observer's attention, however, is the significance of what happens when after our third round of Give and Take, instead of handing the rattle back to me, suddenly Amy turns and offers it to Herschel, who without the slightest hesitation takes it, turns, and with great seriousness offers it to me.

Out of a system that has already taught Herschel so much about the social fundamentals of human communication, spoken language will emerge as naturally and gently as a burp. And, indeed, a few minutes before this tape was made, Amy proudly announced that Herschel had uttered his first word three days earlier. It was—of all things—*shoe.*

## Life Learning

Looking at Amy's and Herschel's tapes, I think it is possible to see why the video camera has made us aware of how the baby's language learning influences his life learning. In the largest sense this is because the meanings a child comes to attach to words like "happy," "sad," "awful," and "wonderful" at two, three, four, or five months reflect what he already has learned about the states those words represent in his exchanges at four, five, and six months. This is why the child who is encouraged to go right to the peak of excitement with his father at six months will view excitement as a positive emotion at six years, while the youngster who was held back from it will think about it in a more negative way later. The same is true for a state like happiness. If through their interactive looks, gestures, and attitudes a mother and father define that feeling as a natural, buoyant state other people help you sustain, that's how their three-year-old will come to understand happiness. But if his early interactions have taught him that happiness is a transient and not completely trustworthy state, resonances of that doubt will color even his most exuberant moods.

The other reason why language learning is so inextricably tied to life learning is that words and their interactive forerunners—expressions, movements, gestures, and vocalizations—are a mother's and father's principal means of demonstrating the human environment's attractiveness to a baby. This doesn't mean an infant has to be actively sold on people; he's already prewired to like them. But the smiles, frowns, and looks of sweet surprise, the happy hi's and hello's, and the triumphant Hey, you did it's that fill his eyes and ears during the first twelve months, as well as the smells and textures that come pouring in through his fingertips, nostrils, tastebuds, and even bottom, are like the elements of a wardrobe. When each item in this wardrobe is cut to fit the baby's tastes and the colors have an eye-catching appeal, over time they coalesce into a general impression of the human environment's allure. And its resonances will continue to reverberate down through the years, coloring how the child, and then the adult, feels about the people who populate that environment.

More specifically, the skills we've watched grow in Herschel over the months will not only help him "crack the code of spoken language," as Dr. Jerome Bruner puts it, each also will (as it does for every infant) have a visible spillover effect into other areas of his life functioning.

A notable case in point is what Herschel's interactions have taught him about intentionality. This is a core characteristic and, when it is nurtured as carefully as Amy and Steve have nurtured and supported it in Herschel, the effects will show up later in such traits as self-confidence and mastery. Indeed, some of its effects already are visible in Herschel's behavior. The baby we saw in that last exchange *knows* he is able to get things done by his communications.

Another case in point is the way Herschel first learns to align his mind in exchanges will influence his response later, at five, when his teacher asks him to line up with the other children for a fire drill, and at thirty-five, when his employer asks him to lead a special team project. To some extent, Herschel's ability to fit into and live by the rules that govern the roles he will be called on to fill later—whether they be that of son, friend, playmate, or spouse—also will be influenced by what he first learned about playing the speaker's and listener's roles in interactions.

In Herschel's case, my own anticipation is for nothing but good things in each of these areas; his exchanges with his parents have been that rich in meaningful communication. But at our center we also see children whose interactive learning experiences have been less nourishing than Herschel's. And this shows up not only in their difficulties in language mastery, but also in related behavioral problems. There is, for example, the disruptive two-and-a-half-year-old in one of our singing groups; she's beginning to learn now that the rules that govern a joint activity, such as singing, are there for *everyone* to follow, but this elementary lesson in cooperation could and should have been taught earlier through the agency of her interactions.

The same is true for the three-year-old who was brought in not long ago for special language counseling. The lessons he failed to learn about intentionality in his early interactions are showing up now, not only in his language problems, but in other areas of his personality as well. And this worries me greatly. Already he has developed a characteristic you see in certain very insecure adults—the ones who, from the moment they sit down in a room, look as if they expect to be asked to leave at any moment.

I think it's important to add that the connections between early language learning and social functioning that we see at the center are one which also have struck other observers as well. Talking about the long-term influence of turn-taking, for example, Dr. Kenneth Kaye of the University of Chicago notes that from this capacity "an infant develops the skills and expectancies that he will apply to other roles in which he becomes engaged in later, including interactions with other adults, with peers and eventually with teachers in school."

Though we have no direct evidence of early language learning's influence on adult-life function, there is a great deal of data to support the proposition that such learning casts a very long shadow indeed. A case in point is a story Dr. Sander tells. In the mid-1950s, while he was teaching at Boston University, he took part in one of the first long-term studies of interactive learning's influence on development. Dr. Sander's group didn't focus specifically on communication, but in examining each test family's general interactive system, as well as the role each participant—baby, mother, and father—carved out for himself within that system, the researchers had an opportunity to learn a great deal about the ways their parents and infants communicated with one another. In the late 1950s, this information was coded and stored away.

As planned, twenty-odd years later a new generation of investigators did a follow-up study among the families. By this point, the former babies were now young men and women and their parents in late middle age, so the new investigators were looking at the families at a more mature point in their cycles. Nonetheless, when the follow-up team consulted the original reports, not only did the descriptions in them turn out to be strikingly similar to the descriptions they had written after their own visits to the study families, what most impressed them was the large number of cases where *the original and follow-up reports used the exact same words* to describe a child's behavior *and* his or her interactive dynamics with a parent.

# SEVEN
# The Building Blocks of Communication
## (Communication—
## Part Two)

ne reason games like Give and Take and peekaboo have become such important tools in video studies over the past few years is that they make excellent vehicles for studying a family's interactive communication system. In the tapes we just watched, for example, Amy's and Herschel's game of Give and Take offered glimpses of all five of the building blocks—myth making, turn-taking, multimodal highlighting, baby talk (parents), and protolanguage (infants)—that parents and infants use to construct these systems. It was also possible to see how each element provided Herschel with a form of learning that one day will contribute to his mastery of spoken language. And it was very evident that each was already enriching his day-to-day exchanges with Steve and Amy.

What the camera didn't (and couldn't) show, however, is how Amy and Steve were able to create a system that served their baby in so many important ways. The reason is simple enough to understand—Amy and Steve built their system around their baby. This is why the end result was a system that fit Herschel very well.

Our experience at the center suggests that while other mothers and fathers also are very good at reading their baby's expectations, sometimes they have trouble translating their understanding into responses. So, in the discussion of the five building blocks of communications that follows, I've included some of the strategies we've developed to help parents fit these elements more closely to their baby's needs.

## Baby talk

One of the risks of putting an activity like baby talk in front of a camera is that the resulting scientific data may end up inhibiting or undermining an activity that is meant to be spontaneous, innocent, and even a little bit silly. Mothers and fathers, after all, are primed to talk whimsically to their babies, and babies are primed to love that whimsicality for a very good reason. Evolution has found such talk to be an efficient way to focus two minds of quite different experience, maturity, and educational levels on a single topic in a way that seems natural and comfortable to both. Which is to say one of the primary things you do when you slip into the hi's, how are ya's, hello's, and hey there's that constitute baby talk, is to establish a frame of reference with your baby. And it's through joint occupation of this frame that the two of you are brought closer together emotionally. At the same time, baby talk also creates a pool of mutual knowledge which allows each of you to know intuitively what the other is thinking and feeling. And since, in the final analysis, that is what true human communication—whether spoken or unspoken—is about, baby talk represents one of the most profound examples of the innate parental wisdom that is every mother's and father's most precious resource.

Do, however, some types of baby talk work better for an infant than others? Yes and no. No in the sense that whether it's spoken in French, Italian, Eipo (a New Guinean language), English, Japanese, or Finnish, baby talk's constituent elements are always the same. Spanish mothers and fathers as well as Nigerian ones spontaneously slow their talk, drop their voice pitch, and exaggerate their words. And yes in the sense that the degree to which baby talk fulfills the roles it was meant to serve does, to some extent, depend on the skill of the individual parent using it.

Thus, the parents who confine their baby talk to short, crisp, clear, engaging words, and repeat them over and over and over again in a musical fashion (a baby can easily tolerate a repetition rate of 60 percent to 70 percent in conversations without being bored) make it easier for the child to track and identify the sounds which parental voices make. And this is one of the ways an infant begins to mark out and remember the sounds that one day will become part of his spoken vocabulary.

Another way a parent can use baby talk to hasten vocabulary building is by getting the ratio of sense to nonsense words right. It's important to echo back the infant's ga ga's, da da's, and other nonsense sounds, and even to build and vary them, since this gives the baby both a sense of mastery (the environment is responding to *him*) and an idea of the magical variations the human voice can create. At the same time, though, the *dialogue you initiate should always and only be composed of real words.* It's no exaggeration to say that these words constitute the child's first dictionary, and while they should be brief and simple, they should also expose him to the symbols he needs to learn to open his own independent dialogue with the human environment. Even in the variations you create of his nonsense sounds, always try to end on a sound that is a real word. Without too many linguistic somersaults, for example, you can transfer "ga ga" into "da da," then into "Daddy." Moreover, this is the kind of natural verbal segue a baby finds easy to follow.

Knowing how to use baby talk to prop up and keep an early exchange flowing smoothly is another example of how your skill at it can make a difference. In the child's developmental cycle, these early exchanges play an important and unique role. But because of the young infant's uncertain grasp on his attention span, he has a tendency to tune in and out of them, with all the consequences that has for his growth. Imaginatively used, however, baby talk can help you shape these exchanges in a way that ensures that if the baby does tune out, he will be able to easily tune back in.

One way of doing this is by building your conversation around *phatics*. That's an anthropological term for short, simple, eye-catching one-word greetings, such as "hi," "hello," and "yeah." Parents already use these words in exchanges. But usually they use them at the beginning of interactions to catch the infant's attention. And while that's how they should be used with an older infant because of the variable attention span of a twelve- or thirteen-week-old, it is a good idea to continue using phatics all the way through exchanges with them. The pleasant sound and high recognition factor of phatics make them excellent reentry vehicles for a temporarily out-of-tune baby who is looking for a convenient doorway through which to slip back into the mainstream of the exchange.

Another way baby talk serves as a stepping-stone to growth, particularly emotional and intellectual growth, is by gearing its *content* to the infant's mental preoccupations. In the first three to four months, his paramount mental preoccupation is with himself and his feelings. So in this stage your talk should reflect this consuming interest through such statements as: "Oh, I'll bet that dry diaper feels sooo good," or: "Oh, look sweetie, you've dropped your bottle." Not only do such declarations put you in emotional tandem with him (in other words, they align your mind with his), *how* you express these feelings also helps the infant to begin to distinguish and identify what he is feeling to himself. While he can't understand the meaning of your words, he can understand the joy in your voice and the smile on your face when you tell him how wonderful it feels to be wearing a fresh, dry diaper, so on some level he begins to associate your positive signals with feeling dry and comfortable. (And that is an association that will have some influence on when and how readily he submits himself to toilet training.) Similarly, your expression of dismay at the strange disappearance of his bottle lets him know that sadness is also a legitimate emotion—one we are all subject to at times of loss and disappointment. In the largest sense, then, your seemingly commonplace baby talk becomes a way for the infant to begin to sort out and characterize the feelings he needs to know about if he is to make sense of and begin exercising control over his inner life. Also important is what it tells him about *you*. It says, "Mommy understands me; I'm special to her."

From the fourth month onward, the environment becomes like a magnet drawing the child's inward gaze outward toward the larger world of toys, objects, and people, and when your baby talk reflects this change of interest, it smooths and enhances his transitions into the great world of things. Now he wants your voice to help him sort out, identify, and explain the function of the doll, the Busy Box, the toy telephone, and all the exciting things he has begun to notice around him. This is why *labeling* becomes such a crucial element of baby talk at about the twentieth week.

As we saw on the tape, Amy was particularly mindful of this. In her conversation, the rattle was always called "the rattle," never "it"; the same principle of clear, unambiguous identification should apply to the other objects that catch the baby's eye. Balls should always be referred to as "balls," blocks as "blocks," and dolls as "dolls." If they are colored in a distinctive way, try to use those colors as part of your identification, as in "see the yellow ball" or "see the red block."

Skillfully used, baby talk can also ease your four- or five-month-old into mutual referencing. As we've seen, this capacity is a forerunner of both cooperation and conversational skills, and one way your talk can be used to enhance the baby's understanding of and skill at conducting it is by using your vocalizations as alerters. Pointing to or directly staring at an object you want the baby to look at are usually not eye-catching enough to arouse his interest, particularly if he is already happily shredding a copy of your magazine.

A better strategy is to brighten and animate your voice with a phatic, such as "hey," first, to arouse and focus him. Then, with your gaze or a pointed finger, gently segue his attention from the tattered copy of the magazine to the Sleepy Bunny book you want to look at with him. If the baby has already got to Sleepy Bunny ahead of you, make sure you label it clearly as a book (and parents who are familiar with this series of books know that their plastic packaging gives them a distinctly unbooklike appearance). Also, make sure you identify the sleepy sweet-faced rabbit on the cover as a "bunny." And be sure that you talk about the book and the bunny in an exciting, engaging voice, since the enthusiasm a baby comes to feel about Sleepy Bunny, or the other books, games, or toys you introduce him to directly reflects the enthusiasm he sees you exhibit.

At first, some mothers and fathers feel self-conscious about producing displays of excitement, particularly when the excitement is expressed in baby talk and its primary object is a baby bunny on a potty seat. But one of the absolutely magical things about babies is that the single-mindedness of their enthusiasm (and their total lack of irony) spins a web of enchantment around even the most curmudgeonly of adults. In time that adult becomes drawn into the child's world in a way that makes him or her care as deeply as the child about the adventures of Sleepy Bunny and, later, Madeline and *In the Night Kitchen.*

One element of adult conversation that never should be a part of baby talk are direct commands. Mothers and fathers don't deliberately act the part of martinets. But sometimes, in the course of, say, showing a baby how to put a block in a box or spin a ball around on its axis, they do unwittingly slip into commandlike language. Try to keep in mind that for a baby a command can be intimidating.

## Multimodal highlighting

In the context of language development, multimodal highlighting refers to the nonverbal channels of communication mothers or fathers use to italicize, underline, emphasize, and energize their spoken words in order to make their meanings clearer to the baby.

Adults employ these channels all the time in their conversations with each other, too, of course. Imagine how hard it would be to talk if you had to keep a perfectly still face. Indeed, it has been estimated that 30 to 40 percent of all the messages we send travel through our body language. The difference for the infant is that such language isn't simply (as it is for us) a way of amplifying points, but a crucial stepping-stone on the road to mastery of the spoken word. Or as Dr. Joseph Sullivan of the University of Colorado put it in a recent study: "The multimodal stimulation a mother or father provides is likely to be of central importance to the course of a child's language acquisition." While I agree wholeheartedly, I also think this is one area where research has little to add to the already enormous fount of innate wisdom that mothers and fathers possess.

Rarely, for example, have I encountered a parent who didn't

spontaneously break into a big, exaggerated grin, an eye roll, or a look of mock surprise on greeting their infant. Rare as well, in my experience, is the parent who does not instinctively use his or her looks, gestures, movements, and vocalizations to add interest and excitement to the rattle, doll, or other toy he or she is presenting. And almost never have I met a mother or father who on referring to a thing verbally didn't spontaneously try to draw the baby's attention to it with a gaze or a pointed finger. Indeed, parents are such naturally good referencers that in a recent study that analyzed more than four hundred individual instances of parental referencing, in only a few cases did a mother or father fail to point or look at the object they had just named for the baby.

In the face of such superb expertise, I think there is very little we can tell mothers and fathers about multimodal highlighting that they don't already know. The one bit of advice I would venture is that when you want to highlight or fasten your baby's eye on an object, try to engage not just his vision, but all (or as many as possible) of his senses.

This is how Amy drew Herschel so deeply into the rattle. The new dimensions she opened up by encouraging him not just to look at the rattle, but to taste it, feel it, rub it, and listen to it, made it much more exciting to him than it otherwise might have been. At the same time, the different kinds of knowledge that emerged from this all-encompassing exploration helped to fix in Herschel's mind the image of the rattle firmly and forever. Which is why, later, when he learns its verbal name, that new bit of knowledge will seem to be simply a logical extension of, and a handy way of referring to, an object that his interactive learning has already taught him a great deal about.

What is true for Herschel is true for every baby. Used with imagination and insight, multimodal highlighting can help to facilitate a language acquisition in the second year by giving the child in his first year an all-around knowledge of an object. After all, for an infant as well as for an adult, it's a great deal easier to learn and remember the name of a thing if the image of it has been an integral part of living memory for months or even years.

## Turn-taking

Understandably, new parents often are baffled by talk of the baby's innate knowledge of turn-taking. Little of it is evident in a three-, four-, or five-week-old's behavior. Indeed, as our first tape of Herschel showed, it is almost akin to an act of faith to describe even a twelve-week-old as a turn-taker. So why then is this seemingly elusive quality considered such an integral part of an infant's preadaptive programming?

A group of exciting new studies by Dr. Kenneth Kaye show that a capacity for turn-taking is indeed present at birth, though in a form only an expert would recognize. Its origins lie in the baby's innate burst-pause cycle of activity. You have probably noticed that your child's behavior comes in rushes interspersed by intervals of quietude (usually marked by head turns and glassy stares). This on-off cycle isn't unique to infants; we adults also behave in bursts and pauses, but it's harder to see because the cycling has been obscured by a veneer of sophistication. Cycling, however, is unique to humans. Wolves, dogs, even primates, such as monkeys and gorillas, don't display it. What Dr. Kaye has done is to demonstrate that the roots of this cycling lie in a biological tendency that predisposes humans to act in a dialoguelike fashion. In other words, the reason our conversations are characterized by two-sided turn-taking with one person talking and the other listening is that we are programmed to behave in bursts (talk) and pauses (listening).

In the case of a parent and infant, the first instance of this two-way dialogue occurs not as mothers and fathers think, in face-to-face play interactions in the second and third week, but in the feeding sessions immediately after birth. Dr. Kaye's video studies show that, in form, these encounters have an unmistakable (again to a trained eye) turn-taking-like structure. At this stage, the baby's turns—his equivalents of vocalizing—take the form of bursts of feeding; during his resting—listening—phase, his mother takes her turn. Sometimes her dialogue is verbal; she will murmur, "I love you." But just as often it is physical; she will gently jiggle her resting baby up and down in her arms. What's most interesting about this protodialogue, however, is that it also has a *content*. Mother and baby are both trying to get the other to do something very specific; but instead of making their case in words, as adults would in a conversation, they are doing it with other modes.

The subject of their dialogue is a negotiation about the length of the pauses between suckings. The babies want to lengthen them because they love being jiggled. Dr. Kaye found that for a few days the mothers go along with this, largely because they don't realize what their babies are up to: angling for more jiggling rather than feeding. But once they do realize, they quickly cut back on the jiggling in order to get their babies back to the more important business of feeding.

Does the outcome of this early form of parent-infant negotiation have any long-term influence on turn-taking? Very likely in some small way, but the most important aspect of this experience is that it gives two people who will be spending a great deal of time together an opportunity to begin learning how to influence, please, and help one another.

The most important forum for what is commonly thought of as turn-taking is the face-to-face play interactions which occur after the eighth week. It is in these exchanges that a parent actively begins to shape the baby's innate burst-pause cycle into something resembling dialoguelike behavior. And as Amy demonstrated in her exchange with Herschel, one common way a parent performs this shaping is by, in a sense, communicating for two. That is, in early exchanges, the mother or father will play both the speaker's *and* listener's roles. The point of this strategy is to provide the infant with a practical demonstration of how both roles are played in conversations. And while it is often a very effective technique, we have created three strategies that can help to augment and enhance it.

The first strategy is *quieting*. The sooner a parent is able to create a cue that tells the baby that it is *his* turn, the sooner the baby's natural bursts will begin to take on a dialoguelike structure. Before a behavior comes to be recognized as a cue, however, a child has to see you perform that behavior enough times so that it becomes a signal to him with a specific message attached to it, like: "It's your turn." And the reason why quiet is recognized as a quicker cue than a facial expression, vocalization, or gesture is—as we've already seen—that it is one parental behavior which *always* rivets the infant. Frequently, a preoccupied baby won't hear a voice or notice a movement, but when you still your face and lower your voice, it brings his eyes to yours in a flash.

Another strategy that helps to shape the baby's behavior into a dialoguelike structure is *back channels*. Even an infant who is able to identify a cue that signals his turn may require a few moments to organize himself to the point where he is physically able to produce the behavior or sound that is meant to constitute his turn. This is why in exchanges with infants under four or five months, there are—as every parent knows—intervals of dead time. Filling them with short utterances, such as "yeah," "hey," "come on," or just "uh-huh," is a way of keeping the action moving and the baby's attention focused until he is prepared to take his turn. Another advantage of these sounds is that they are unobtrusive; they don't distract the child or make him feel he is being elbowed out of his turn.

A third and related strategy is what we call *chorusing*. No matter how hard he tries, sometimes a three-, four-, or even five-month-old just isn't able to produce the sound he wants. It's as if the noise got stuck in his vocal cords and just an extra bit of help is needed to get it unstuck. An open mouth with no sound coming out of it is a sure sign of such trouble. A parental "ahhhh" or "ohhhh" at this point usually provides just the extra bit of push the baby needs to dislodge that trapped sound and send it traveling up and out through his mouth. Chances are that even before you have finished your "ahhh-ing," he will already have chorused in with a happy "ahhhh" of his own.

## Protolanguage

This is the name for the familiar coos, oohhs, and ah-ah-ahs which, though they forever delight, also puzzle parents. Principally, of course, because mothers and fathers wonder if these sounds have any meaning. "Is the baby trying to tell us something?" Hanŭs and Mechthild Papoušek were no different than other new parents in wondering about this; except that being research psychiatrists and having the resources of the Max-Planck-Institut (where they both teach) available to them, they were in a better position than most mothers and fathers are to satisfy their curiosity when their baby daughter, Tanya, began making these sounds. The exciting new insights that emerged from their work with her, moreover, is only one example of the several new ways research has added to our understanding of the protolanguage phenomenon and its place in the infant's growth cycle.

We know, for example, that protolanguage is a two-track phenomenon. One of the tracks is composed of the short, squeaky sounds that begin appearing between the third and sixth week. Usually, these are described as being vowel-like in nature, though I must confess that to my ear they sound closer to squeaks. Their emergence is a great source of pleasure and excitement to the baby, which is why infants never tire of making them. The Papoŭseks reported that at ten weeks, little Tanya, without any encouragement, would happily babble alone in her crib on waking, for up to an hour at a time.

While these short sounds continue throughout the prelanguage period, between the fifth and sixth month, a new series of syllablelike sounds—for example, "duh, duh" or "ga ga ga"—appear, and as the months pass, these syllablelike utterances begin to be strung into what sounds like multisyllablelike vocalizations. Don't be surprised, however, if a syllable or group of syllables you are accustomed to hearing one day suddenly disappears from your baby's vocabulary. Tanya Papoŭsek's tendency to drop a sound for a week or two is a habit most babies share.

Increasingly, there is agreement among linguists and developmental psychologists that the sounds Tanya's parents so eagerly recorded do have meaning. The Papoŭseks, in fact, reported that as early as the third week, a baby who is stumped by a learning task will emit a series of vowel-like vocalizations, and on solving that task will emit squeals and squeaks of delight. As the Papoŭseks also note, however, there are easier and much more reliable ways to monitor a two-week-old's developmental progress than by tracking his sounds.

Indeed, the feeling among language specialists generally—

and it's a feeling I share with them—is that the correct interpretation of protolanguage requires such a highly skilled technical knowledge that mothers and fathers should avoid trying to squeeze out meanings from the baby's every utterance. If you focus on his *general drift*, this will tell you all you need to know about his happiness, sadness, playfulness, or distress. At the same time, it will also tell the baby that *you* know what's really on his mind. And a recent study by Dr. Beatrice Beebe of Yeshiva University in New York found that mothers and fathers who are skilled at drift interpretations had by the end of their first year established an unusually rich bond with their babies. There are two other points to keep in mind about protolanguage:

1) *Always echo back the baby's sounds.*
   Having already seen how thrilled an infant is by parental echoes of all kinds, it should come as no surprise to learn that the more you echo back the baby's protolanguage to him, the more of this language he will produce. What may come as a surprise, however, is the difference your direct eye contact can make in his echoing rate. Recent studies show that a combination of direct parental eye gaze *and* vocalizations increase a baby's production of protolanguage by a significant rate.

2) *Create variations within your echoes.*
   A variation is a rearrangement of familiar elements in a way that allows us to see them in a new light. For a one-, two-, or three-month-old, your principal way of illustrating the magic of variation and the special grace it lends to the human environment is through sounds. By combining the baby's vocalizations with your echoes of them, you not only create a startlingly and dazzlingly new (for the baby, at least) sound, you also give him a hint of the ways imagination and playfulness can join to illuminate our understanding of an object, idea, or image in an unexpected way. Later, he will discover this himself when he looks at his first painting by Miró or photograph by Eugène Atget, or listens to his first symphony by Mahler or to a composition of Philip Glass's. But his appreciation of these

works and the extraordinary perspectives on the ordinary which they offer will be that much deeper because he has already been exposed to the magic of variations.

## Myth making

Those of us who have spent our lives working with mothers and fathers have always been intrigued by this phenomenon of myth making. I remember my own equal measures of surprise and delight at first encountering it in the early 1970s, while doing a study with some colleagues from St. Luke's Hospital in Manhattan. Watching the mothers and fathers in our study group, I was struck time and again by the way each of them seemed to use the exchanges we had recorded to act out the little stories and myths they had created about their infants. I remember one young father in particular—I later learned he was a comedian at one of the local New York clubs—who responded to each of his four-month-old's gurglings as if it were the punch line to a long, elaborate, and very funny joke. The father would laugh uproariously, then snuggling up to his son, would whisper conspiratorially in his ear: "Listen, kid, that's dynamite stuff. Who's writing your material. I need a guy who thinks that funny. Could you give me his telephone number?"

As I pointed out earlier, this enchanting parental trait is what breathes life not just into a baby's skills, but into his humanity. At the roots of the infant's ability to act intentionally lies his mother's and father's unshakable belief that from the very moment of birth onward, *their* baby is full of purpose, motivation, and intention.

You might almost say that evoltion's real genius lies not in the way it has programmed or preadapted the infant to fit into the human environment, but the way it has programmed his parents to believe that their baby is just a little bit smarter than he really is. This belief is why in the first few months, parents are not only happy to communicate for two—so real is the image of the competent baby in their minds—usually, they don't even realize they are doing it. And, of course, it is because mothers like Amy and fathers like Steve believe in their infant's competence, that the baby, like Herschel, eventually attains the competence and skill his parents have been attributing to him all along.

Another part of evolution's special genius is the way it has ensured that these parental myths and dreams are held *lightly*. You can hear the lightness reflected in the way mothers and fathers talk to their infants. Though occasionally you will hear a parent make a direct, boldface statement, such as: "Boy, what a smart guy you are," more typically parental attributions of knowledge and skill are made in a more oblique and, I think, more winning way. A good example is the fragment of a conversation I recently overheard in our playroom.

Looking in one afternoon around five o'clock, I found a father and his baby daughter seated on the floor. Suspended a few feet above them at the top of its arc was a whiffle ball, which the father had just tossed into the air. Reaching out to catch it, he missed and the ball hit the floor, then bounced a full foot or so up into the air. From the way the father snapped back his head, this obviously surprised him. (It surprised me, too; being plastic and full of holes, whiffle balls *aren't* supposed to bounce, which is why we had bought them.) But he reacted as if this unexpected bounce hadn't at all surprised his six-month-old. Looking at her with an expression of mock indignation, he declared: "Suzanne, you little devil, you knew that ball was going to bounce, why didn't you tell Daddy?"

Attributions of knowledge, wisdom, and emotional sophistication eventually give birth to these qualities and to the intentionality needed to express them. Very likely, aside from their inspirational and motivational value, these parental attributions and the myths and dreams they reflect are probably also a reflection of the mother's or father's own general nurturing skills. Whatever the case, there is a correlation between the positiveness of the fantasies and myths a parent creates about her baby and the child's later development. Another element that is essential to the beneficiality of these myths is that they also be held *lightly*.

This is why I've been greatly disturbed by all the current

talk about building "superbabies." It isn't accidental that interactions were evolved as the primary forum for infant learning.
Natural, spontaneous, unstructured, they offer a pressure-free
environment specially fitted and suited to the baby's emergence
into personhood. Never, I think, has there been an apter example of the hand-in-glove metaphor. That is not, however, true
of the infant learning centers which recently have begun appearing. Their chief self-recommendation that they can mass-
produce superbabies with IQs in the 140 to 160 range is as
offensive as it is distressing. Furthermore, no rigorously controlled scientific study has found evidence to substantiate their
claims. Structured learning experiences—in the form of flash
cards and other vocabulary builders—perhaps have their place
in the life of a four-, or a three-year-old, but thrusting a five-,
six-, or seven-month-old infant into such a high-pressured,
achievement-oriented environment puts him at risk for emotional and intellectual shutdown.

Parents should be left free to create their own myths and
fantasies about their babies. The only legitimate role we experts
have in this myth-making process is to help them interpret
the often surprising meanings behind their baby's smiles,
frowns, gestures, and other behaviors, so that when they respond *as if* to him, their response will accurately reflect what
the child is thinking and feeling. And it is through such accuracy that a baby is brought a little closer to using his innate
vocabulary of cues and signals *in order* to communicate those
thoughts and feelings.

# EIGHT
# Cries, Cries, and Signals
## (Communication—
## Part Three)

**A** hand already punctuated the air as I finished my talk. "Dr. Sanger," said its owner, a ruddy-faced young man whose head began turning away from the outstretched microphone as he tried to illustrate his query, "what does it mean when my little girl goes like this?" Before I had a chance to reply, a husky female voice from the other side of the auditorium answered for me. "That's an aversive reaction." Then, unexpectedly, a voice from the front row chimed in to amplify the point further: "It means your baby doesn't like what she's looking at.'

In the lectures I give to new parents from time to time, questions about the meanings of the baby's cues, signals, and cries are an invariable and, for me, enjoyable part of the question and answer sessions. Over the years, I've also come to think of these questions and the deep knowledge and concern that forms them as a special kind of tribute to the innate parental wisdom I've referred to so many times in these pages. Special in this case because for years, in the face of nearly unanimous expert opinin to the contrary, mothers and fathers insisted that their baby's looks, movements, gestures, and even body posture had meaning. And the introduction of videotape technology has proven them right. Analyzed frame by frame, even a two- or three-week-old reveals himself to possess a fairly extensive behavioral vocabulary—one to which he will continue to add throughout his first year.

At the same time, I think our newly developed ability to decode this infant language represents another example of how new research enriches the biological wisdom parents already possess. One way is by helping mothers and fathers to enhance their baby's sense of attunement with the human environment. Nothing makes an infant feel more in synch with his parents than the feeling that his wants and needs are being accurately read. And while a one- or two-week-old is still many months away from an awareness that these feelings can be conveyed to others through his looks and gestures, he already is acutely aware of whether the environment's responses are in tune with him—that is, producing responses we would define as accurate, out of tune, or inaccurate—or whether it is producing no response at all. Thus, long before a more finely tuned system of communication emerges, a mother who is interpreting her baby's needs correctly is already sending him a global message, and it is one which even a three-day-old understands, since it simply says: *"I love you and I am sensitive to your needs."*

In recognition of this, a number of cues and signals I have included in this chapter are ones which never become transformed into true communication symbols. Responding to a baby's sneezes as if they were signals of distress—which is what they often are—won't prompt him one day to sneeze in order to tell his employer or his wife that he or she has just upset him. But a child's knowing that *you* know what he means when he goes "achoo" will make him feel supported and understood.

The other reason a knowledge of signals and cues is important, of course, is that it facilitates the transformation of the behaviors that one day will be used for communication into true, meaningful symbols. In a very real sense, one of the most important things a parent does with his or her as-if responses is help a baby to complete his thought. Watching you smile to his smile, the infant gradually comes to realize: "Oh, yes, that's what I mean when I smile—I'm happy and I want Mommy to share in my happiness." And so over the weeks, the baby begins to learn how to use his smiles to state that thought by himself.

How smoothly and quickly this lesson is mastered, however,

is dependent on how accurately the baby sees his feelings and thoughts reflected back to him. A child may not yet be able to define to himself why one response to his cues seems right on the mark—correctly echoing the joy or sadness he feels inside—while another, say, a frown, seems puzzlingly inappropriate or gratuitous; but his biology tells him which of these responses is right and which is wrong. This is why a smiling baby beams even more brightly when he sees his happiness reflected in his mother's smile. It is also why a sad or distressed baby turns away from that same smiling maternal face as if to say: "No, no, you got it wrong. I'm feeling sad, not happy."

Stepping up to the microphone in a pair of bright pink running shoes, which seemed to wink slyly at her tailored blue business suit, my second interrogator on this particular evening was the owner of the husky voice that had helped me earlier. "Dr. Sanger," she declared, "what puzzles me is how even a misunderstood baby is able to learn to use his facial and body language. If what you say is true, I would think such a baby would never develop real language skills."

I explained that given the potential number of adult models available and his own native intelligence, eventually even a misinterpreted infant, on his own, begins to figure out that the things he does and says communicate meanings to others. But, I also added, the child who is left to puzzle this out on his own often develops language skills later than a child who is actively helped "to crack the language code."

New research indicates that infants appear to be preadapted to learn certain things best at certain points in their growth cycle. And while this does not mean that skills won't develop later, it does mean that the emotional and biological factors that would have been available to facilitate and enhance their emergence had they appeared on schedule will no longer be present in the same nurturing constellation.

To illustrate the consequences I told my audience about Mary Ann, the little girl I mentioned in Chapter Six. She is the child who is having such difficulty getting along with her peers in singing class. I pointed out that her present problems with Ann, who is leading the singing class, and with her playmates in the class are in part due to her failure to master the skills of joint action and cooperation in her early exchanges. I told the audience that I'm sure that with help and encouragement, eventually Mary Ann will master these skills. What remains a possibility, however, is that no matter how well Mary Ann learns to get along with others, the role of partner or helpmate may not feel as natural or as comfortable as it would have had her understanding of cooperation and joint action sprung out of her exchanges with her parents.

I pointed out that in the case of cue and signal learning, the baby's biological timetable appears to be tied to the first year. Our experience at the center suggests a correlation between the emergence of an ability to use body language meaningfully to express feelings and thoughts in the seventh, eighth, and ninth months and a smooth passage into spoken language between the thirteenth and eighteenth month. There's one other characteristic we have also noticed among our children who develop communication abilities on schedule. And it is important to mention because it illustrates what I said earlier about the connection between language learning and life learning.

We have found that our two- and three-year-olds who are most comfortable in turning to others for help and are good at implementing the advice they receive have parents who were good at accurately interpreting their cues and signals as infants. I think that what we are seeing now in their ability to reach out naturally for assistance is a carry-over effect from that earlier experience of being accurately read. Having learned at *the* most impressionable point in their growth cycle that the human environment is available to support you—even to communicate for you when you don't know how to do it for yourself—these youngsters have developed a fundamental, and quite wonderful, expectation. When you don't understand how to do a thing yourself, there will always be another person available who does and who can be *trusted* to help you.

My last interrogator on this particular evening—a tall, distinguished man with an eye-catching mane of silver hair—earned such a lusty round of applause when he announced, "Four months ago, at the age of fifty, I became a father for the first time," that I had to ask him to repeat his question. Surprised by my statement that purposeful cue and signal use doesn't emerge until the seventh or eighth month, he said: "I know I sound like a doting father, but from the way my four-month-old, Jessica, behaves, I would have thought this capability developed much earlier." I told him that, in fact, there was some disagreement on this point.

Dr. Colwyn Trevarthen of the University of Edinburgh believes he has seen what he calls "intentions to communicate" in infants as young as two months. Dr. Kaye, on the other hand, takes a much more conservative approach. He argues that intentional cue use doesn't emerge in any recognizable or meaningful form until the ninth or tenth month. From my work with infants at the center, I would come down somewhere in the middle. I think a baby's use of cues and symbols becomes intentional sometime in the second half of his first year. However, the question of when in the second half a child begins smiling in order to get his father to smile back depends largely on how knowledgeably a parent uses his or her as-if responses and, of course, on the baby's own native ability.

I told my interrogator that the signs of communication he had seen in Jessica were probably examples of her preadaptive linguistic abilities. So remarkable and sophisticated are these capabilities that it's very easy to attribute conscious meaning to them. For instance, we know from studies that if a mother makes a depressed face, her four-month-old will respond with a big smile. And while that smile may look like a deliberate attempt to brighten up sad Mom, what's really speaking in the smile is the baby's biology. Infants are primed to smile at the human face.

One indication of the breakthrough into intentionality, which occurs in the second six months, is that if you place a nine-month-old in front of a depressed mother, he not only smiles, his smile shows a clear and purposeful intention to soothe. This is to say that what is speaking in a nine-month-old's smile is his *mind*. Another indication of the enormous intellectual leap that takes place in the second six months is that the infant develops the ability to distinguish between what a person says and what he means. Daniel Stern and his colleagues at New York Hospital-Cornell Medical Center demonstrated this capability a few years ago in a remarkable study.

According to their research, sometime between the sixth and ninth month a baby begins to grasp what the Beatles meant in their song "Hello Goodbye," that sometimes *how* a person says something is a better measure of their true intentions than *what* they say.

Since the route to this skill, as well as to virtually all of the baby's other communication skills, has as its starting point his belief that his thoughts and feelings are understood, let's now turn to the dictionary of infant cues and signals, which is the principal subject of this chapter. In order to make the list as comprehensive as possible I've drawn not only from our own work at the center, but also from that of other investigators as well, including Barry Lester and T. Berry Brazelton of Harvard Medical School, Philip Sanford Zeskin of Virginia Polytechnical Institute, Heidelise Als of the Child Development Unit, Children's Hospital, Boston, Hanŭs and Mechthild Papoŭsek of the Max-Planck Institut, Robert Emde of the University of Colorado, Kenneth Kaye of the University of Chicago, Tiffany Field of the University of Miami, Kurt Fischer of the University of Denver, and Daniel Stern of New York Hospital-Cornell Medical Center.

Before we begin, one word of caution: The following signals and cues constitute *a representative sample.* While they are a part of most infants' vocabularies, they are not universal. Some infants may use only a few, others a great many of the signals that follow. Still other children may put such an idiosyncratic spin on a cue that as used by them it bears little relationship to the description we've provided. Keep these admonitions in mind as you read.

# Cries

### Precursors
Though fussiness is the most reliable sign of imminent crying, a number of other indicators—some remarkably subtle—also may signal that tears are near. Among them are clenched fists (usually both hands will be tightly knotted), especially if held for twenty seconds or longer, and rapid flexing and stretching of the arms and legs. Abrupt marked changes in facial

color, from a normal tone to a red also serve as reliable storm warnings.

Appearances of any of these signs should prompt you to make a quick mental inventory. Is it near the baby's feeding time, is he wet, did a favorite toy animal just fall out of the crib? Did something unusual happen outside the house? For example, did a passing car emit a backfire? Usually, the precursors I have listed precede crying by thirty to sixty seconds, which means if you know your baby well and are able to think quickly, you have enough time to identify the source of distress and eliminate it before tears begin.

### Healthy Cry

Its principal distinguishing characteristics are a full-throated robustness and rhythmicity, which is why of all the baby's cries this one can almost be described as pleasant to hear. While loud, it has a definite rhythmic quality that is not unlike the rhythmic quality of a speaking voice. The irritating harshness and intervals of high-pitch wailing, which mark some other kinds of infant cries and which makes listening to them like hearing a piece of chalk scratched across a blackboard, are almost completely absent from the healthy cry.

Though it can have a number of causes, infants most commonly use the healthy cry when they want human companionship. The baby is asking for an interaction; and almost any response that acknowledges his desire for human contact will bring it to an end. However, recent studies show that of all the naturally happy endings a healthy cry lends itself to, the one the infant likes best is being picked up and held. Not only does this satisfy his desires for the exchange and the body contact, it also provides him with a bonus. From the vantage point of your shoulder he has a perfect spot from which to examine all the interesting things in the environment.

### Anger Cry

While an anger cry has the same basic structure as a healthy cry, which is to say it also sounds full-throated and robust, it is at once noticeably more agitated and less rhythmic. Listening to a mad baby wail, you can almost hear him say: "Hey, stop that, I don't like it." Another way of distinguishing an angry cry is by its inconsolability. Only rarely is it soothed by parental rocking and walking; to produce contented coos, generally you have to identify and remove the source of the baby's anger.

Given this distinct profile, I was a bit surprised when the results of a recent poll we conducted among our parents suggested that mothers and fathers found the anger cry among the most difficult to identify. As I thought about this irony, I realized that anger isn't an emotion that mothers and fathers—especially if they are first-time parents—associate with a baby. Particularly if he happens to be under six months. So when the child cries because a favorite routine is interrupted for a changing, or a favorite toy is put away because it's feeding time, or when he's placed in the crib when he really wants to be in your arms, his angry cries of protest are usually interpreted as signs of stress, pain, overtiredness, or colic.

The special advantage of knowing how to identify an anger cry is that it makes it easier to remedy its cause. For example, a game can be continued on the changing table, the toy may be left clenched in his arms while he feeds, or his body snuggled securely in your arms as you gently rock him to sleep in a rocking chair. (Rocking chairs, I think, are a must for families with infants.)

### Pain Cry

Its most identifiable characteristics are a sudden, long onset and the length of its opening sequence. A healthy cry usually opens with a nice, even "wawa-wawa-wawa," an anger cry with an uneven, disjointed "wawa-wa-wa," but the initial sequence of a pain cry has an unrelenting, unbroken upward thrust to it. The baby's "waaaaaaaaaa" being roughly equivalent to the adult's "ouch!" on being unexpectedly pricked by a pin. The longish interval between the first and second pain cry is usually due to the large amount of air the baby took in during his first wail; once it's discharged, another long, unbroken, full-blooded cry will follow.

Since 99 percent of the mishaps that produce pain cries are minor, often the first impulse is to get the baby's mind off his discomfort by smiling at him, bouncing him up and down, or offering him a toy or another distraction. But the bath water that was a little too hot or the head that banged against the crib post a little too abruptly really did hurt, and to deny that hurt by switching to another response mode is to deny the infant's pain. He may not understand why such a response makes him feel isolated, but it does. This is why I said earlier, always start from where the baby starts, and if his starting place is in pain, place yourself next to him. Respond to his discomfort with quiet sympathy; in this case, a look of concern and a series of soft vocalizations which through their empathetic tone tell him you know how he feels.

### Random Whimpering

As most mothers and fathers know, such whimpering seems to have no clear starting place and no clear end point; nor does it usually build into a full-throttled cry. It is just there, like the Muzak in an elevator or the buzz of a neighbor's power saw. Though it may not seem so, this whimpering, along with the fussiness and crankiness that accompany it, are usually limited to the first three months. Rising to a crescendo of intensity between the fourth and six week, the whimpering begins to taper off around the seventh week, disappearing completely in many cases between the thirteenth and twentieth. Though it may be hard to believe, whimpering even constitutes a compliment of sorts. It's a one-, two-, or three-week-old's way of telling you he enjoys your company *so much*, he would like to be picked up and held.

### Stress Cry

You only hear this cry among infants at risk, and the words most commonly used to describe it are high-pitched, irritating, excessive, and urgent. Though its grating quality is so distinctive that even a first-time listener can distinguish it from other infant cries. The organic problems that put a baby at risk in the first place, such as low birth weight or prematurity, are what give the stress cry its uniquely harsh quality. And while those organic problems have long been a source of concern, we are now beginning to realize that the cry itself may also have serious consequences.

In studies of interactive failures, what I'll call high-risk families show up in disproportionately high numbers. And there is a growing feeling—one which I share—that a main reason for their higher profiles in such studies is that the disturbing, raucous nature of stress cries often establishes a disturbing emotional cycle between infant and parent.

Having usually endured a difficult pregnancy, mothers of at-risk infants come home from the hospital already emotionally and physically depleted. This means they are especially vulnerable to the irritating, insistent, plaintive quality of stress cries. Adding further to the danger of an interactive breakdown are the often secret feelings of guilt and inadequacy which these women harbor. Thus, along with the cries, the unspoken fear that she has let her baby down sets the stage for a serious parent-infant conflict—one which can permanently affect the tone of a mother's and baby's relationship.

This is why high-risk families require immediate aid, whether from the hospital's pediatric outpatient service, from a psychiatrically trained social worker or nurse, or from the family pediatrician. In form, we find that one kind of help that is most valuable is simply making the mother aware that her baby's illness is real and one she bears no responsibility for. Often, once a woman realizes this, she is able to hear the child's stress cries as expressions of the organic problem that they really are and not as the accusations of guilt or incompetence that she takes them for. Another factor that can make life easier for everyone in a high-risk family is arranging chores in such a way that the mother gets the sleep she needs. In our work with these families, for example, one of our first priorities is to get the husband deeply involved in changing diapers, bed-making, and washing the baby.

## Infant Cues & Signals

### BIRTH TO THREE MONTHS

#### Head

##### *Head Slumped on Chest—Eyes Glazed*
Seeing a baby's head in this position always brings to mind a photo I once saw of Winston Churchill slumped in an easy chair about to fall asleep. Like the very elderly, the very young have muscles so slack that in this position the head doesn't so much rest on the chest as collapses on it. While it may

be a sign of tiredness, the presence of the glazed eyes also may signal a mildly aversive reaction to an environmental element which the upset baby is trying to escape by tuning out. Your best way to distinguish what's bothering him is through situational cues. Is it near nap time or bedtime? Is there a lot of light and sound in the room? Also, check the toys near the baby; one of them might be upsetting him.

### Head Slumped on Chest—Eyes Alert

On the other hand, this is usually a sign of awakening interest and curiosity. The baby is trying to organize himself to the point where he will be able to begin engaging the world. The fact that his head is resting on his chest and not held erectly on his neck, however, indicates that he is having trouble organizing and needs a bit of parental help in the form of an organizing stimulus. While sights and sounds sometimes work, we find that a baby in a preresponsive mode usually needs something more physical to rouse his awakening alertness. The telltale sign is the slumped position of his head; it suggests a need for large-muscle stimulation, like stroking and gentle rocking. Or you can try to lift the baby's head or urge him to move it from side to side by whispering in one ear and then the other.

### Head Turns

Since there are several reasons why a baby may turn his head away from a parent, in order to decode the meaning of a particular head turn you have to be aware of the characteristics that define different kinds of turns.

*Cyclical turns,* for example, can be distinguished by their frequency; they are a normal part of interactive behavior. Commonly, they are characterized by brevity, a lack of sharpness, the incompleteness of the head turn, and the willingness of the baby to turn back to his partner. An infant in a normal cyclical turn doesn't have to be wooed back into an exchange; he will return voluntarily.

*Aversive head turns,* on the other hand, are very sharp. Often the baby will turn a full 90 degrees to the side, and if the person or thing upsetting him follows him into the turn, he will keep turning as if he were trying to swivel his head a full 360 degrees. The extreme emotional distress that underlies

# Cues Infants Use to Signal Desire to Open or Close an Interaction

| Vocalization | Face | Hands | Body Movements |
|---|---|---|---|
| **Indirect Cues (these usually precede direct-request signals):** | | | |
| None | Widening of eyes, elevation of eyebrows, opening of mouth, brightening of face, or other signs of growing alertness | Open fingers, slightly flexed | Head raised |
| | Elevation of eyebrows | | Slight raising of arms with loosely fisted hands held upward |
| **Direct Requests for an Interaction:** | | | |
| Giggling Babbling | Smile, infant looking at parent's face Non-distress cry Direct eye contact | Reaching out toward parent | Smooth, cyclical movements of arms and legs Head turned toward parent |
| **Indirect Cues (these usually precede attempts to break off an exchange):** | | | |
| Whimpers Hiccups Sneezing Snoring | Increase in blinking, lips compressed or grimaced Brow lowering as if into a frown Protruded tongue Attempts to avert gaze | Join hands together Clasp self Put hand to ear, back of neck, stomach, or mouth | Kicking Arms held straight along sides Head turned and lowered Legs tensed Shoulders shrug |
| **Direct Attempts to Suspend Interaction:** | | | |
| Crying Whining Fussing Spitting | Crying face Brow knit | Held outward away from body with palms facing parent as if to say, "Halt" Pounding surface with fists | Arching of back Pushing away Head shaking in a "no" movement Overhead beating of arms |

this signal is often indicated by the baby's reluctance to resume the exchange. Frequently, he won't turn fullface again until whatever has upset him is removed. If that happens to be a doll or stuffed animal that has been waved too closely to his face (which is a common source of aversive turns in young infants), put it down or, even better, *put it away*. A parent who has unwittingly produced such a head turn should quiet himself or herself and wait for the baby to make a response. No matter how difficult it may be to see him straining his head to the side to get away from you, he needs time to collect himself. And it's important to both of you that he be given that time.

*Ambivalent head turns* are characterized by a turning toward and turning away from a person or thing, and such turns mean what they look like they mean: The baby can't make up his mind whether he likes or dislikes the object or person in front of him. Unless he's provided with a way out of his dilemma—by removing the object or moving it farther away from his face—this ambivalence usually ends in confused tears.

*A bobbing or floppy head* signifies disjointedness, and the rubbery, floppy quality it lends to upper body movements is normal; don't let it upset you. Around the third or fourth week the baby will begin to hold his head erectly. And by the sixth or seventh week he will begin to use his head and neck together—as if they were part of the same organism; not, as has been the case for his last five weeks, as if each leads a totally independent existence. The most visible sign of this new physical control will be in the baby's manner of looking. Instead of shifting his gaze toward an object, he will now begin to turn his head *and* eyes together toward the object. Each of these changes is an important physical benchmark. It means the baby's biological organization is proceeding smoothly.

## Facial expressions

### Quiet Alertness

This expression makes its appearance in the first two to three weeks and is the young infant's equivalent of a look we would

call curious or interested. In this state, the baby's *eyes* have
the same *focused, expectant quality* yours might have if you
were to run into an old friend who had an interesting piece
of news for you. Another way of identifying this expression
is by the condition of the facial muscles, particularly the cheeks.
While they are relaxed—mirroring the baby's own relaxed inner mood—they are not flaccid or slack. Everything about
quiet alertness bespeaks openness, receptivity, and interest. The
baby is alive to the world in all its rich possibilities. This is
why a quietly alert infant is also an infant who is perfectly
primed for an exchange.

Let me add one cautionary word. While approaching or
in an *open space,* a baby wears a look much like that of quiet
alertness. So before making an opening bid, examine the child's
eyes (from a distance so as not to be obtrusive). A preoccupied,
alert gaze indicates the presence of an open space. Another
way of identifying these intervals is through situational cues.
Usually open spaces *follow,* rather than precede, interactions.
In an open space, of course, a baby should be left undisturbed,
though occasionally you might want to try to nudge him gently
with a technique we will discuss later, called menu offering.

### Strained Alertness

On an adult, this expression would be described as tense or
uptight. The eyes are focused, but they look fixed and concen-
trated the way a student's do during an exam. Tense or stiffened
facial muscles is another telltale sign of strained alertness. You
see this state most often in infants who are having difficulty
organizing. Your response should be one of supportive quiet.
An attempt to open an exchange now would lead to further
disorganization and might well produce tears.

A passive expression also indicates a young infant in difficulty. Stand in front of a mirror and let your facial muscles
go slack: notice how everything—from cheeks to chin—seems
to ooze downward on your face. When a baby's face looks
this way, usually it's because he wants to tune out. The glazed
gaze is another expression of the desire to shut down. Often,
very sleepy infants will look this way, but the expression also
is a common sign of overstimulation. So if it is not near bedtime,

chances are the baby wants the interactive "volume" lowered.

A third indicator of an infant in difficulty is *rapid changes of expression*. A baby whose look quickly goes from strained to glassy to averting to unfocused and floating is nearly always experiencing distress. Before responding, however, wait and see what state the baby ends in, then choose your reaction accordingly.

### The Smile

This appears sometime between the sixth and tenth week and is, for most parents, an infant's first truly human expression (though that distinction probably more fairly belongs to quiet alertness). While the happiness and pleasure signaled in a smile are obvious, babies, like adults, have different kinds of smiles, each with its own special meaning and message.

For example, *a smile that bares the gums and brings the tongue just behind the lips or directly onto the lips* indicates not only extreme pleasure, but also extreme receptivity. You can almost hear this smile's full-throttled chortle: "Hey, let's have fun together," is what the baby is shouting. It is his way of saying he wants not just an exchange, but an exchange that's full of mischief and excitement.

In contrast, a smile where *the tongue remains in the mouth cavity* is closer in meaning to our adult social smile. It says, "Oh, that's nice," and often it is found on the waking baby who opens his eyes to find a parental face hovering quietly over the crib guard, or on the child who sees his mother taking his favorite toy out of the toy box.

The *pursing of the baby's lips into an O shape,* while not a smile, has a smilelike meaning. It and the contented coos that accompany it are cues that a child feels relaxed and receptive.

## Random sounds

### Hiccuping, Gagging, Sighing, Coughing, Sneezing, and Yawning

These are among the infant's most misread cues, primarily because parents think they have the same meaning for the baby as they have for themselves. And while there is some overlap—for instance, a child also yawns when he is tired and coughs if something gets stuck in his throat—for a baby, these cues can be signals of stress.

The key to reading them accurately lies in context. A child who coughs or hiccups when a parent puts her face right up next to his is signaling distress at the invasion of his personal space (and infants not only have a sense of personal space, they guard it as protectively as adults do). Coughs, sneezes, or sighs also may indicate stress, whether from tiredness, coldness, discomfort (see if his diaper is wet), or overstimulation.

## Body language

Although a baby's relative physical immobility in the first three months limits his vocabulary of body language, he does employ several significant gestures and movements. It's important to be aware of them not only because they reflect his inner feelings, but also because they reflect his developing progress as well.

### Smooth Versus Jerky Muscle Movements

While a certain amount of jerkiness and uncoordination are inevitable in the first twelve weeks, smooth muscle and limb movements should gradually begin to predominate. The ability to put a hand to the mouth or to sit up alertly for a moment or two are more than signs of physical progress, they also indicate intellectual growth. A baby who is able to coordinate all the muscles needed to sit up or put his hand to his mouth is demonstrating that he has the *mental* capacity to make his body do what *he* wants it to do.

### Smooth Versus Rapid, Disordered Breathing

One of the best indicators of a calm, relaxed state—smooth, even breathing—is most often seen in quietly alert babies or those in an open space. Rapid, jerky chest movements, in contrast, usually signals organizing trouble or stress. Jerky breathing should prompt a check of the environment for disruptive noises or potentially frightening objects. (Clown masks, for example, often upset infants because of their distortion of the human face.)

Facial coloring also can provide a cue to the baby's mood. *Blotchiness* is generally an indication of a distressed, about-to-cry baby, while a glowing, pink tone is, of course, a sign of tranquillity and receptivity.

Other movements that indicate calm in a young infant include:

- Hand playing with mouth

- Clasping parental finger in hand. Sometimes a baby will also try to use his foot to clasp a finger

- Sucking rhythmically on nipple, bottle, or pacifier

- Movement of hands and feet toward the center of the body. This also indicates that central nervous system organization is proceeding well.

## Hand signals

### Open Hand Extended Toward Parent
This is a signal of alertness and, usually, also a cue that the baby is ready for an interchange.

### Clenched Fist
This may signal general distress, though it also is commonly a sign of anger, and whatever its source, it is nearly always an indication that tears are imminent.

### Hand Held Partially Open, Wrist Limp
This may indicate that the baby is having trouble organizing and is in need of comfort. It is also a sign of a tired child. Situational cues will tell you which.

### Hand Held Limply at Side
This is usually an indication that the baby is ready for sleep.

## FOUR TO SIX MONTHS

In these months, the first change parents notice is in the baby's facial expressions. They begin to look more like real smiles, frowns, and expressions of interest. Usually, this is also the time when the child starts to look just like Uncle Henry when he's angry or Aunt Claire when he is surprised.

Another change that becomes apparent in this period is the

greater clarity and nuance in the infant's communications. The child knows (or, at least, he is learning) that an emphatic eyebrow flash is an excellent way of italicizing a message, and that a well-placed hand or leg movement can add an extra resonance to a smile or frown.

One reason for all these dramatic changes is that a baby has, or is in the process of acquiring, a whole new group of cues and signals in these months. The other reason for the change is simple practice: With experience he has gained a new expertise and dexterity in employing the cues and signals he has been using throughout his first three months.

## Head

### *Lifting Head While Lying on Belly*
In this position an infant looks like a swimmer surfacing for air. His back is arched into a U-shaped curve and his head is thrust upward into a kind of exclamation mark. Attempts to assume this stance have been going on since the eighth or ninth week, but it's only in about the sixteenth or seventeenth week that mastery of it is firm enough to make it a clearly recognizable cue. The alertness and interest it signals is the infant's way of asking: "Hey, Mom and Dad, how about some company?"

## Gaze

### *Looking At and Moving Hands*
Watching a baby perform what usually is called *hand regard* is like watching a skillful mime tell a story with his hands. Slow and fluid, the infant's hands move with the same choreographed grace as the mime's. Indeed, like the mime, the infant also is telling a story with his movements. He is saying: "I've just found these two fascinating objects—my hands." The momentous discovery this represents for him is hard to exaggerate. The child has now identified one of the places where he ends and the world begins. And, quite understandably, he would like to be left alone to ponder that mystery as well as to enjoy and marvel at those two dynamic objects at the end of each arm.

The other reason hand regard should be left undisturbed

is that its emergence signals that a capacity for self-amusement is developing. And though—given his notoriously short attention span—the ability of the baby's hands to keep him amused quickly wanes, hand regard itself is a sign that his hand-eye system is now switched on. Placing another object in that system at this time, such as a rattle or a block, while the motor is still humming, allows the infant (by bringing, say, the block up to his eye rather than the hand he has grown bored of) to practice hand-eye coordination in a new and,

## Arrival Times of the Most Significant Human Facial Expressions

*Present at Birth:*

Interest

Disgust

Distress (in response to pain)

Startled response

*Four to Eight Weeks:*

Social smile (not to be confused with the neonatal smile, which is present at birth and is a tension releaser.)

*Three to Four Months:*

Disgust

Surprise

Wariness

*Five to Nine Months:*

Anger

Fear

Sadness

Repulsion

Avoidance

Curiosity

Joy

*Nine to Twelve Months:*

Petulance

Elation

Confidence

## How Emotions Grow During First Year

| | | | |
|---|---|---|---|
| *Birth*<br>(The two<br>primal<br>sensations<br>from which<br>all emotions<br>arise) | | Excitement | |
| *One month* | | ↓<br>Distress | |
| *Three to Four Months* | Disgust | Wariness | Rage |
| *Five to Nine Months* | ↓<br>Dislike | ↓<br>Fear/Sadness | ↓<br>Anger |
| *Nine to Twelve Months* | ↓<br>Repulsion | ↓<br>Anxiousness | ↓<br>Petulance |

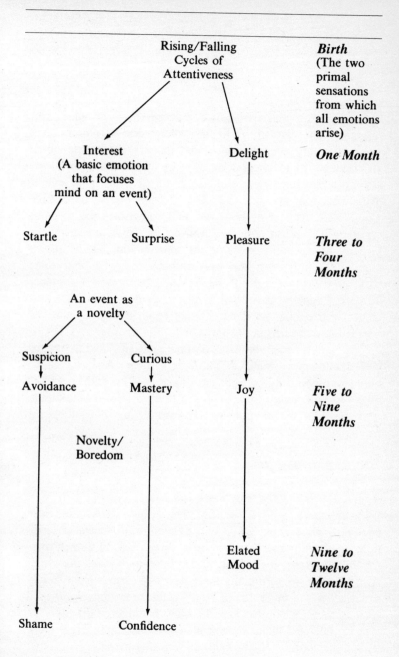

Rising/Falling
Cycles of
Attentiveness

*Birth*
(The two
primal
sensations
from which
all emotions
arise)

Interest
(A basic emotion
that focuses
mind on an event)

Delight

*One Month*

Startle                Surprise

Pleasure

*Three to
Four
Months*

An event as
a novelty

Suspicion          Curious

Avoidance          Mastery

Joy

*Five to
Nine
Months*

Novelty/
Boredom

Elated
Mood

*Nine to
Twelve
Months*

Shame          Confidence

for now at least, more interesting way. At the same time, the imaginative ways you show him how to use this system provide him with ways of amusing himself when you are not there to inspire him.

### Looking at Objects

This is a sign that the baby's universe has expanded from his immediate care givers to the wider world of objects. And since you only need to follow the infant's eye to the object he's looking at to know what's on his mind, it's also one of his most readable cues. He wants you to bring your eye to that object too; and he wants you to comment on it for him. You should be aware, however, that sometimes the meaning of a baby's gaze isn't quite as clear-cut as it may appear. While he may be spending most of his time looking at the rubber dog directly in front of him, his real interest may be the teething ring on the other side of the room. The reason his glance only occasionally goes to it is that already he can track distances well enough to know it's not reachable, while the less interesting dog in front of him is.

For parents, the corollary of this kind of looking is that you should try to track *all* the baby's gazes. And if you see him looking fitfully at a distant object, get up and bring that object to him. Don't think such sensitivity is lost on the infant; it shows him the environment is working to fit itself to his needs.

## Facial expressions

### Anger, Surprise, Sadness, Fear and Joy

Like the smile which preceded them, these looks are close enough to their adult equivalents to require no special descriptions or definitions. Whether on a forty-year-old's or a four-month-old's face, joy, anger, and sadness look much the same. Also like the smile, initially these new expressions exist simply as reflections of inner moods. Only as their meaning is mirrored back in *as-if* responses does the baby begin to realize that he also is making a social statement and can use these expressions to tell the world: "I am happy," or "I am sad." The other role *as-if* plays is to help the infant begin to define general

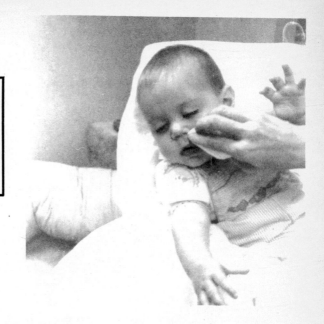

**N**egative
face—head
averted,
hand raised

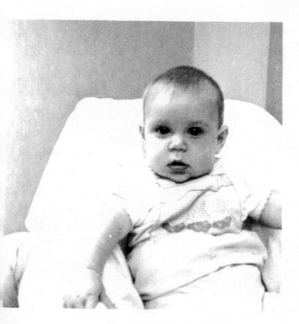

**C**ontemplation
(open space)

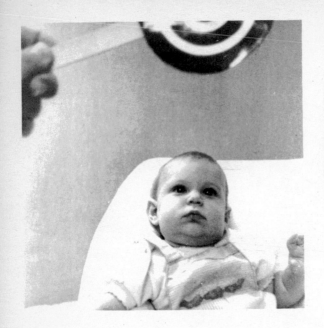

Intense study
(open space)

Deciding
whether a
strange face
is a friend

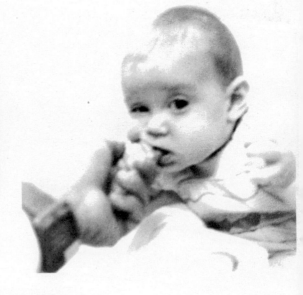

Deciding a strange face is a friend

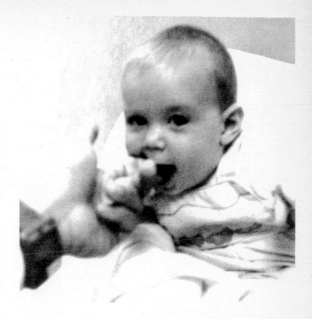

My mommy and me

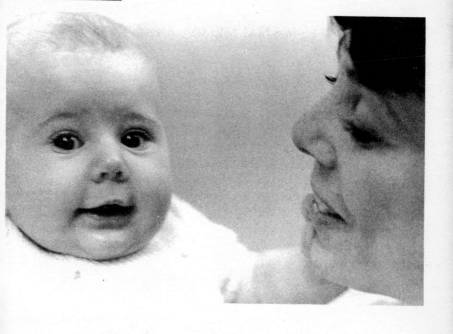

**Y**awn indicating baby rejecting my bid for attention

**S**trong interest

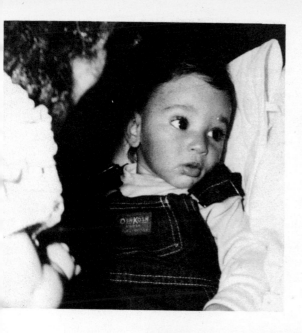

**A**version
(turns away
from doll)

**E**xcited interest,
focused
and alert

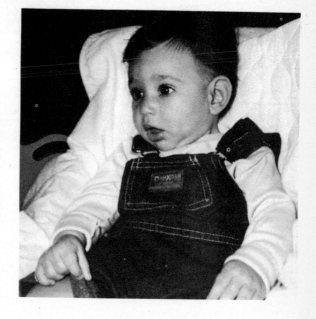

**S**neeze to shut out unpleasant stimulus

**E**xpecting a good thing

**S**avoring a
good thing

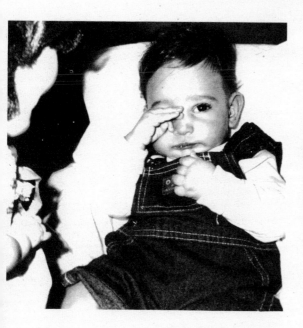

**S**top
stimulating
me

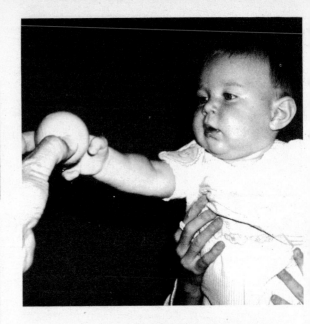

**S**imultaneous
exploration
with hand
and eye

**E**arly
puzzlement

feeling states, such as distress, in more specific ways. As he watches your responses, for instance, he learns that sometimes his distress is due to anger and sometimes to sadness.

This is why it's important to respond with *as-if* to negative, as well as to positive, facial expressions. And while this doesn't mean parents should jump into anger or sadness the way they would jump into joy or surprise, it does mean they should both acknowledge them and help the baby to define those feelings to himself. Your looking sad in response to his look of sadness, for example, is one of the ways he learns that the distress he feels has a specific name—sadness—and that it affects those around him in specific ways. And those are both important pieces of information for an apprentice communicator.

Also important is to identify what it is that is saddening, frightening, or angering the baby. If you know, for instance, that what scares him about the wind-up alligator you brought home today is the way it scurries furiously around the floor, or the funny little clang its metallic engine makes, that will tell you that self-propelled toys should be kept away from him until he is a little older.

## SIX TO TWELVE MONTHS

Though a few new facial expressions have yet to be added by the start of the seventh month, the baby's innate vocabulary of biosocial expressions and signals is largely in place. Predominating in the second half of the first year are what we call developmental cues. These are the signals an infant uses to announce new emotional or intellectual breakthroughs that he would like you to begin reflecting in your responses.

### Movements

#### Bringing Feet to Mouth
Usually a six- or seven-month-old does this while he is lying on his back in the crib or on a blanket. It's an important signal to take heed of because it's the baby's way of saying, "Now I'm ready to understand and identify objects by their size." Earlier, his primary way of knowing a block, a teething

ring, a mobile, or a book was by its color, feel, taste, or sound. Whether it was large or small largely escaped his notice, just as the dimensions of his own body did. The discovery of his feet—which is what the bringing of his foot to his mouth means—signals that has changed; the infant now has a clear idea of where he stops and where he starts, and hence, he also is ready to begin discovering where the things around him stop and start. Now is a good time to begin introducing larger toys, such as stuffed animals. That way the baby will have an opportunity to practice his newly developed sizing skill by comparing his big, new acquisitions against the smaller objects he already has been playing with for months.

### Grasping Small Items Between Thumb and Forefinger

A signal that the baby's coordination is becoming fine-tuned, generally this capability emerges between the eighth and ninth month. And though it tends to be thought of largely in physiological terms—the baby can now hold up a toy horse by grasping one of its feet rather than by grasping it on the trunk—this new mechanical dexterity also has significant social implications. Now that he can hold small objects comfortably you can begin introducing solids so that he can at least try to feed himself. Such self-feeding not only enhances his sense of competency and independence, it brings him one important step closer to the experience of eating as a social experience. Now is also a good time to begin introducing more sophisticated social games, such as Give and Take. That way, the infant's new mechanical dexterity can be made to further enhance his social and communication learning.

### Crawling

This emerges between the sixth and ninth month (physically precocious youngsters may begin as early as the fifth month) and, similar to looking, it is one of the baby's most self-explanatory signals. Generally, all you have to do is look toward the direction the infant is heading in to know what's on his mind. Since babies sometimes lose the thread of their thoughts, just the way adults do in the middle of conversations, make sure you get a firm fix on the thing the child is darting toward.

That way if a bump in the rug or a tangled leg so distracts him that he forgets what he was crawling toward (inexperienced crawlers are particularly prone to this kind of forgetfulness), you will be there to remind him by picking up the object and saying: "Hey, here's the block you were after."

### Ability to Hold Larger Objects Firmly in Both Hands

Generally, this motor skill appears between the eleventh and twelfth month, and like the earlier emergence of the capacity to grasp objects with the thumb and forefinger, it also should be treated as an announcement that the baby has attained a new level of social and psychological maturity. In particular, it means he would not only like to, but he is physiologically ready to assist you in dressing himself. That, of course, means that for the next eighteen months or so, dressing is going to be a long, complicated, and sometimes heartbreakingly tangled affair. As your apprentice learns how to distinguish shirt and T-shirt sleeves from neck openings, seemingly whole days can be lost. But it's worth the extra time and effort since an infant's participation in such activities as dressing are important way-stops on the road to personal competency and independence.

### Vocalizations

While protolanguage in the form of musiclike babbling makes its appearance as early as the second or third week, until around the sixth month (in some infants it may occur a few weeks earlier), it is used primarily as a form of self-entertainment. The baby is exercising his talent to amuse himself. Around the sixth month, however, protolanguage takes on a new and markedly social dimension. One sign of this change is that the pauses between sounds, which occured randomly before, now start forming a discernable pattern while also increasing in number. This is the child's way of inviting a parent into his sound making. In these pauses he wants you to echo back his sounds to him.

By the ninth month he will be able to return the compliment by echoing back your vocalizations. The emergence of this capacity represents an important building block of language, since it is one of the ways a baby learns to handle the complicated syllables that make up words. You can help him attain this mastery by creating little volleys of noise between the two of you. If, for example, he says, "baba," you say, "baba dada," then quiet and see how well he does in trying to mimic your more complicated sound. If he has trouble, drop one of the das from your next echo and see how well he handles that simplified, but for him still complicated, sound.

## Facial expressions

### Boredom

The songs, pictures, games, tricks, or toys that cause half-drooped eyelids, a glazed look, and a general slackening of the facial muscles in a six- or seven-month-old should either be dropped from the parental repertoire or be varied in an interesting new way. That this doesn't happen as often as it perhaps should, I think is in part due to the fact that boredom is often mistaken for sleepiness, which it resembles, and in part due to the fact that parents assume babies don't bore. They do, and an occasional expression of this feeling should not be taken as a failing on your part.

After all, being human, infants are just as likely to grow tired of something they already know well as an adult is. Furthermore, boredom provides you with an opportunity to teach an important lesson. The specific strategies you adopt now, such as replacing the mobile over the crib with a new toy, temporarily moving your interactions to (for the baby) a relatively unfamiliar room, or introducing new games, or simply varying play with a familiar toy, may not be applicable when an infant is two or three. But the general principle you illustrate with these strategies—that boredom can, with a little imagination, be defeated—will be applicable then and for the rest of the child's life.

### Shyness

The six- or seven-month-old who averts his gaze, drops his head, and seems to draw up inside himself (nervous fussing may also be present) in the presence of a new or relatively new face is having a first attack of shyness. The presence of a favorite toy in that unfamiliar person's hands helps to ensure that the bout won't be as distressing as it otherwise might have been.

Usually, recognizable looks of *shame* also begin to appear around the sixth or seventh month. But this emotion and its expression are so individual that no one group of characteristics can be said to adequately define its presence in infants. Developmentally, the most significant thing about both shame and shyness is that both—especially shame—are almost purely social expressions (in the sense that they are almost always directed at another person), compared to smiles or looks of anger, which aren't.

### "No"

The tight-lipped pursing and/or vigorous head shaking that mark the baby's "no" usually appear toward the end of the ninth month. And both gestures present themselves so emphatically, it's almost impossible *not* to understand what the baby is saying. What mothers and fathers sometimes tend to forget, though, is that the ability to understand no's meaning cuts two ways. Now that the infant understands what he means by "no," *he also understands what you mean by "no"*—"Don't do that." That puts your interactive discourse on a whole new plane. Instead of just taking away the cereal he's tossing around, for example, now you can *tell* him: *"Don't throw it."* And while instant miracles are not going to spring from that admonition, eventually, as your no's are repeated with variety, the baby will stop throwing the cereal.

One word of caution: Angry, emphatic no's are never a good idea, but they are particularly inappropriate in the first twelve months, since the acts of deliberate defiance they usually are aimed at curbing are beyond the powers of a young baby. Consequently, they end up frightening without also enlightening. The baby wonders: "What did I do that was so wrong?" Light, playful no's still allow you to get your point across, but in a more reassuring way.

# NINE
# Memory, Individual Differences, and Fitting In

**P**erched on my knee on a parsons bench outside the playroom is eleven-month-old Evan, who in his flaming red jump suit and black cape looks this morning like a miniversion of Captain America. From the suspicious patch of wetness spreading across his pants, however, I would guess that the real Captain America probably keeps his diaper drier. And I'm sure he keeps his cape cleaner. Despite its relative newness, Evan's already looks like it has had one hair-raising adventure too many. By way of explaining its presence, earlier his mother Eileen told me that on leaving the house two alternatives had been presented to her: "Evan let it be known that we would take the cape or he would have a temper tantrum. I let him take the cape."

As a twinkle lights up Evan's eyes, I look up to see Eileen approaching us. A few moments later the three of us are inside the playroom, and a now drier Evan, happily ensconced on his mother's lap, is staring fascinatedly at a toy stage much like the ones puppeteers use in Punch and Judy shows. From top to bottom the stage measures three and a half feet, and it is painted blue. On its now shuttered curtains the face of a clown smiles brightly at the world.

Transfixed by the clown's beguiling smile Evan barely notices the heartbeat monitor which I attach to his chest as Eileen, who still holds him in her lap, soothingly strokes his head. Looking like a large Band-Aid, the wireless monitor signals a recorder in our control room. Dr. Philip Zelazo, who created the technique with Dr. Richard Kearsley, is a consultant at the center and director of the Department of Psychology at the Montreal Children's Hospital. What we are measuring today isn't really Evan's heart, which is robustly healthy, but how it reflects his *central-processing agency*.

The "CPA" is the portion of the brain where information from the environment is stored, processed, and retrieved; a parent would call it her baby's mind. Its centrality to our mental life is why since the early 1980s, measurements of the CPA have begun replacing traditional and narrower measurements, such as activity level (the familiar quiet, average, active categories) and sensorimotor-based IQ tests, as a way of defining how babies are different. The reason why an index of CPA function provides us with a broader and more accurate gauge of the *individual differences* among infants is that the CPA is fundamental to the baby's active memory. And as with quiet and the role of social learning in language learning, the videotape camera also has taught us to think about infant memory in a new way. *Specifically, we now realize that a child's recall function influences more aspects of his thinking and behavior than do any of his other capabilities.*

One case in point is the relationship between infant IQ and infant memory. Work by Dr. Zelazo, Dr. Jeffrey Fagan of Rutgers University, and other memory investigators, shows that a baby's ability to identify an object and then recall it later is a very accurate measure of his overall intelligence. Designers of adult IQ tests realized this a long time ago, which is why the ability to draw from memory designs just seen in the IQ tests given students taps precisely this capacity. The extension of this insight to infancy has not only provided us with a more reliable tool for measuring a baby's intelligence, but has also helped to solve one of developmental psychology's great challenges—why our current baby IQ tests have been such poor predictors of later intelligence. Sensorimotor ability (that is, the capacity to identify a stimulus and move eyes and hands in a coordinated fashion) measures a complex phenomenon—intelligence coupled with eye-hand-finger coordination. For example, a bright child who happens to be clumsy will have a low score.

Even more exciting than the work on IQ—and, I think,

potentially even more significant—is the important correlation the new memory research has uncovered between the infant's *recall ability* and what might be called his *life functioning;* in other words, his ability to enjoy, participate, learn, and be emotionally enriched by his interactions with the human environment. Initially parents express surprise at the new significance attached to this connection. But once they have had a chance to think about it, they realize why active-recall memory would be so important to social behavior generally, and interactive behavior specifically.

One example of how it works is the way a child's recall function influences his ability to open exchanges. When in the first year these important infant initiatives begin appearing is contingent on how quickly the child is able to remember it is his smiles that always catch his mother's eye and his excited kicking and arm waving that catches his father's. Once these memories are firmly encoded in the CPA, seeing Mommy automatically triggers that sort of recollection, as if to say: "Oh, yes, I know how to make Mommy light up, I'll smile"; while Daddy's presence makes him remember: "Daddy always laughs and wants to join in when I kick."

Much the same correlation operates between infant memory and the ability to read parental cues. The better the baby's recall, the sooner he comes to recognize that a finger waved across his nose means "no," and that the creak of the opening toy box signals that he and Daddy are about to play. A baby who learns how to read his parents' signals is not only quicker to develop games and routines with them, he also enjoys an important advantage when it comes to skill development. This is why the child who is able to remember from one exchange to the next that the flow of uhuhs his mother uses to keep the action moving also are cues for him to take his turn usually is much quicker to master the speaker's and listener's roles than a child who has to be reminded each time what those maternal uhuhs mean.

Even a baby's capacity to be soothed and to soothe himself can be a function of memory. This emerges very clearly in recent studies which show that an important reason some infants are easier to calm than others is that they are better at remembering the cues that soothe them. Thus, if that cue happens to be being pressed against mother's breast, what I'll call the high-recall infant begins calming the moment he feels the warmth of her skin against his head, because he remembers it as a calming cue and now knows what to expect next: Mother will rock him gently and whisper comfortingly in his ear. Low-recall children, on the other hand, because they don't remember these maternal behaviors as cues, have to rediscover the wonderful soothing quality each time they are upset. And since that discovery takes time to make, they cry longer and are harder to calm.

At the center, we are using this new memory data in a novel, and I believe pathbreaking, way. Since recall capacity influences a baby's behavior across a wide range of measures, we have created an interactive index, which uses memory function specifically, and central-processing-agency function generally, to measure what we believe is the most important infant individual difference: *fittability into the interactive environment.*

Our index's two principal categories are *Alpha,* for babies whose minor memory sensitivities may make them more difficult to fit in, and *Beta,* for infants whose recall capacity makes them easy interactive fits. While these ratings are meant to help us and parents anticipate the arc of a child's developmental curve, *these designations are not judgments nor do they fix a baby's course.*

One of the happiest findings to emerge from the work of Dr. Zelazo and other investigators is that recall capacity can be enhanced and strengthened. In fact, one of the most important things we do at the center is to help babies move from Alpha to Beta status. Our principal tools are a series of memory exercises which we will look at later in this chapter. In order to determine who is and isn't in need of such exercises, however, we first have to determine a baby's basic "fittability." And one of the ways we do that is through Dr. Zelazo's miniature stage, which despite its clever disguise is really a test of infant recall function.

Its special grace is the deftness with which it taps into and measures memory and recall. Though Evan can't tell us when he has memorized a person, place, or thing, there are two ways to determine when a memory engram implants itself on his CPA. One is by monitoring the ebb and flow of his looking, smiling, and squealing. Each of the test's first six trial runs repeats the same sequence of events—a toy car knocks over a series of Styrofoam balls. We will be able to know when Evan's memory of this sequence is firmly fixed because at the middle of a trial run, after the action has been repeated, he may squeal and smile in delighted anticipation. By monitoring his responses, we can tell when repetition makes the action in the sequence overly familiar, because not only will Evan's smiling and squealing eventually decrease, he will begin to turn away from the stage with what we would call in an adult a bored look.

The second way we examine the memorization process during the procedure is through heart beat; it too has its own pattern. By recoding the ups and downs in Evan's pulse, we can tell when he has committed an event to memory, and even when he has developed a set of expectations based on that memory.

As the test starts, the cardiac unit we are using to monitor Evan's heart rate indicates a beat well within the normal range. But as the stage's curtains are drawn back, the machine records a sudden drop—a pattern characteristic of a child who is focusing his attention. And, indeed, as I look up from the monitoring unit, I see that Evan is riveted by what the curtains have revealed. As he studies the half-foot-high incline on the stage and the tiny blue car perched on top of it, you can almost hear him thinking, "Hmmm, that looks very interesting." Since the incline is in profile, the little roadway that runs down its middle isn't visible, but when I slip behind the stage and give the car a starting push, it will shoot down the roadway and ram into a group of brightly colored Styrofoam balls.

After this happens a few times the image of the car crashing into the blocks so arouses Evan that he squeals in delight; simultaneously, the cardiac unit records a sharp increase in his heart beat. At this moment, Evan is a very excited little boy. In each of the trial runs that follow, however, like the waves in a receding tide, the upward shifts in Evan's heart beat recorded by the monitor grow progressively modest.

In fact, by the time we reach the fifth of the six trial runs that make up the test's first phase, not only does the sight of the car careening down the incline fail to produce a flicker of change in Evan's heart beat, during the crucial crash he actually looks bored. This indicates that somewhere in Evan's CPA the image of the car, the stage, and the balls now have been firmly encoded. Three months ago, when Evan was first exposed to the test, it took a full seven trial runs to produce evidence of definite memory formation. The fact that only five trial runs were required to produce the same result today suggests an improvement in Evan's memory function.

I say "suggests" because we won't be able to gauge the true measure of that improvement until we conduct the second and most important part of the test. While this portion also consists of six trial runs, it is built around a mild discrepancy or variation. During the first three runs in this sequence, after hurtling down the incline, the toy car will not—as Evan expects—knock over the balls. In the last three runs, the original sequence will be reintroduced. The aim of this variation is to measure Evan's ability to retrieve and make use of a memory. Will he be able to overcome the confusion produced by the three discrepant trial runs and "remember" the original sequence—the car knocking over the balls—when it is reintroduced?

Inclusion of this sequence is designed to measure an infant's capacity to retrieve a memory from his CPA. This capacity is not only the most important aspect of memory function, it is one we all—adults as well as infants—use dozens of times each day. In the infant's case, an example of a real-life situation where retrieval is called for is what happens when Aunt Claire, who visited him last week in a red dress, visits again wearing a blue one. Her different-colored dress is the equivalent of the test's discrepant runs. Just as the baby's ability to overcome the confusion produced by the variation in the runs and recognize the original sequence is dependent on his retrieving the memory of that original sequence, e.g., his ability to identify Aunt Claire is dependent on his retrieving a recollection of her that will allow him to transcend the confusion produced by her new blue dress, and to be delighted when yet a week later she appears in red.

Later in the first year, a baby will recall Aunt Claire no matter what the color of her dress.

This growing capacity is known as recall identification. And it was Evan's below-average score on it during his first exposure to Dr. Zelazo's test several months ago which suggested to me that many of the seemingly unrelated interactive problems that had brought Evan's parents to the center for an initial consultation might be due to Evan's minor memory deficits.

During that first meeting, Evan's father, David, had described Evan's behavior as "a little puzzling." Then, pausing as if carefully measuring the impact of the words shaping in his mind, he added, "I suppose a professional would call Evan an unresponsive child." Knowing how painful it is for a parent to make such an admission, I felt an immediate pang of sympathy for David and for Eileen.

At the same time, studying the video we made of Evan and Eileen the next day, I understood why David had chosen that word. At several points in the exchange, Evan did appear unresponsive. This was particularly apparent during Eileen's attempts at paragraph building. Usually, these enticing strings of signs, sounds, and movements cause a baby to reach a new pitch of interactive excitement. Evan, however, has visible trouble holding on as each of Eileen's paragraphs build momentum. It's not that they are overstimulating; but rather, that he has difficulty following them. While he brightens at the start of each new paragraph, often midway through, his face abruptly clouds over as if he had just realized: "Oh dear, I've forgotten the next step in the dance." During these memory lapses, Evan's almond-shaped eyes make him look like a little lost elf. His inability to recognize Eileen's cues also gives the exchange a disjointed quality more typical of interactions with very young infants.

In exchanges with two- and three-month-olds, this bumpiness is normal because the baby's memory span is short and he and his parents are still developing the cues that later will allow them to move smoothly from one interactive routine or game to another. Around the fourth month, however, a noticeable synchronicity and smoothness should begin emerging. And by the sixth month, mother, father, and infant often become so in tune that they come to resemble one of those legendary vaudevillian teams renowned for their flawless timing. Here, each partner should have so memorized the potential menu of interactive games and routines and be so quick at identifying each other's cues that they are able to move effortlessly from a finger game to an eye game, up to the changing table for a diapering, back to the floor for a conversation about a nearby doll, and then return to the finger game, all in the course of a single exchange and without missing a beat.

Though the sense of attunement (and knowledge of each other's cues) which creates this seamless flow was missing from Evan's and Eileen's interaction, I saw nothing on the pretest tape to indicate that Evan's unresponsiveness was a reflection of or a reaction to Eileen's behavior. Throughout the exchange Eileen was engaging and imaginative without being overstimulating. I noticed that at every opportunity she waited or quietly urged her baby to take the lead. Even more striking was how, even in the face of Evan's frequently ambiguous cues and signals (possibly due to by-product of minor memory deficits), Eileen still was able to make herself a reliable and inventive echoer of her baby. On this and the subsequent tapes we made of this family, there also was no evidence that Evan's behavior was intended as a form of rejection (a commonly held secret fear of all parents).

At the end of Evan's fourth month, a full-time baby nurse had been employed so that Eileen could return to work. And now both parents worried that having perceived this change as a rejection of him, Evan was responding by rejecting them. Understandably, introducing a full-time care giver into a baby's circle is a source of great concern to working parents. And given the central role such care givers play in an infant's life (we will explore how a care giver influences a family's fit in Chapter Thirteen), she should be selected with great care. But having met Dothlyn, the lovely Jamaican woman who had been selected to look after Evan, I was confident that David's and Eileen's fears on this score were unwarranted. Dothlyn was what every care giver should be—an imaginative, supportive, loving presence in Evan's life.

Aside from a lack of other possible causes, there were three incidents on the tape that actively suggested that Evan's "disinterest" was really due to minor memory deficits. The first was the disjointed quality of the exchange itself; its flow should have been much smoother. The second was Evan's response to Eileen's paragraph building; at this stage her paragraphs should have been easily recognizable as cues and alerted Evan to his mother's next interactive move. The third was Eileen's difficulty in bringing Evan's eye to a nearby plastic bowling pin. By the seventh month (Evan's age when the tape was made) usually such mutual referencing is so ingrained as a part of a family's interactive repertoire that the baby instantly recognizes what the parent's gaze signifies. His response to the cues in the eye dance that follows this initial reference is as instinctive as ours when another adult says, "Hello."

Evan had no difficulty with the reference's opening sequence; his eyes immediately chased Eileen's to the plastic bowling pin. Two other steps follow in a complete reference, however. After gazing at the object, parent's and infant's eyes return to one another. Generally, this is the time when they do most of their commenting about the object under mutual scrutiny. Then, in the third step, their eyes again return to the object. Somewhere between the second and third step in this dance, Evan appeared to forget the meaning of Eileen's eye cues, and his face abruptly clouded over with that same "I think I've forgotten where I am" look I had seen during the paragraph-building episode.

The results from Dr. Zelazo's test confirmed the presence in Evan of the memory deficits. On our interactive index, Evan's test score placed him in the Alpha category, which indicates a level of recall function that may make a baby susceptible to fitting-in difficulties. In the months that followed, much of our work with Evan at the center, and Eileen's and David's work with him at home, revolved around a series of recall strategies we began developing in the early 1980s. These grew out of our desire to translate the exciting new work on memory into a series of practical aids for the parents of Alpha infants. But since their goal—to allow a baby to tap his recall function fully—is as applicable to Beta babies as it is to Alphas, recently we have begun incorporating these strategies into our work with Betas as well. These techniques require no special expertise to apply. I think you will find that they can be integrated into your exchanges easily and naturally.

### Create Contextual Cues

We have all had the experience of hearing an old song that brings us back to the person we first heard it with. The song is a good example of a contextual cue and how it acts as a subtle memory trigger. What makes these cues especially important to a baby is that the more of them that are available, the more opportunities he has to practice memory retrieval. And memory is no different than other skills in the sense that the more opportunities a child has to work his recall muscle, the better he will be at remembering. While anything, from a favorite song to a toy to a game, can be transformed into a subtle contextual cue, there are two aspects of the immediate environment that make particularly good cues.

One aspect is *time*. Even though a baby doesn't yet have our adult notion of time, he does have a biological clock, and setting aside a special hour for the two of you to be together has the effect of creating a memory aid. Say six in the evening is the time you reserve. Within a week or two, this clock may be so regulated that the child will be able to gauge your arrival to within a few minutes. This means that at five-fifty, memories of you and yesterday's time together will be flooding through his mind.

In selecting an hour for your special time, keep in mind that infants, like adults, have high and low points in their daily cycle. So as much as work, chores, and other commitments allow, try to place your hour in or near the baby's peak period. That way he will be at his best and, hence, more likely to remember what the two of you did and which new cues you created together today.

The second aspect of the environment that lends itself to cue making is *place*. Combined, time *and* place can be made into a pair of mutually reinforcing reminders. High-recall Beta babies are less in need of this twining of reinforcements. In fact, after the fourth month, it's a good idea to begin varying their settings, since too much sameness and repetition bores them. But for Alpha babies, the addition of place to time provides a backup cue. That way, if your presence at six o'clock fails to stir the baby's memory, what will is being brought to the corner under the window that you set aside for your special encounters. Seeing that the two of you are once again in your favorite corner, the baby thinks: "Oh yes, now I remember what Mommy and I are going to do."

### Activity

The use of activity can further reinforce this recollection. One way to use it is by setting aside a special group of toys which are brought out only during these special encounters. Another way—and this applies to all infants—is by centering these encounters around special activities. At my suggestion, for example, David and Eileen used their special hour with Evan for teaching-like tasks. Even though Evan still is much too young to distinguish instructional activities from the other things he does with them, over time he will come to think of these encounters as the occasions when Mommy and Daddy show him how to do things, such as how to roll a truck across the floor or operate a Busy Box. This means that through David's and Eileen's consistency, over time, activity also will become a contextual cue for Evan.

### Create Memory Sequences

As in weight training, where slow, incremental increases in poundage are used to develop muscle strength, slow, incremental increases in the number of recollections a baby associates with a particular event can be used to develop his memory strength. A good way of doing this is by taking an already familiar activity, such as feeding, and developing a specific sequence of events that lead up to it. You don't have to duplicate the sequence exactly each time you use it, but in order to lay down memory tracks of each item in the scenario, before feeding repeat each item in approximately the same order and at approximately the same pace. Thus, if there are four items in your sequence—say, a song, a rocking, a stroking of the head, and then nursing or a bottle—the more consistent you are in repeating each in the same order, the quicker the baby will be to memorize the sequence. After starting the song, you will be able to see from the anticipatory gleam in his eye that he already is three steps ahead of you and thinking about your milk. Another example of sequence building—this one for a slightly older baby—might include washing his hands, putting on his bib, singsonging "We are going in to eat," placing him in the high chair, and announcing "Here we are."

A second advantage of sequencing is that it adds the sense flow that was so palpably missing from Evan's and Eileen's exchange. Over time, as the sequences begin to run into and become cues for one another, they tend to give the child's and parent's time together a seamless quality. Their entire day begins to seem like one long, happy, uninterrupted interaction—one which has no discernible starting or ending point. Thus, on hearing the song that starts off your prefeeding sequence, the baby may think of the several items that follow the song. He also is reminded that *after* feedings he and Daddy always play together. That is a recollection to set off another happy train of memories.

### Create Memories That Tap All the Baby's Senses

Though recollections are often visual, our other senses stir a good many of our memories. This is why allowing an infant to experience with his ears, his nose, his fingertips, and his skin—with as many different senses as you can involve—not only increases his knowledge (which makes later recall easier), but also gives him several different pathways by which he can retrieve his memory of the experience later and bring it back to the surface of his conscious mind.

Technically, this is known as *intermodal memory making*, and to illustrate how it can be used to build recall function, take the "brrrr" sound parents make by vibrating air through their lips. Babies love this; it makes them giggle with delight. A way to enhance this delight is to put your lips to the baby's arm or leg, then vibrate them. Aside from adding to his enjoyment, this experience will create a *tactile* (the feel of your lips against his skin) memory of your sound making to add to the auditory one he already has. Which means that later, not only will certain sights and sounds make the baby recall the pleasure your noise making gave him, but also certain kinds of touches (like shaking his toes).

In explaining the use of intermodal memory making to Eileen and David, I pointed out that it is also a way of introducing a social element into such experiences as feeding. Dining, as opposed to eating, is a preeminently civilized activity. And one of the things that makes it so is that food is experienced not just through the palate, but through *all* the senses—eyes, ears, nose—and even through the emotions. This is why to most of us, dining not only means eating, it also means good conversation, tantalizing smells, imaginatively presented food, and, of course, the companionship of good friends. These appreciations don't just spontaneously appear. They have to be *presented/introduced.* And while it isn't until toddlerhood that the social and emotional aspects of dining are paramount, you can prepare for this introduction by dressing up the baby's feeding hours with engaging sights and sounds, and warm, good company. That way, when he sits down at the table at two or three, the images in his mind won't be simply of food, but of all the delightful things that accompany it, such as good talk and loving company.

### Help the Baby to Remember Tactile Experiences

You can do this by tapping a special mechanism in the infant's recall function. If you are about to introduce an object you want him to form a tactile memory of—say you want him to remember that a tennis ball feels fuzzy or that a lacquered wood surface (like the kind used on many wooden toys) feels smooth and glossy—you are more likely to imprint a memory of that object's feel if your introduction is preceded by a rich visual, then a rich auditory, stimulus. These two elements enhance a baby's capacity to remember tactile sensations; sight and sound help an infant to locate himself in a room, and in turn, it is easier for him to perceive and remember an object's feel. To sense himself in space is thought to help him sense objects. That is the hypothesis.

Whatever the precise reason, these two forms of introductory stimulation do enhance a child's ability to form tactile memories. In practice this means that if you start with some singsong talk, then make a few exaggerated faces, then introduce a tennis ball, later when the baby sees the tennis ball lying on the floor at the other end of the room, he is more likely to act as if he is saying to himself: "Oh yes, now I remember, that's the tennis ball Mommy showed me. It feels fuzzy."

### Notice What a Baby Likes

He is more likely to mark and remember the things, people, games and activities, gestures, sounds, and colors that touch him in a special way. A corollary of this is that a child is more likely to recall the sequences you build and the contextual cues you create if they employ these special likes of his.

One way a baby declares his preferences is through his smile, but infants also use more subtle cues. If, for example, on reaching for his box of Bunny Builders you notice that the baby suddenly quiets, opens his mouth, widens his eyes, and looks expectant, these are indications that he holds the Bunny Builders in special regard. Another behavior that signals a special preference is if it helps an infant to organize. I noticed, for example, that Evan was much more likely to look at Eileen's face after playing peekaboo with her. That exploring behavior of his is an indication of organization. This means that for Evan, the physical stimulation of peekaboo has an organizing effect. For other infants, the stroking of an arm or leg can produce organization, or a special sound—sometimes even a song—can do it.

In a multifaceted program, such as the one Evan underwent at the center, it is impossible to single out the influence of any one element. Nonetheless, those of us who worked with Evan, David, and Eileen believe that many of the behavioral changes we began noticing on the tapes we made during the family's visits to the center were due to the influence of memory exercises. This visual evidence of improved recall function is why Evan's many friends at the center are optimistic about the results of today's test.

Indeed, I notice that a small group of staff members has quietly assembled at the playroom doorway as Evan is being prepared for the retest. I attach the cardiac transmitter as Eileen soothingly strokes her baby's head. Then I position myself near one of the windows so that I can monitor Evan's reactions. However, as before, we will use heart rate as our primary indicator of how long it takes Evan to re-identify the events on the stage, which he saw a while ago. While he searches his memory for similarities, Evan's heart beats evenly as if he were saying to himself, "Hmmmmmm, where have I seen you before?" The "Oh yes, now I know," which he mentally shouts when he makes the match is reflected by a sudden jump in his heart rate.

In the last portion of the test, there are three separate trial runs, and from my monitoring of Evan's looking, I think I know why the technician is smiling when he slips out from behind the monitoring unit at the end of the third trial, walks over to Eileen, and whispers something in her ear. Evidently, so too do the four happy faces in the doorway who, much to Evan's delight, burst into applause.

# TEN
# Menu Offering: A Parent's Guide to Alpha and Beta Infants

$\boxed{\text{L}}$ ike Evan, many infants have central-processing-related sensitivities. And also like Evan, often their sensitivities take the form of minor memory deficits. But since the CPA controls several aspects of the baby's functioning, central-processing weaknesses also may cause problems independent of or in addition to recall. One is a *hypersensitivity* to moderate levels of noise, light, or tactile stimulation. Another is *weak signaling,* or the incapacity to coordinate facial and body movements into a single, uniform, unambiguous signal or cue.

At the center, these three sensitivities (memory is the third) designate a child as an Alpha infant. And in addition to sharing a CPA-related sensitivity, Alphas also share one other characteristic—the problems that may make them challenging to fit *can be overcome.* Alpha families have a wide number of resources available to them. Examples of these resources are not only the memory exercises, but many of the other strategies (especially those related to quiet and predictability) we have looked at in this book. Used with love, patience, and understanding, these exercises can raise many Alpha infants to their full intellectual and emotional potentials.

At the same time, there are a growing number of facilities, like our center, that offer professional support and guidance to Alpha children who may need special help. A key element in the helping process, however, is early identification. Prema-

191

turity and birth trauma are high on the current list of suspects. It is important for *you* to be aware of the behavioral patterns that mark Alpha and Beta infants.

To help you, we have created a strategy called *menu offering*. It represents a structuring and formalization of what you and other mothers and fathers already do in exchanges, which is to offer the infant a series of options: Do you want to play an eye game? Do you want to look at a block? Do you want to talk? Do you want to just sit quietly and look at one another? Over the months, you and other mothers and fathers create a set of routines and ways of presenting those routines in the form of options, which allows the baby to select the activity he wants. At the same time, infants develop their own idiosyncratic ways of making choices. Some use primarily facial expressions, others use hand and arm movements. Nonetheless, there are general aspects of a child's interactive behavior that, if you know how to identify them, indicate whether he is an Alpha or Beta infant.

## Alpha Infants

Among the four menu behaviors that characterize an Alpha child's interactive responses are:

1) *Difficulty in Reading the Menu*
   The doll you hold up as an enticement to play and the block you offer as a next option are essentially memory cues. In order to bring them to life, the baby has to consult his memory; which is to say, in order to read your menu of options he has to think to himself: "Now, what did Mommy and I do last time we played with the block and with the doll, and which toy was more fun to play with?" Depending on his recollection of each item, the infant will then signal his choice. An Alpha infant has trouble doing this because the agency of memory, which immediately brings a block or a doll to life in another infant's mind, doesn't work as effectively in his case. So the Alpha's response tends to be like Evan's. The disinterested expression on his face is due to the fact that he can't remember how he saw the doll or block before.

Hence, his lack of enthusiasm at the prospect of playing with them.

As a parent, what you should be watching for when you offer options are *overall patterns* of such blankness. All babies forget, and young ones have an especially slippery grip on memory. But a consistent pattern of forgetfulness—as manifested in situations like the one I've just described—should alert you to the possibility of a recall deficit.

2) *Inability to Clearly Indicate Menu Selections*

Characteristic of a weak signaler, this kind of menu behavior arises from organizational difficulties. The baby's cues appear unclear and ambiguous because he hasn't yet achieved the physiological control necessary to shape his gazes, facial muscles, and arm and leg movements into a single, unambiguous message.

An example of a weak signaler is the six-month-old who can't coordinate his gazes and neck and head movements (don't expect such coordination from a one- or two-month-old). Thus, at the beginning of a mutual reference, his eyes move to the right but his head does not, so his parent, who is trying to bring his attention to an object, is left wondering: "Is my baby looking at it or isn't he?" A second example of a weak signaler is the child whose arm goes limp just as it is about to point to something; that final bit of organizational effort is just too much for him. A third example is the infant who twenty to twenty-five minutes after nap time still looks half-asleep. "Should I try to rouse him with some exciting stimulation," wonders his puzzled father, "or should I put him back in the crib?" A fourth example is the baby who goes from sleep to crying and vice versa without intermediate steps, such as fussiness or whimpering.

Weak or confusing signalers require parents to be, above all, patient. Study their eyes, look at the direction their arms and legs seem to be headed in. Though a weak signaler often can't put all of these aspects of his behavior together, individual movements and changes of gaze will give you a hint of what's on his mind. Also important is to make your own signals as clear as possible. Slow down your gazes, exaggerate your arm and leg movements, and repeat these over and over again until the infant notices them. Be sure, too, to reflect and amplify his weak signals by, for instance, calling attention to the feelings he is trying to express with them. Over time, as the child watches how you create signals, and as his own biological organization advances, his cue-making capability will improve.

**3)**   *Unable to Tolerate Certain Menu Offerings*
Commonly an indication of a hypersensitive infant, at its root also is an immature organizational system, which makes the baby unable to absorb and process stimulation at levels other children find easily tolerable.

If there is, for example, a hypersensitivity to auditory stimuli, a parent may find that a vocalization, sometimes pitched just barely above normal speaking range, produces crankiness and fussiness, while a startling background noise, such as the sharp ring of a telephone or the insistent buzz of a stove timer, results in a burst of tears. One strategy that often helps such infants is to adopt an especially quiet singsong voice in exchanges. Another is to ensure that the settings for your interactions are free of *any* potentially disturbing background noise.

A hypersensitivity to visual stimuli signals itself more subtly, so you have to be more alert. Notice, for example, how the baby responds when you turn on the light next to his crib. Does he wince and become fussy? A reaction is normal to a sudden flood of light, but if the child is still wincing and fussing ten minutes later, it may signal a visual hypersensitivity. One strategy that often helps such infants to acclimate themselves to visual stimuli is careful preparation. Before switching on a light or exposing a baby to bright sunlight, rock him for a few minutes. The soothing swaying will help to prepare him for the organizational challenge that lies ahead. Rocking and quiet, in fact, are two of an Alpha parent's greatest aids, because they facilitate organization for *all* difficult-to-organize infants.

**4)** *Difficulty in Coping with New Additions to the Menu*
This is characteristic of all Alpha babies generally, but
for different reasons. A hypersensitive infant resists a new
menu selection if it contains a stimulus too potent for
the baby to absorb. A case in point would be the visually
hypersensitive child who howls when a clown abruptly
pops out of the box just placed in front of him. A weak
signaler, on the other hand, leaves a parent uncertain about
the pleasure he takes in a menu offering. So, lacking a
clear-cut signal one way or another, that parent makes a
mental note to herself. In the future, avoid finger games
because they don't seem to inspire much excitement.

Infants with memory deficits resist menu offerings for
a different reason. What allows a baby to play knowledgeably with his new Busy Box—even though he has never
seen a Busy Box before—is that he draws on his memory
of other toys and other kinds of play and uses those recollections to guide his behavior with the Busy Box. This
is called a learning transfer and it is one of an infant's
most important strategies for coping with the new. Memory deficient children have more difficulty making such
transfers because of their lack of recall facility. So instead
of inciting enthusiasm, such an infant will look puzzled
and turn away from the box because he doesn't know
what to do with it.

Because these characteristics make Alpha infants demanding interactive partners, not uncommonly an Alpha
mother will tell me that sometimes exchanges with her
baby leave her feeling frustrated and incomplete. In her
very next breath that same parent will then express remorse
and guilt for even suggesting such feelings. *There is nothing
abnormal about these emotions.* Interactions with Alpha
infants are challenging, and their parents wouldn't be human if they didn't feel occasional twinges of frustration
and doubt.

At the same time, helping an Alpha baby overcome
his disabilities—watching him grow into a zesty, inquisi-
tive, loving child who, with your help, is able to realize
his full potential, offers a special satisfaction few parents
are fortunate enough to experience. There are two maxims

that all Alpha parents should keep in mind. One is: *Be kind to yourself* You are doing everything you can to aid and support your baby. The other is: *Be patient*. With help the infant will catch up, but right now he already is dancing as fast as he can.

## Beta Infants

The Beta category also grows out of what we have learned recently about the value of CPA function as a mark of individual differences among infants. At the same time, the category also reflects our (and a growing number of other investigators') dissatisfaction with the traditional ways of measuring individual differences. The two most important indexes in all of these differences—to the baby himself and to his parents—are interactive fit and intelligence. And of the two traditional ways of distinguishing how infants differ, the first, activity level (quiet, active, and average), tells us nothing about either fit or intelligence.

Sensorimotor measurements, on the other hand, are designed to have a predictive value. The two infant capabilities they measure are physical coordination and the capacity to identify a stimulus. Follow-up studies, however, show that sensorimotor-derived IQ scores bear little or no relation to a child's IQ at two or three. As Dr. Jeffrey Fagan, one of our leading memory researchers, notes, "These measurements have been characterized by poor to inconsistent validity." Dr. Zelazo is even blunter: sensorimotor IQ tests, he declares, "have little or no predictive value."

A major reason for the poor validity is that physical coordination only dimly reflects IQ. Just as there are a great many physically awkward adults who are superior in intelligence and emotional adjustment, there also are a great many physically clumsy babies who are superior as well. And while these two qualities fail to be picked up by sensorimotor measurements, they emerge very sharply when a baby's behavior is examined through the prism of CPA function. This is why, like the proverbial absentminded professor, there are some Beta babies who are physically awkward and by sensorimotor measurements might be categorized as below average in intelligence. But what these infants share with all other Betas is a normal to superior recall function and signaling ability, and also a normal tolerance to stimulation. These qualities are what make Beta children such easy fits. They are quick to learn about themselves, about their partners, and about the human environment generally.

At the same time, this very quickness makes a Beta infant a demanding, if stimulating, interactive partner. Seeing you pull out a toy the two of you played with two days ago, he may now turn away because he is already familiar with it and wants a new toy to test himself against. Similarly, the clarity of his signals allows a Beta to express himself directly and emphatically. If he doesn't like something you do, he will tell you straightaway. The Beta baby is growing as fast as his biology and the interactive environment allow, and his quickness to catch on to things is reflected in his menu behaviors. For example, because they do master things easily and bore quickly, Betas demand the following:

1) *The interactive menu must be continually changed and updated.*

For a parent this means that a Beta babys rejections should never be taken as final. Games, toys, and routines that only a few weeks ago were spurned as too complicated should be kept in reserve, ready for reintroduction to the interactive menu at the appropriate moment. An example of the Beta child's desire for menu changes can be seen in the way his preference for interactive games changes in the first year.

A case in point is Gotcha, the game where a mother or father swoops back and forth in front of the infant for a moment or two, then suddenly darts in close and gently pokes the baby's stomach with a finger. For an eight- to twelve-week-old, the stimulation level in this game may be too high. It can be played with him, but at best the infant will be a passive partner, and he may even break into tears.

Pat-a-cake, on the other hand, provides just the right amount of sight and sound for a young Beta infant. The

## Games Babies Love to Play

| *One to Six Weeks* | *How to Play* | *Goal* |
|---|---|---|
| Follow Me | Lay baby on back and move a doll or rattle back and forth in front of him at eye level; call his attention to its location with a gentle voice. | To improve eye-ear coordination, also practice for mutual engagement. |

| *Seven to Twelve Weeks* | | |
|---|---|---|
| Ten Little Indians | Jiggle fingers or toes in turns while singing, "One little, two little, three little Indians," and make the tenth a special jiggle accompanied by a final "Girls, boys," name of baby. | Encourages eye-hand-ear coordination with a sense of the importance of the hand and body connections. Also presents rhythms in synchrony with melody, smiling, and predictive mutual touch. |
| Whoops Johnny | Touch each fingertip and say, "Johnny," with the "Whoops" reserved for the thumb-index-finger joint. | To encourage a love of laughter and a sense of mutuality. |
| Tickle, Tickle Little Star | Walk fingers up baby's body slowly while saying, "Tickle, tickle little star," and ending with a gentle, under-chin touch, saying, "How I wonder how you are." | |

| *Three to Five Months* | | |
|---|---|---|
| Pat-a-cake/Peeka-boo | Bring baby's hands together in midline, singing, "Pat-a-cake, pat-a-cake, baker's man." When this becomes boring, then cover baby's eyes with | Introduces baby to the concept behind hello and good-bye. Baby through his own control with hands, eye-blinks, or object can make a loved one ap- |

his two hands and part them, saying, "Peekaboo." Baby might then enjoy blinking, or a cloth covering his eyes, or your disappearing and reappearing as further variations of this game. You can accompany this activity with a singsong "Where is mommy? Here she is!" pear and disappear. These games are linked with the ability to hold objects and examine them using both hands.

## Five to Nine Months

### Gotcha

Starting as with Tickle, Tickle, add the uncertainty of your finger in the air while saying, "I'm gonna getcha," then gently poke baby's tummy, allowing him to grab your finger.

Adds the element of uncertainty to a game, plus the challenge of encouraging baby to find the finger and control it. This is pleasurable excitement and calls his attention to your hands.

### Early Hide 'n' seek

Conceal objects under a cloth and ask where they are; if baby is hidden behind something, ask where he is, then exclaim, "Here he is!"

Peekaboo has now developed into seeking objects together and actively mastering disappearance.

## Ten to Twelve Months

### Give 'n' Take

Whatever the baby has in his hand, or a special toy, can be asked for and then given back. A back-and-forth pattern can be established, accompanied by a rhythmic singing of "Back and forth"; this can progress to "May I have _____?" "Thank you." "Here is your _____back."

Makes it fun to share an object. Stretches the baby to tolerate the frustration of waiting to have the item returned. Creates gradual tension of waiting for the return and then of repossession.

| Let's Dance | To singing or music on a record player, move baby's arms and body, encouraging a back-and-forth motion accompanied by words with repetitions. Encourage baby to move his hands and arms in unison with yours. Ring around the Rosie, with both of you "falling down." Asking the question, "How big is _____?," and both of you then saying in unison, "So big!," can be an interchange without music. | To foster a musical, conversational interaction that either one can start which incorporates all the earlier pleasures adding a sense of love and pride in independence. |

three or four vigorous claps of the parental hands which it provokes are exciting and rousing without being overwhelming. In fact, recent studies by both Dr. Alan Sroufe and Dr. Tiffany Field of the University of Miami show pat-a-cake to be *the* game of choice for babies between three weeks and three months.

By the fourth month, however, a Beta baby's interest in pat-a-cake declines visibly; he may even turn away from the parental hand claps as if he were saying: "Hey, I already know that game, Daddy, how about something new?" Now more mature cognitively, he wants an entertainment that reflects his new intellectual scope. From the third to the fifth month, the game that does this best is peekaboo. And because it gradually introduces the infant to the idea of pleasant surprise from a suddenly appearing familiar object, it also helps to prepare him for the previously spurned Gotcha, whose main feature is the suddenly appearing tickling finger.

In the seventh month, as the first glimmerings of intentionality light up his behavior, the baby requests a third change in the game menu. From now until the end of the first year, he prefers interactive games that are more social in the sense that they give him an active role to play beyond that of pokee or onlooker. In other words, a role that allows him to display and practice his new skill for behaving intentionally. This is why he shows less interest in a menu where the only dessert listed is Gotcha, and a great deal of interest in a menu where the featured dessert is Give and Take.

Another update parents should be alerted to involves play styles. Vigorously swing an eight- or twelve-week-old around in your arms and he may break into tears; in fact, he almost certainly will. The amount of physicality involved in swinging is too great for him. Six to eight weeks later, however, that same child will not only be delighted at being swept up in your arms and swung around, he will begin asking for it by stretching his arms out in front of him when he sees you approaching. Furthermore, at this stage his requests will reflect a real biological need, since activities like swinging enhance dexterity and coordination in a baby.

2)  *Use a menu that reflects his preferences.*
Because of the Beta's recall ability, by the third month your presence in his doorway already has become a contextual cue for him. And to some degree, the amount of enthusiasm he offers you in his greeting mirrors how closely your menu offerings have come to reflecting his own emerging set of likes and dislikes. When the two match, your menu not only draws the child closer to you—who wouldn't want to spend time with a person who knows what *you* like?—it also becomes a kind of advertisement for the human environment's attractiveness. You show the infant how much a sensitive social companionship enriches life. This is why taking note of and incorporating the baby's preferences into the interactive routines you create not only becomes a way of enriching individual exchanges, but also a way of demonstrating the possibilities for support, sympathy, and playfulness available from other people.

In the first three months, however, even a clear-signaling Beta infant has difficulty making his preferences known.

To discover what he likes requires careful observation. You have to notice where his eyes go, and, even more important, what quiets and soothes him. These two behavioral changes signify that there is some unique property or thing about what he is doing, what you are doing, or what the two of you are doing together that helps him to organize, and the ability to organize is the most profound declaration of a preference a two- or three-month-old can make.

At this age, his preferences usually are limited to different modes of stimulation. He notices and may especially like the sound, look, feel, touch, or smell of a thing, but pays little attention to its substance. In the early months, accordingly, your attention should focus on his responses to the sensory modes you offer him. Does he seem to like sound better than sight? Or is he especially fond of the way a thing feels? In the fourth and fifth months, this information can be used as a guide to creating interac-

## Ten Toys That Help the Infant Grow

*Each toy on the list shares two qualities: (1) It is contingent in the sense that it can be operated by the infant; and (2) It presents a potential challenge that he must stretch himself a bit to meet.*

### 0 to Three Months

Balls of different sizes, colors, and textures
Mobile over the crib (one that can be "worked" by baby)
Rattle with transparent handle showing moving object

### Four to Seven Months

Soft ball
Chinning ring or bar over crib
Complex rattle

### Eight to Twelve Months

Mirror
Busy Box (simple version for this age)
Flashlight
Teddy bear that makes noise when turned

tive games and routines. While these activities should reflect what you have learned about his special tastes, all
the baby's sensory modes need to be regularly exercised.

To illustrate the point, say the infant displays a painterly
eye. Though all babies cherish bright, bold, eye-catching
colors, he is especially enchanted by them. You notice,
for example, that whenever you are wearing an eye-catching checked blouse, his eye immediately goes to it. Or
on being placed on the floor of a friend's living room,
the first place his eye goes is to the window and the striking
green-blue curtains that frame it. To incorporate this preference into your interactive menu, you might buy some
brightly colored paper or balloons. Or to enliven your
games of peekaboo, you might hide your eyes behind some
brightly colored swatches of cloth rather than behind your
hands. Once the child reaches his seventh or eighth month,
see how he reacts to your introducing crayon and a sketch
pad into exchanges. While the figures you create with the
crayons may still be beyond his comprehension, the color-
ful marks of the crayons won't be.

Alternately, if sound is what attracts the baby, singing
should be made an important part of exchanges. You might
also try to introduce this infant to light music. You should
know about a recent experiment conducted at the City
of London Maternity Hospital by Dr. Michele Clements.
Her subjects were a group of seven- and eight-month-old
*fetuses,* and she found that classical music not only had
a soothing effect on the unborn children (she determined
this by monitoring fetal heart rate), they even had a favorite
instrument. As judged by the soothing effect its sound
produced, these unborn babies most enjoyed listening to
the flute.

# ELEVEN
# Parental Flexibility
# Exercises

**B**y now it should be clear that it's essential that the *baby* be allowed to set the tone in an interaction. *His* needs have to be expressed; *he* has to determine the flow and direction of the interaction. It's *his* individuality that has to be recognized and encouraged—that has to become the centerpiece of the interaction. Everything you, as a parent, do should be aimed at building and enhancing who *he is* not who you, for one or another reason, *want* him to be.

Although most parents would unambivalently agree with—even applaud—this goal of child-determined growth, in their actual day-to-day interactions with their children, sometimes they let hidden agendas get in its way, *often without realizing they are doing so.* What are some of these hidden agendas?

One is the parent's own developmental timetable, which he or she is superimposing over the child's. Your use of adult language rather than baby talk because you want to hurry along the infant's language skills is an example of this.

A second hidden agenda could be your acting out *your* parents' conception of what "good" parents should do—a conception left with you by memory, or by their reminders. "My mother always talked about how she peopled a whole little fantasy world for my brother and me," says one woman who is relentlessly trying to interest her ten-month-old in talking to the plastic Disney characters he would much rather eat.

Many parents implement these agendas with the use of now-fashionable early-childhood training "aids": flash cards, educational toys, special classes for babies in everything from motor to social development. And while these vary in value, the best and most effective teaching tool remains what it has always been—*a parent's own emotional receptivity to the child as he is.* This is how the baby learns to be a three-dimensional human being—not simply an academic star—and when he learns this lesson well, mastery of individual abilities, such as social adeptness and language, follow naturally.

This is why the only appropriate developmental goal for an infant is *authenticity*—to be who he is. And it is also why the most important way you can help your child to achieve it is by building your fantasies and myths around him and his needs, not around your own dreams. At the center several years ago, we developed a series of exercises to help our parents make such distinctions, and because it has been a great success with our families, we've created a modified version of it for this book. The exercises take the form of a series of questions; they aren't meant so much to be directive—in the sense of telling you what to do—as simply to alert you to and put you in touch with any preconceptions that may be subtly disrupting or inhibiting your family's fit. As you read over each question, stop for a moment and ask yourself two things: First, does this apply to you and your baby? And second, if it does, what steps can you take to make yourself more open and accepting?

1) *Begin by making a mental (or, better yet, a written) list of your baby's qualities and characteristics. Think—what is he really like?*

Be as objective as you can. Imagine he were the child of a friend or acquaintance. How would you describe him to yourself. Make this list your reference point. Whenever you find your normal, healthy fantasies about your baby taking a grandiose turn, refer back to the list.

2) *Do you exaggerate your baby's attributes?*

Say he's musically inclined. Do you turn up the volume on the stereo each time you see him begin to beat his foot in rhythm to a song? Or, if he's a frequent waker, will you bring him out to meet your guests since he's up anyway? These are examples of *leading*, and the danger in leading rather than following an infant is that the qualities being led may unnaturally come to dominate the child's personality.

3)  *How comfortable are you in just echoing your baby?*
One of the things an infant most wants you to do is react to him. Or to put it into the idiom of developmental psychology, he wants to make your responses contingent on his behavior. This is one of the key ways he develops a sense of mastery and competence, and in order to do so in the way a parent would wish, he requires an accomplice who is not only an easy and natural listener and sounding board, but who is also able to make his or her ego the smallest in the room. In practical terms, this means a parent who is able to greet the baby quietly with a smile, instead of a loud "OH LOOK, YOU'RE UP," on waking. And it also means a mother or father who knows how to avoid *overriding* in exchanges.

At the center, we see this phenomenon most often in very conscientious first-time parents. Feeling that responsibility for keeping an interaction flowing smoothly rests entirely with them, they will override, or redirect, the baby's spontaneous behavior. These redirections are attempts to keep the child actively engaged and interested in the exchange, but the effort produces so much self-absorption that often the parent overlooks important cues and signals, or interferes with the infant's attempts to take his turn.

4)  *Do you try to "gray out" your baby's emotional swings?*
Graying out is something parents often do in self-defense when they are feeling particularly—and usually understandably—frazzled by the baby's daily cycle of ups and downs. Instead of continuing to follow him through his mood swings, they will flatten out their responses in the hope of putting him on a more even emotional keel. Most often, however, this flattening has the effect of breaking

the mutuality of an interaction, and that, in turn, leaves the baby feeling that he has no one to share his daily triumphs and crises with. Even if it takes an effort—and sometimes it does—stay on the baby's roller coaster.

5) *To what extent can you resist criticism and be your own parent?*

On occasion every parent's authority is challenged, and usually the challenge comes from one of two sources: either visiting grandparents who wonder why the baby isn't smiling, walking, and/or talking yet, particularly since *you* were such an advanced child; or friends who express frank surprise at how fat or thin he looks, or who gently suggest that he seems a bit spoiled. Don't let these critics upset you or, even more important, undermine your belief in yourself. A healthy degree of self-confidence is an essential part of every good parent's equipment. Besides, no one knows your baby as well as you do; hence, no one is in a better position to judge how well his needs are being met. You deserve all the nice compliments you can think of to pay yourself.

6) *Can you comfortably share your baby?*

One of the most important social lessons an infant learns—or rather, needs to learn—in his first year is how to admit a third person into an interaction without disrupting the flow of the exchange. And one of the most important ways parents can help him to learn it is by avoiding a subtle form of competition we call the look-at-us syndrome. It goes something like this: On returning home, the working spouse, instead of being invited into an ongoing exchange, is made to sit and play audience while the baby is put through his paces. Ostensibly, the point of these performances is to demonstrate the day's developmental breakthroughs, but they may constitute a subtle form of competition: Can the observing parent make the baby repeat his triumphs? And aside from the unhealthy sense of competitiveness this fosters between a mother and father, it also leaves the infant with the mistaken impression that the only way to admit a new person into an exchange is by stopping the flow of action and putting on a performance.

7) *Can you allow your baby to regress?*
No infant marches uninterruptedly from one developmental milestone to the next. Growth is a series of progressions and partial regressions. And while this sometimes makes for disappointments (it may be a week or two before you hear the baby utter "Mommy" or "Daddy" again), it is also important not to force march a child from gain to gain. He's already dancing as fast as he can, and pressure from a parent—however well meant—can only risk disturbing the delicate balance of physiological and psychological forces that combine to make developmental leaps possible.

8) *Are you able to tolerate a certain amount of mystery and ambiguity in your baby's behavior?*
By their very nature, some of the things a child does are unknowable. Why your infant woke up from his afternoon nap crying today and smiling yesterday is one example of infancy's many inevitable mysteries. Since such behavioral riddles can have a hundred different causes— or no real cause at all—it's not worth disturbing yourself or the child in a frustrating and fruitless search for explanations. Accept the fact that in the course of his first year, every baby is the subject of dozens of obscure, self-correcting problems. And *trust yourself* enough to believe that if anything major does develop, you are sufficiently in tune with him to spot it quickly.

9) *Do you feel you always have to be "up" around the baby?*
In addition to being a parent, you are also a human being, which means you are prey to moments of anger and depression. Don't feel guilty about these feelings, or deny yourself the right to have them. After all, some of the things babies are prone to do, such as breaking objects or pulling hair, can be anger provoking. Just as some of the situations new parents find themselves in, such as being caught on what seems an endless treadmill

of diaperings and feedings, can occasionally be depressing. Besides, properly handled, your feelings can be transformed into an important object lesson for the baby. You can, for example, show him that your emotions aren't a threat to your relationship with him as they are under control.

**10)** *Are you embarrassed by the way you behave around the baby?*

If the answer is yes, the next time you feel self-conscious because you've been caught by another adult in the middle of a stream of baby talk or while making a silly face, remind yourself of three things. First, these behaviors are a necessary and important part of the baby's emotional, social, and intellectual growth; second, think how much sillier you would look if you were seen talking to him as if he were a grown-up. And third, keep in mind that the baby needs to know you are the same person wherever the two of you may be. So don't, for instance, be afraid to set limits in the supermarket the same way you would at home.

**11)** *Do you sometimes confuse your vulnerabilities with your child's needs?*

One indication that you might be doing this is overreaction. So if you find yourself quick to anger at his every little instance of ill-discipline, or are too easily embarrassed by his behavior, it's probably a good idea to sit down and try to figure out why you are so touchy. In making this mental inventory, however, keep in mind that there is nothing necessarily wrong or abnormal about having vulnerabilities. The point of your self-examination is simply to help you identify those issues or conflicts in yourself that are inhibiting the fitting-in process between you and your child.

# PART III
# Figures
# in the Square

## How Mothers, Fathers, Care Givers, Day-Care Centers, Brothers, Sisters, Grandparents, and Significant Others Affect the Fit

# TWELVE
# Parental Ecology: How Mothers and Fathers Make the Fit

**T**he Eipos are the people who time forgot. Locked in the dense tropical rain forests of New Guinea, they inhabit a world our hunting and gathering ancestors would instantly feel at home in. The steam engine, the timepiece, even the wheel are discoveries whose resonances have yet to touch the Eipo way of life. All this is why their culture made an ideal laboratory for a question that began shaping in the mind of the German anthropologist Dr. Irenäus Eibl-Eibesfeldt, in the late 1970s. As the new interactive research started emerging from laboratories in Europe, America, and Japan, Dr. Eibl-Eibesfeldt found herself wondering about its deeper significance: Specifically, she wondered if the camera caught a relatively new cultural phenomenon, or had it opened our eyes to a pattern of child rearing that, though earlier overlooked, was deeply embedded in human biology?

Traveling through the rain forests of New Guinea, Dr. Eibl-Eibesfeldt found answers to this question all around her in the form of parent and infant behaviors that would be instantly recognizable to developmental specialists in Munich, Los Angeles, Milan, or Tokyo. Eipo mothers use pieces of tree bark instead of rattles, but the game they play with their tree bark was one Dr. Eibl-Eibesfeldt had no trouble identifying as Give and Take. And although, as far as she could tell, Gotcha is not a part of Eipo language, she reports that the game as played by Eipo mothers is essentially the same as the version played by German and American mothers. There is the same feigned parental mock attack, the same tickling and finger pointing, and the same ability of the game to reduce Eipo babies to delighted laughter also is the same. They are just as enchanted by all the feinting, bobbing, and touching as German and American infants are.

Isolated by the barren wastes and brutal heat of the Kalahari Desert, the *!Kung* (the sound ! is produced by clicking the tongue) tribes of central Africa have stood as resolutely outside of time as the Eipos. Though the !Kung parents Dr. Eibl-Eibesfeldt encountered during her visit, as the Eipo parents she had met earlier, displayed the same innate grasp of interactive play's importance. !Kung mothers and fathers, she reports, show as instinctive awareness of *as-if's* importance in responding to their two- and three-month-olds' smiles and frowns. And they are as conscientious about providing such responses as mothers and fathers in advanced societies. Instinctively, too, !Kung families know about the importance of joint action, and so a great deal of the time they spend with their infants is devoted to showing the child how to align his mind with theirs. The only difference is that the !Kungs use sticks, rocks, and pieces of animal bone as objects of focus instead of dolls, Busy Boxes, and blocks.

!Kungs, Eipos, Australian aborigines, and the other primitive societies that have been subjects of cross-cultural studies like Dr. Eibl-Eibesfeldt's also show an instinctive understanding of baby talk's importance. The most striking thing about this aspect of the research, however, isn't that baby talk as spoken in these primitive societies is similar to baby talk as spoken in ours, but rather *how* similar. Whether in a jungle clearing or a high-rise apartment, whenever a mother or father turns to talk to an infant, instinctively they drop their voices a few decibels and raise the pitch.

Next to the universality of interactive behaviors, the most significant finding to emerge from the recent cross-cultural work centers on the way mothers and fathers use these behaviors. Gender, this research shows, makes no discernable difference in how a parent funnels a baby's burst-pause behavior into turn-taking, draws his eye to an object, or responds as if to his looks. Eipo and American fathers have as much *potential* competence and sensitivity in these areas as Eipo and American mothers.

But this new anthropological work has also identified several other areas where a parent's sex does make a difference. And this suggests that in designing the fit, nature created a division of labor between the sexes—one meant to ensure that the baby's needs for organization, nurturance, excitement, and competence training would be met in different but complementary ways by mothers and fathers. The nature of these sex-related differences is the subject of this chapter. We will look at the special contributions the mother and father make to the fit, how those contributions can be enhanced when they work together, and how the fit itself is affected when a mother works.

## Mothers

One of the best ways to measure the special depth of the mother-child bond is through a paradox that puzzles mothers and delights fathers. Why, given the amount of time a woman spends with her baby, is "Daddy," not "Mommy," more often the baby's first word. Not that mothers resent this, it just makes them feel a bit unappreciated, understandably. But they should also know that in his word choice the child is actually paying them the profoundest of compliments. Starting at birth (and very likely before) and continuing through the daily cycle of feedings, diaperings, and baths that follow, mother and infant share such a commonality of experience that *the baby comes to think of the mother as a part of him;* in other words, he doesn't point to her first and say, "Mommy," for the same reason he doesn't point to his arm first and say, "arm." In his mind, these elements are indistinguishable from him. Father is in a different category because he is usually the first aspect of the exterior environment that the infant notices. And because in his first year one of the baby's priorities is distinguishing between himself and the environment, usually somewhere between his eleventh and fourteenth month he will point to that exterior element who always seems to be hovering nearby and say, "Daddy."

The reason a mother comes to occupy such a unique place

## Five Stepping-Stones to Sensitive Parenting

### 1. *Mutual Supportiveness*

Mother and father respect each other's parenting styles and view one another as competent. This is especially important for women, since studies show that the more husband perceives wife as a competent, maternal figure, the more competent she becomes.

### 2. *Self-Confidence*

Feel pride in role as parent and confidence in ability to fulfill it without letting it overshadow other aspects of life.

### 3. *Commitment to Infant*

Are willing to give his needs priority over such other "desirables" as an always-clean house and large amounts of leisure time.

Result:

Happy, resourceful child who is capable of being productive when alone and engaged and responsive with others.

### 5. *Ability to Read Baby*

Can identify the cues he uses to signal his needs and wishes and is able to select appropriate response and implement it immediately.

### 4. *Acceptance*

Comfortable with infant's sex, physical appearance, temperament, helpless, crying, and physical needs.

in the infant's mind is, of course, tied to her role as nurturer. And the fact that it is a role that women in all societies play— and as far as history allows us to judge, always have played— strongly suggests that its roots lie in a biological predisposition. Having once experienced the child as a part of her, a woman has a special sense of both the baby's vulnerability and his unfolding on an immediate day-to-day level. And it is these feelings that are behind the woman's four special contributions to the fit.

In interactive terms, one of the most important of these contributions is *maternal patience*. Studies on parental modeling of tasks—for example, how to pile one block on top of another—have demonstrated that while fathers are roughly as likely as mothers to initiate such modeling, they don't stay with the tasks as long. If after the second try the baby still can't get one block on top of the other, a father usually tries to change the subject either by introducing a new task or by moving on to a game; a mother won't. She will model the activity again and again. How much of this remarkable patience arises out of biology is impossible to say. Though as a veteran observer of it I've often been struck by how neatly maternal patience fits the baby's need to have learning tasks continually repeated.

Women's interactive *play styles* also reflect their nurturing roles. The memory of the biological bond, and especially of the baby's frailty in the womb, gives the mother a special sense of his vulnerability, and this shows up in the great gentleness of her play. A case in point is a recent University of Illinois study which found that while mothers sometimes roughhouse on the whole, their physicality is limited to touching. And often they eschew even touching for a gesture (a pointed finger) or an object (a toy). The greater rates of maternal smiling and vocalizations in exchanges also reflect this desire not to overstress the baby physically; whenever possible, a woman prefers to use a nonphysical "instrument," whether it be in the form of a gesture, a toy, a gaze, or a sound, to engage her child.

Is it coincidence that these behaviors, especially maternal gaze and sound making, also correlate with infant intelligence at one year? Possibly, but as with maternal patience, the correspondence between a woman's predisposition to smile and vocalize with the baby and the baby's need for these behaviors suggests that we are looking at another response that evolution instilled in mothers.

The third special contribution mothers make to the process comes as something of a surprise; in part because it involves a quality we don't usually associate with maternal nurturance, and in part because it contradicts one of the most deeply held tenets about infant development, which is that competence training is a special province of the father. Since we actually have begun to look at how parents play with infants—as opposed to theorizing about it on the basis of adult memories—the mother has emerged as the parent involved most in *skills training*.

Social skills, such as cooperation, and mechanical skills, such as putting a block in a box, quite literally are learned at a mother's knee. Another notion recent research challenges is that mothers aren't as demanding of the baby as fathers are. Videotapes of mothers involved in skills training shows them to be rigorous, thoughtful, and result-oriented taskmasters. While they are quick to support and encourage the baby's efforts in every instance, they also are careful to key their praise to the amount of *real* progress he displays. Unsuccessful attempts to, say, get a block inside a box, earn supportive smiles and murmurs, but authentic praise is withheld until successful completion of the task being shown.

Though fathers also function as skill trainers, I think that what makes this role a greater maternal priority, and also what accounts for a mother's great ability in filling it, is the special quality of her myth making. I suspect one important purpose of these myths is to help inspire a mother to create challenges that stretch the baby just the right amount. If you watch a mother model a skill (or if you think about the way you do it), I think you will see what I mean. Instinctively, mothers often know how to create learning situations that are a bit beyond the baby's current competence, but not so far beyond it that he feels overwhelmed.

The fourth quality that is usually considered part of a mother's special contribution to the fit is the special sensitivity said to grow out of after-birth bonding. As I pointed out at the beginning of this book, over the last ten years, several dozen studies have failed to find any evidence that this contact has a *long-term* influence on either mother or baby. While still not entirely clear, research does suggest, however, that such contact may have a *short-term* influence on maternal sensitivity. Thus, it may well be that bonding evolved as a kind of special grace period of seven to ten days during which a mother's heightened awareness of and sensitivity to her baby's behavior set the stage for their later, long-term fitting-in.

## Fathers

The "rediscovery" of father and the new importance attached to his role is a good example of how social and scientific trends sometimes converge in a fashion that illuminates a familiar subject in an exciting new way. In the case of fathers, the social trend involved is the rise of the two-career family. With an increasing amount of a woman's time being taken up by work outside the home, care-giving chores have become more evenly divided between the sexes. And though this trend toward a more egalitarian division of domestic labor isn't proceeding as fast as many women (and some men) would like—according to a recent British study, women actually do *more* housework in the six months *after* the birth of their first child—fathers do play a greater direct role in the infant's life than they did a generation ago. Hence, the feeling among researchers that we needed to know more about the role men play in shaping and nurturing that life.

Scientifically, the reason for the new emphasis on the male is in great measure due to the way videotape studies have changed our thinking about the parent-infant equation. While both early psychoanalytic and developmental theorists held that the feeding—and in particular, the breast-feeding—experience lent a special, unmatchable dimension to the mother-child bond, actual observation of families has failed to support this notion. Which is to say, film studies have failed to find evidence that feeding leads an infant to look at the person feeding him in a unique light. But what *does* make a critical difference to the baby, these studies show, is the degree of sensitivity and responsivity he encounters in his interactions; in other words, the aspects of parental behavior we have looked at in this book. And in these areas—sensitivity and responsivity— men possess the same potential for competence as women.

We know this in good part thanks to Dr. Ross Parke, whose pioneering work has been a major influence on the current rethinking of the father's role. Looking at each sex's innate competence to read and respond to cues, Dr. Parke, who is a professor of psychology at the University of Illinois, found that men are as able to interpret accurately such infant distress signals as sneezing, coughing, and hiccuping as women are, and also as likely to respond to those pleas quickly and appropriately.

Like mothers, however, fathers also contribute to the fit in special ways. The most immediately visible of these contributions—at least to mothers, since they are the ones who usually have to calm the excited baby afterward—is the unique paternal interactive *play style*. While mothers like to play, fathers *love* to play; so even though in absolute terms they don't spend nearly as much time with the baby, proportionately a far greater amount of the time they do spend is devoted to play. A recent study by Dr. Milton Kotelchuck of the University of Massachusetts makes this point eloquently. His study mothers spent an average of nearly an hour a day cleaning and slightly over two hours a day playing with the baby. Dr. Kotelchuck's study fathers, on the other hand, went right to dessert. On the average, they devoted nine minutes of their daily time to cleaning and nearly an hour and a half to playing with the baby.

Nor is this trait unique to American men. The English fathers whom Dr. Judy Dunn of Oxford interviewed were just as playful as Dr. Kotelchuck's American fathers. Dr. Dunn reports that her male subjects devoted 90 percent of their interactive time to playing with the infant. These findings explain another paradox, which also puzzles mothers and delights fathers—why, at around the eighth month, not just boys but girls as well begin to show a preference for interactions with their father. For the baby, fun-loving Daddy represents an ice cream sundae and a fudge parfait all wrapped up into one.

It's less the amount than the *style* of paternal play, however, that represents a man's unique contribution to the fit. While mothers rely on indirect instruments in the form of a voice, a look, or a toy to stimulate and arouse, fathers use their bodies; which is to say they are primarily physical. In most families, it is the man who is the baby tosser and the rough-houser. And though sometimes this can be heart stopping for a mother to watch, babies not only love it, it seems to be an important source of emotional growth for them.

A recent study by Dr. James Herzog of Harvard Medical School, for example, suggests that paternal excitement is one of the mechanisms through which an infant gains homeostatic control. Challenged by a father's play style, which is not only physically but verbally arousing, the infant is forced to stretch his organizational capabilities, and provided the stretch imposed is not too great (in which case he either turns away or cries), Dr. Herzog believes these challenges raise a baby's stimulation tolerance. This means that his next exciting encounter with Daddy is that much easier for him to tolerate comfortably.

Another way paternal physicality may serve the baby—especially if the baby is a boy—is by teaching him how to express his physical drives in a *healthy way*. This suggestion comes from Dr. Parke: "As a result of experiencing competent physical play with fathers at an early age," he says, "boys may learn how to regulate their physical aggression in ways that allow them to later play physically with peers without causing harm. In fact, effective peer play generally may be learned through interactions—especially with fathers."

While men also contribute to the family fit by facilitating *sex role identification*, this male contribution is selective; it only operates in the case of infant *boys*. And it reflects a general paternal pattern: Men become more directly and intimately involved in the care-giving process with a son. Though sex makes no difference in a mother's responsiveness, even in the newborn period men already mark out sons for special attention. Recent studies show that they look, talk, and touch more when the newborn is a boy; reports on three-, six-, thirteen-, eighteen-, and twenty-four-month-olds show that this preference not only continues, but intensifies.

Men feel they have a special part to play as role models for their sons. And, indeed, allowing a boy to partake in what to his small eye looks like Daddy's greatness and protective powers does make a difference to him. You can hear this difference in toddlers' conversations. Three- and four-year-old boys almost never say, "When I am a man," but rather, "When I am a daddy." Little boys are also much more prone than little girls to brag about their fathers' prowess—whether it comes in the form of a warning to a playmate, as in: "If you hit me, I'll tell my daddy," or in the form of a boast about a father's accomplishments, as in: "My daddy can count to one thousand."

You also can see the special difference a father makes in a boy's life in the results of child-rearing studies of single households (headed by women). These reports show that while a father's absence has no measurable effect on a baby girl's subsequent social and cognitive performances, boy babies reared in such homes often score below average in cognitive tests. Nor is this finding simply a reflection of the fact that male infants have one less partner available to interact with. Even when there is an aunt, an older sister, or another figure to supplement the mother's teaching and guidance, male infants still do less well later on in developmental tests. Fathers and sons have their own special fit.

A father's third unique contribution to the family's interactive dynamic lies in his *role as a husband*. As his wife's main source of emotional support, a man has an enormous influence on her perception of herself as a competent, nurturing, sensitive care giver; to put it more directly, if a man thinks of his wife as a good mother, she is much more likely to think of herself that way too. And while this involves *direct* support of her in the form of praise for her maternal skills, it also means other, more *indirect* forms of support some men aren't as mindful of as they might be. One notable case in point is a willingness to assume some responsibility for household chores so that distracting visions of unmade beds and dirty dishes don't fill his wife's head when she is with the baby. Another example of such support is satisfying her needs for a stimulating and supportive adult relationship. No matter how devoted we are to our children, we can't be our best selves—to the baby or to ourselves—unless we have another adult presence, one we can confide in and consult with—whether it be a husband, a friend, or a close relative.

Those of us who work with families know from experience how much of a difference masculine support makes in a woman's mothering. Often, just by observing a husband's and wife's dynamic in conference, I can tell how responsive the woman will be later when I watch her with her baby. We also know from studies what an important difference a man makes. Candice Feiring of the Educational Testing Service of Princeton, for example, found a direct correlation between the amount of support a mother felt she was getting from her husband and her responsivity and involvement in exchanges with her baby.

## Working Together

The most striking thing about the new research on mothers and fathers is that when it is brought together it begins to tell a story. It says that when parents work together for the baby's benefit, the contribution of each to the fit not only complements the other's, *it enhances those contributions;* for example, a father's play style becomes even more beneficial when it is framed by a mother's smiling and vocalizing. This *enhancement effect* has been identified by a half dozen studies—a notable example being a recent report by Dr. Alison Clarke-Stewart of the University of California. Briefly, Dr. Clarke-Stewart found that the two parental behaviors that correlate most closely with a baby's intellectual competence are: maternal expressions of warmth and positive emotions (both of which might be defined as nurturance), and a father's engagement of the child in play. Like the two key pieces in a jigsaw puzzle, when these qualities are available to a baby, the other elements of the fit seem to fall naturally into place.

At the same time, this doesn't mean, as some parents think, that they are prisoners of biology. The same flexibility that

allows the fitting-in process to serve the !Kung and Eipo families as well as American, French, and Italian ones—with all
the vast cultural differences implied in that comparison—also
allows it to serve families where the man and woman have
chosen to fill their parental roles in less traditional ways. Indeed, there are positive benefits when a father becomes more
of a nurturing figure by assuming some of the nurturing-related
chores, such as washing, feeding, and diapering, and a mother
infuses more excitement and adventure into her play style.

At the center we call this strategy *cross-fertilization,* and
one advantage of it is that it helps to eliminate the parental
jealousies that can arise when a family takes a rigidly tradition-
alist view of the mother's and father's roles. An example of
how this *strict constructionist* view of parenting can feed such
jealousy is what happens when a man limits his role to playmate. Over the months this transforms him into a play cue
for the infant, so that even Daddy's appearance at the doorway
signals "fun" to the baby. And as he excitedly crawls away
to greet his playmate, Mother, who has spent the day feeding,
cleaning, washing, and changing him—in other words, in performing all the humdrum but essential chores that are integral
to the infant's well-being—is left sitting alone on the floor
wondering, "My God, am I that boring?"

A man falls prey to a similar kind of jealousy when the
distressed baby spurns his attempts at succoring. This happens
for the same reason. Over the months, a mother's consistency
in fulfilling the succoring role leads her to be typecast in the
child's mind as the *only* person who can relieve his upset.
And so it is she he demands when he hits his head a little
too abruptly against the couch, or when he is feeling colicky,
or even when he just wants some gentle rocking to soothe
him. Not long ago a father told me that when he goes into
his ten-month-old's room at night, the baby simply looks at
him and then points to the door. "The only time Jerry stops
crying," said the father, "is when he pulls himself up on the
crib rail and points for my wife."

Cross-fertilization allows a parent to avoid being stereotyped
this way because it *broadens* the infant's perception of the
number of roles his parents can play in his life. As he becomes

accustomed to occasional episodes of rousing maternal play, for example, the infant not only sees a new and appealing side of Mommy, he comes to look forward to his zesty encounters with her (and, of course, his quiet ones as well) as much as he does those with Daddy. Alternately, as he becomes accustomed to his father's bathing, feeding, and changing him—in other words, Daddy's relieving and soothing him—he becomes more willing to accept Daddy's comfort when he is in real distress.

Shouldering more of the nurturing chores also has another important effect on a man. It gives him a greater understanding and appreciation of what his wife has quietly achieved over the months as she has molded and shaped the baby's undisciplined emotional and biological urges not only into a predictable pattern of feedings and sleep times, but into the beginnings of a defined and disciplined personality. Often, even very sensitive fathers don't grasp what an enormous accomplishment this is or how important it is to the baby's development. A more intimate involvement in the kind of care-giving chores that are the stepping-stones to such organization opens a man's eyes to it and to his wife's skill as a care giver, as well as allowing him to enjoy his baby's triumphs in a new and much richer way.

A father who focuses narrowly on play usually doesn't notice when his child's daily schedule begins to solidify into a coherent pattern or realize what it represents when the infant suddenly begins smiling *in order to.* A nurturing father does; so he is able to see and to savor these quiet triumphs as the important developmental milestone that they are. He also is more mindful of the need *not* to disrupt those delicate and still fragile patterns by overexciting the baby an hour before bedtime, or beginning a game of Gotcha a moment before a scheduled feeding.

## Women, Work, and Fitting-In

Powerful new social trends are like tidal waves; as they sweep through a society they touch everything around them, including the nature of the scientific work being done. Nothing illustrates this point better than the literature on the working mother. In the early and mid 1970s, as women began entering the work force in large numbers, they were accompanied to their new jobs by a group of reassuring new reports that claimed to find no difference in the skill or quality of care between working and stay-at-home mothers; a few investigators even reported finding work to have an actively positive influence. Because a woman felt more fulfilled as a person, she made a better mother to her baby.

More recently, the tide has begun to move in the other direction. Along with the mini-baby boom of the early 1980s have come another new group of studies that report that staying at home optimizes development. Working mothers, according to this literature, tend to smile and vocalize less in exchanges, and to develop a more aggressive interactive play style. Lately, a number of investigators, most prominent among them Dr. T. Berry Brazelton of Harvard, also have raised another concern: the possibility that work may impair a mother's myth-making capacities. Pregnant women who know they will be going back to work *after* the baby's birth, say these investigators, don't seem to fantasize as eagerly, as often, or as richly about their infants as mothers who know they will be at home afterward.

In what seems to be rapidly shaping into a debate about the influence of work on mothering, I think the first thing that has to be said is that the extraordinary thing isn't that juggling the competing demands of work and a baby sometimes causes difficulties, but rather, how many mothers are able to do both not only successfully, but effortlessly. If the late twentieth century has an unsung heroine, it surely is the working mother. The other thing that has to be kept just as clearly in mind is what is being debated. A careful reading of the seemingly conflicting reports shows that the real issue is not whether a woman works or not, but rather how well she is able—and helped—to combine the roles of worker and mother.

Our experience at the center reflects this. A good many of our mothers are professional women whose careers as doctors, lawyers, teachers, editors, and financial analysts place great demands of time and energy on them. Yet they still are able to provide the quality interactive time their infants need. We also see working mothers who are less successful at this, and looking into their situations, very often we find that the reason they are less successful has nothing to do with their desire for or competence at mothering, but rather, in organizing their lives they have overlooked the two elements every working mother must have.

The first is a reliable support system. A woman can't have the *peace of mind* she needs to be a relaxed, open, receptive care giver unless she knows that directly behind her stand a group of dependable figures whose function is to serve and enhance her relationship with her baby. In practical terms this means that on leaving the house in the morning, she must know that whoever is with the child during the day—whether it be a nurse, a person at the day-care center, an older sibling, or a grandmother—is competent and trustworthy. It also means that on returning at night, she must know that the dishes, the floors, the bed, and the other routine household chores are largely taken care of. With the geometry of everyday life mastered, a woman can then give her undivided, undistracted, and *unhurried* attention to her baby.

The second element essential to a working mother's success is knowing how *not* to let the pressure of work affect her interactive style. On one point, all the recent research does agree; and it is that when a woman returns to work, her interactive style is subject to change. It tends to become more directive, task oriented, instructional, and physically active, and less open-ended and free-flowing. Mother and baby are less likely to *be,* and more likely to *do.* Given the pressures she is under, the reasons for this change are certainly understandable. Often a working woman feels, first of all, the need to prove to herself, but also to her husband, to her parents (especially *her* mother) and to society at large that her competency as a mother has not been diminished.

However, the problem with the make-every-minute-count style, which tends to arise in response to these competing pressures, is that it disrupts the delicate balance of an exchange. Instead of action flowing primarily from infant to mother (as it should) it flows from mother to infant. And with this redirection often comes a change in the way a child sees his mother and himself. Instead of viewing her as a nurturing figure who sometimes is a teacher and entertainer, he comes to see her as a teacher and entertainer; a powerhouse who sometimes is a nurturer.

The new busyness and briskness of the interactive environment also offer him fewer opportunities to initiate responses and fewer opportunities to see them echoed back. And as his chances to play the role of initiator diminish, so too often do his ideas about his personal competency and mastery. A new study by Dr. Sarale Cohen of the University of California is one of a number of recent reports that have highlighted the risks of the make-every-minute-count interactive style. Dr. Cohen's subjects were a group of working mothers, and she found that though they tried very hard to make exchanges with their babies meaningful and enriching, the amount of self-absorption involved in this effort had an unwitting effect: It made them less responsive. Preoccupied by their own initiatives, they failed to notice their infants' bids.

This is why *interactive quiet* is an especially valuable resource for a working mother. Allowing the baby to set the pace by echoing his movements and gestures not only ensures that action flows in the right direction (from child to mother), it also allows both partners time to just be. And that serves a working mother in three important ways:

1) *It ensures that she remains the primary nurturing figure in the baby's eyes.*

   This role isn't allotted on the basis of time, but of responsiveness. Instinctively, a child assigns it to the person in his life who seems most in tune with *his* need to be an initiator. And if his exchanges with his mother are the place where he finds his needs uniquely understood, encouraged, and supported, the amount of *physical* time those exchanges occupy in his day will matter less. In the best sense, this is what quality time means: creating moments so rich, enticing, and in tune that the baby feels most loved in them. By putting the child firmly and securely in the center of the interactive universe, interactive quiet nurtures this feeling. As he looks around, the infant sees that everything is responding to *him* and at *his* pace.

Thus, the very slowness and stillness that quiet creates enhances the limited amount of time a working mother has to spend each day with her baby.

The make-every-minute-meaningful approach, on the other hand, has the opposite effect. Studies show that by becoming *too* active, a woman threatens her status as nurturer. As she becomes more like a teacher in exchanges, the baby responds by turning to someone else in his immediate circle for nurturance. It may be his baby nurse, his day-care worker, his grandmother, an older brother or sister—whoever he perceives as being most responsive to and supportive of his need to express himself. The result is that there become three primary figures in his life, each playing a different role: father is seen as the entertainer, mother as the teacher, and this third figure as the nurturer.

2)  *Quiet encourages the skills that the baby of a working mother needs most.*

New people and new situations are a bigger part of the landscape for an infant whose mother goes to work every day. He encounters them at the day-care center, at his grandmother's house, or in the form of the baby-sitters and baby nurses who are part of the family's support system. And, in large part, how well he responds to these new situations and, especially, new faces is determined by how well he has learned to feel comfortable with others and extract information from them.

One of the information-collection routes a baby uses is body contact. This is called *proximal* style, and it means that through touching and being touched he comes to know the other person. This style is fine for becoming acquainted with a parent, but it is an alarming way to meet a new face, since it requires touching and being touched before he knows how safe that new face is. The second, less-threatening way a baby extracts information is by looking and listening. This is called the *distal* style, and what makes it less disturbing is that it allows an infant to maintain a reassuring distance while he learns who the new person is.

Both of these information-collecting styles—proximal

and distal—are shaped in exchanges. A physical father is the primary teacher of the proximal style, and a mother, through her natural predisposition toward interactive quiet, helps mold an infant's knowledge of the distal style. Watching the way she uses her eyes and ears as tools, the baby learns to use his eyes and ears that way too.

Though this knowledge of how to look and listen makes it easier for him to meet new faces, we know that another effect of work is that it makes a woman's interactive style more *proximal*. In other words, she touches and is more physically playful, and looks and listens less. And while this change arises out of a mother's understandable desire to be entertaining and fun, it places her baby in a dilemma. Just at the time when he needs to learn *more* about how to use his eyes and ears as information extractors, he starts learning *less*. In this case, interactive quiet is a way of ensuring that a woman's own natural predisposition to use looking and listening isn't lost by her return to work. It is also a way of ensuring that her baby is given an opportunity to continue learning about new faces in a way that allows him to feel comfortable.

**3)** *Quiet enables a working mother to monitor her baby's progress.*

While you were at work today the infant may have learned a new way of using his eyes as a cue, or for the first time turned his head and eyes in unison, or managed to sit up erect, or began using his smiles *in order to*. Such developmental leaps tend to occur all at once—in a flash. And though a sensitive and observant care giver will notice and tell you about some of them, you also need to monitor the baby's behavior during your times together in the morning and evening for signs of change and progress. Interactive quiet is your ally in this process for two reasons. First, it gives the child the time and space *he* needs to announce his latest triumphs; and second, by freeing you from your preoccupations, it puts *you* into the kind of responsive frame of mind where you will notice those changes.

# THIRTEEN
# The New Sociology of Infancy

I magine, for a moment, that we had a time machine that magically could whisk us back for visits to 1860, 1900, 1930, and 1960. Traveling through the years we would encounter many changes in the nature of infancy. Around 1900, for example, we would find more and more infants being born in hospitals, and arriving in 1930, we would see delivery rooms already beginning to acquire the ominously high-tech look, which in the 1970s would lead to a worldwide parental revolt against the "medicalization" of birth. At home, many alterations in the baby's environment also would be apparent. Visiting his room in 1930, for instance, we would hear for the first time strains of music drifting in from the family's new radio in the parlor, and on our next visit in 1960, the new television and hi-fi sets would have added to the din.

Amidst all these changes, however, we would find one constant: the nature of the baby's social network. In 1960, as in 1860, its principal figures would be mother, father, siblings, and perhaps a grandparent. And therein lies the reason why the years since 1960 represent such a sharp—I am almost tempted to say revolutionary—change in the nature of infancy and parenting. During the past two decades or so, this social network, the most steadfast feature of the baby's life for the past one hundred—indeed, for the past several thousand—years has altered beyond recognition, and largely for a single reason: the rise of the working mother.

Thus, while only 18 percent of women with young children worked in 1960, by midpoint through the 1970s that figure had already risen to 35 percent, and by 1984 it had increased a further 11 percent to 46 percent. Put another way, this means that *nearly one out of two American babies now spends a good portion of his day in the care of someone other than a parent.* And if, as seems likely, present employment trends continue, we can expect that by the end of the 1980s, as many as three fifths will.

What is true for American families, moreover, also is true for German, French, Swedish, Japanese, Italian, and, to a lesser extent, British families.* Worldwide, mothers with young children are returning to work in unprecedented numbers, thereby creating what a colleague recently—and I think very aptly—described as a new sociology of infancy. To grasp what he meant by that phrase, and also what unique challenges and rewards this new sociology offers, let's consider for a moment how much more demanding the last twenty-five years of social changes have made in the life-style of today's baby.

One key, and easily identifiable, difference between him and, say, a child born in 1960 is, of course, in the nature of their care givers. In 1960, a baby's principal companion, both night and day, was more than likely to be his mother; now a child is almost equally likely to divide his day between his mother and a surrogate—whether it be a day-care worker, a baby nurse, or a grandparent. A second major difference is in the size and nature of the baby's social network. Two decades ago, outside of a few close family friends, a baby rarely encountered a new adult face during his first year; today, the network of day-care centers, which are a main source of support for working families, not only bring an infant into daily contact with a wide variety of new grown-up faces, but—what was even rarer a generation ago—they also bring him into daily contact with his peers.

Changes in parental expectations also have contributed to changes in the baby's life-style. Think, for example, of how

---

* Interestingly, British mothers have been most resistant to the current back-to-work trend. While their numbers are increasing, at present only 7.5 percent of U.K. moms with children five or under work outside the home.

uncommon it was twenty years ago to see a three- or four-month-old jauntily carried along the street in a backpack, or to hear two mothers at a party discussing the comparative advantages and disadvantages of their six-month-olds' play groups. Today, if both situations are commonplace, it's because the emergence of the "competent infant" from video research has altered the expectations of parents generally, whether they work or not, about their baby's ability to cope with diversity and thrive, whether it be represented by a new face, a new place, or a new situation.

Are these expectations justified? Or, as some authorities worry, are such experiences as maternal employment, day-care attendance, and the greater social and physical mobility of today's working and nonworking families alike creating demands that push a three- or four-month-old, and even a nine- or ten-month-old beyond his competency to cope?

Unquestionably, there is legitimate reason to be concerned about the way some recent social trends are affecting the infant. One case in point is the finding that work outside the home may adversely affect the quality of mother-infant interactions. Another new piece of data that also is worrisome is the suggestion—raised in several new reports—that regular day-care attendance may promote unruliness and aggressiveness in an infant. This research, however, only tells one side of the story. The other side can be seen in studies that suggest that such experiences as maternal employment and regular exposure to peers produce many, many positive benefits, including a healthy sense of independence, an eagerness to explore, and—what may be most important for long-term development—they give a child a head start in mastering the difficult art of friendship.

What accounts for these seemingly contradictory findings? Simply put, it is because infants vary enormously in the ability to benefit from the advantages and avoid the hazards of today's increasingly active life-style. And while there are a number of reasons why they do, the most important are the baby himself and the way he is reared to meet the challenges of this life-style. In saying this, I don't want to oversimplify. There is not one set of experiences that can ideally prepare a four- or five-month-old for the shock of separation he experiences when his mother returns to work. Just as there is not one way that can be devised to avoid the disruptions that often accompany a child's first few encounters with three or four noisy, rambunctious peers. Nonetheless, a baby is quicker to adjust to these and other new situations, and, even more important, quicker to begin turning them to his advantage if his parents have prepared the ground.

1) *Promote a distal style.*

In the last chapter we saw why such a style is important to a socially active infant. The ability to use his eyes and ears as intelligence-gatherers gives a child an important advantage when the time comes to be introduced to a new day-care worker or baby nurse. Both of these encounters, as well as others with unknown adults, are fraught with potential anxieties. But unlike the proximal baby, who must touch or feel a new person or place to know it, the distal baby's capacity to extract information from sights and sounds means he can learn from and even enjoy new encounters without having to leave the security of his mother's or father's lap. In terms of promoting a distal style, the most important thing to keep in mind is that it can *only* be learned in exchanges with *you*. Watching the way you use your eyes and ears to learn about him, the baby develops the ability to use his eyes and ears to learn about others.

I stress this point because one of the most common reasons parents give for wanting their baby to join a play group at the center is that they believe the regular exposure to new faces which it provides will enhance his ability to get along with others. And while regular contact with adults and infants does indeed foster social competency, it does *not* teach a baby the skills he needs most to turn those contacts to his advantage. This is why infants with already developed distal styles usually are immediately able to fit into one of our groups, while those who haven't acquired this skill at home sometimes continue to have difficulty even after months of regular exposure to other adults and children.

**2)** *Know how to introduce new faces in a nonthreatening way.*

Like a distal style, knowing how to choreograph introductions also helps to increase receptivity to strangers. But how do you tell a four-, five-, or six-month-old that this new person standing over him imposingly is safe? Mothers and fathers usually are told that the best way to make a baby feel at ease is by responding warmly themselves to a new person. This advice is based on the notion that if an infant sees a parent reacting in a friendly way, he also will assume the stranger to be a friend and, hence, will relax too. The problem with this advice, as many parents already know from experience, is that it rarely works. And it doesn't because it overlooks an elemental fact of developmental physiology: For most of the first year, a child doesn't have the cognitive sophistication to tell how a parent is behaving—warmly, coolly, or neutrally—toward another person.

A better way to put your child at ease during introductions is by aiming your friendliness *directly at him,* not at the stranger. What a baby has no trouble reading is a parent's attitude toward him, and when that attitude makes him feel good, he will automatically feel good about the new person he is meeting.

An example of the difference this more direct strategy makes in a child's receptivity toward strangers can be seen in the results of a study by Dr. Michael Lewis of Rutgers University. In the first part of the experiment, Dr. Lewis told his mothers to use a conventional introductory approach; that is, he instructed them to direct their positive emotions at the stranger he sent to visit them and their infants. In the second phase, the mothers were asked to change their emotional focus. While they were instructed to offer the stranger a cordial hello, they were directed to aim most of their attention at their infants.

Dr. Lewis used an especially ingenious way to measure how these two types of introductions influenced a baby's receptivity. Like the rest of us, when he is feeling loved and secure, an infant wants to reach out and share that good feeling with others; so Dr. Lewis reasoned that if one of his young subjects offered the stranger a toy during their meeting, it meant the baby felt relaxed and comfortable. In the first part of the experiment, very few such offerings were made. But during the second phase, Dr. Lewis reports that the babies were put in such a good mood by their mothers' cooing and smiling that the laboratory workers who played the part of strangers found themselves deluged by offerings of rattles, rubber ducks, teething rings, and other tokens of affection.

**3)**    *Use significant others to enhance your family's fit.*
I think you will have a better idea of how to use these important figures as allies if we first look at the part they play in the fitting-in process. A significant other usually is defined as anyone other than a mother or father who the baby forms a close emotional bond with. That can be a grandparent, a day-care worker, a sibling, even, if one is willing to stretch the point a bit, a peer. These figures are the major actors in what I earlier called the new sociology of infancy. And from a parent's perspective, perhaps the most reassuring thing we have discovered about them concerns the nature of the bond they form with the infant.

A theme that occurs again and again in my conversations with mothers who are planning a return to work is a fear that they will be displaced in the baby's affections by his new surrogate care giver. Research, however, shows that this fear is groundless. A case in point is the result of a new study by Dr. Michael Lamb of the University of Utah. While Dr. Lamb found that the bond a baby forms with a loving nurse or day-care worker indeed can be quite deep and rich, it does *not* affect the bond he already enjoys with his mother and father. Even a three-month-old has such a large reservoir of love, he can sustain several important relationships at once.

In developmental terms, what makes a network of significant others beneficial is that they not only can enhance a baby's social competency, but, even more important, they can provide a rich array of what developmental psychologists call attachment paradigms. By that they mean that the alliances a child forms with nonparental figures serve (like parental relationships) as prototypes, which influence the infant's self-image and the relationships he comes to form later with playmates, colleagues, and even with his spouse and his own children.

This represents a new and important discovery, since it means that just at the critical moment when an infant is fashioning his social and personal selves, he has available for guidance his learning experiences not just from one relationship (that with his parents, as we had already known), but from several. One key advantage of this multiplicity is that it offers exposure to a wide range of positive personal qualities. Few mothers and fathers, for instance, can match the nearly infinite patience of a loving grandparent. So exchanges with a grandmother or grandfather can supplement parental exchanges by serving as the baby's primary source of learning about the uses of patience as a social skill.

A satellite relationship also can sometimes help a child to see or learn about a thing in a way a parent can't. An older brother or sister (or day-care acquaintance) who inspires toy play is a case in point. Studies show that a baby learns much more about the use of a rattle or a block from watching a three- or four-year-old play with it than from having a parent demonstrate it, because the older child brings an uninhibited gusto and enthusiasm to play which makes the toy seem singularly enticing. Seeing his "big" sister toss a new ball into the air, a baby thinks, "Oh boy, that looks like a neat thing to do," in a way that he doesn't when a mother or father tosses it, because their adult cautiousness takes all the zip out of the throw.

Since the day-care worker who is too harried to provide one-to-one exchanges and the baby nurse who spends her time at the park talking to other baby nurses also can be sources of negative learning, how do you ensure that your child's contact with these significant others in his life is always and only enhancing? When one of our parents asks me that question I tell him or her that the best guarantee is knowledge: You have to know which qualities make another adult or child a good (or bad) companion for your infant. So for the remainder of this chapter we will focus on the four most-significant others—day-care workers, baby nurses, grandparents, and peers—in the infant's social network, and the qualities that make them allies in your family's fit.

## Day Care

America's thirty-two thousand day-care centers serve as surrogate care givers for an approximate two million children who are three years of age and younger. What proportion of these youngsters are infants is unknown. One recent estimate put the number at a half million, another at three quarters of a million. On one statistic, though, there is general agreement: By 1990, half or more of children twelve months and younger will spend some part of their first year in one of these centers. And while recent research would seem to make this a trend parents and professionals alike can applaud, since that research tells a happy story about the effects of day care, there is a growing suspicion that the tale it tells also is a highly selective one.

No one doubts the findings that on emotional and cognitive developmental indexes day-care infants score as highly as stay-at-home babies, or that on indexes of sociability they come out ahead—often *far* ahead. The problem is that these results are derived from studies done almost exclusively at university-affiliated day-care centers. And generalizing from this work contains the same risks of distortion as generalizing about the overall quality of the American educational system from test scores of Harvard, Yale, Berkeley, and University of Chicago students.

Beneath the pinnacles of excellence represented by the university-connected and -subsidized centers, quality varies widely. Some privately run facilities offer care as good as any to be found on a college campus; others, it is generally agreed, are little more than warehouses for the very young. The reason for this distressing and bewildering disparity in quality is that, alone among advanced nations, the United States has no federally mandated and enforced day-care standards. One consequence of this oversight is that currently, only a quarter of day-care workers have any training in child development, psychology, or a related field. Another is that staff ratios at some facilities are as high as eight to one. Such ratios not only makes it unlikely that a baby will ever be regularly exposed to one-to-one exchanges, they constitute a physical risk to him. As Dr. Edward Zigler of Yale pointedly asked in a recent *New York Times* article: "How can one caregiver even be expected to get eight babies out of a burning building?"

Because of the lack of other standards, a few years ago we assembled a series of guidelines to help our families facing difficult day-care decisions. I think you will find many of your concerns and questions about day care addressed in it.

### At What Age Should a Baby Start Day Care?
While there is no generally agreed upon date, I think the absolute minimum age is three months. And, if possible, I would delay enrollment until between the fourth and fifth month. This is because the fourth month is one of the two developmental touch points that occur in the first twenty-four months. These are periods when developmental breakthroughs create a special receptivity to change. And the principal reason the fourth month qualifies as one such point is that it precedes the onset of the stranger anxiety, which can make meeting an unknown face such a trial for a baby a few months later. The other touch point occurs around the fourteenth month and grows out of the baby's newly acquired mobility. So many exciting avenues of exploration are opened up by the discovery that those two appendages under his trunk can hold him erect and hurtle him through space that a child often relishes the challenges posed by a new physical setting.

### What Physical Attributes Characterize a Quality Day-Care Center?
Some are obvious. The facility should be clean, attractively decorated, appropriately lit (while it shouldn't be dark and gloomy, neither should it be bathed in a glare of fluorescent

light), and temperate (too much air conditioning or heat can almost be as bad as too little). Space is another important criterion. In a recent joint study of day care, Dr. Zelazo and Dr. Jerome Kagan of Harvard concluded that at a *minimum* a center should provide each child with one hundred square feet of crawling and walking space. And while this isn't the kind of information a visual inspection yields (unless you happen to be an engineer or an architect), you can determine a center's per-child ratio by asking what its total square footage is and dividing that number by the number of children being looked after. If, for instance, it has twenty infants, it should have two thousand square feet of floor space.

Other things to check for are a facility's rocking chair to playpen ratio—a preponderance of the former suggests babies are routinely held and cuddled, of the latter, that they spend a significant amount of time restrained—and the number of room dividers, sliding walls, and other space dividers it uses. Every facility will tell you it divides its infants by age group, but the presence of dividers is visible proof that this center has a special area set aside for three- to six-month-olds and another for seven- to twelve-month-olds.

### What Qualities Should I Look for in Day-Care Staff?

At or near the top of every parent's list should be continuity of care. High staff turnover—because it makes attachment to a single figure difficult—can be a source of serious infant anxiety. Even facilities that rely heavily on part-time help—if this means that the baby's week will be divided between two care givers—should be avoided. The daily presence of the same reassuring face is the single most important element in your baby's successful transition to day care. And, as a parent, it is also your best guarantee that the person looking after your child will know him well enough to be able to identify subtle but important behavioral changes. Dealing with the same person also makes communication easier since it ensures that you and the day-care worker are able to exchange the maximum amount of information in the minimum amount of time during your conferences at the beginning and end of each day-care day.

Another important benchmark of a staff's quality is the child-to-adult ratio. For infants it should be three-to-one. This ensures that a care giver will have enough time to provide each baby with individual attention.

A third benchmark is a staff with a high preponderance of psychology and child-development degrees, though I think that a day-care worker who has children of her own has at least as good a feel for her charges as a young man or woman with an academic degree.

*Is There Any Special Information I Should Get from a Center?*
Yes. You should ask for the names and telephone numbers of other parents who currently have children at the center. Be wary of facilities that refuse to provide this information or discourage unannounced visits from parents.

## Baby Nurses and Other Supplementary Care Givers

The figures in this category range from the licensed practical nurse who has specialized training in infant care to a loose network of retirees, neighbors, teachers, and friends who use baby-sitting as a means of supplementing their incomes. Together, the women in this category constitute one of the largest sources of surrogate care in the United States, serving an estimated quarter of working families with young children. This means that a significant number of readers already have found, or will in the near future find, themselves in the position of interviewing one of these surrogate care givers. What qualities should you look for?

The best way to answer that question is to start not with the care giver herself, but with you and your feelings. I say this because a full-time surrogate has a way of acting as a lightening rod, bringing to the surface, sometimes with an unpleasant jolt, a woman's unconscious ambivalences about her dual role as mother and breadwinner. There is nothing unusual or abnormal about such conflicts.

Nonetheless, for the tug not to become a source of friction, these feelings should be identified and worked through *before* the care giver arrives. As part of this internal stocktaking, I advise our mothers to begin by reminding themselves that a surrogate is just that—a surrogate. She is there to facilitate and augment your role as mother, *not* to supplant it. You remain the principal figure and yours is the primary relationship in the infant's life; whatever his bond to his care giver, quite literally, you remain the love of his young life.

Also important to realize beforehand is that there are certain duties—particularly nursing functions, such as bathing and feeding—that will largely become the responsibility of the care giver. Rather than let this become the source of jealousy, let it be what it should be—a reason for peace of mind. With your baby in competent hands, now you can give your full energies to the work day.

Resolve, too, that you won't allow a care giver's skill and knowledge to become intimidating. First-time mothers, especially, can feel overshadowed by the competence and authority of an experienced care giver. If you find yourself a bit awed by the nurse's diapering or soothing skills, remind yourself that her competencies are a tribute and direct reflection of your *own* skill in choosing her for your child. Working mothers deserve every nice thing that is said about them, even the nice things they say about themselves.

In selecting the care giver herself, there are three factors you should pay particularly close attention to.

**1)** *References*
You will, of course, want to ask the surrogate's former employer-families about her honesty and skill. But, in addition, you also should try to find out how comfortably she operated within the context of their fit. Though highly skilled and reliable, some care givers have disruptive personalities. Either they try to put one parent against the other or use their relationship with the baby as a lever in negotiations about pay, hours, or duties. Anyone with a history of such tactics should be avoided, as should a care giver whose spans of employment average six months or less. A change of surrogates, in the first year especially, can be a source of great anxiety to a baby. So you want someone who will see your child through his first, preferably, his second twelve months.

**2)** *Trial Period*

While qualifications and recommendations are important before making a final hiring decision, I advise our parents to set up a trial period of three to four weeks. Usually this is enough time to decide whether you can establish a smooth working relationship with the care giver, are comfortable having her in your home eight to ten hours a day, and—what should be your most important consideration—can tell how receptive she is to the baby. During these weeks be especially alert for signs of her growing involvement with the child. Your best insurance that he will be well looked after is the depth of the care giver's attachment to him. And a care giver who spontaneously begins entering his room to check on him when he is asleep and makes suggestions about his care is evidencing signs of such attachment. And, of course, the ultimate test is the positiveness of the infant's response to the care giver.

**3)** *Make Sure the Care Giver Shares Your Values*

Another advantage of a trial period is that it allows you to tell to what extent a care giver shares your philosophy of child rearing and family life. The initial interview will give you some hints about her views, but sometimes there is a disparity between what a surrogate says to a prospective employer and what she truly believes in her heart of hearts. Not long ago, for example, one of our mothers discovered that despite her explicit instructions to the contrary, on her return to work, the care giver put her baby on a four-hour demand-feeding schedule. "It was so infuriating," the mother told me. "I specifically instructed her not to do it, but now Isabele's become so accustomed to the schedule, I'm afraid to take her off of it."

Not uncommonly, parents and care givers also have different views of discipline. If you believe (as I do) that questions of right and wrong have no place in the first year of life, you should be wary of a surrogate who speaks of a former charge as being "too demanding" or "spoiled," or who thinks the best way to establish authority over a baby is "to let him cry it out." A care giver who is uneasy at the idea of paternal involvement in the care-giving process also should make you hesitate, since she is likely to resist your husband's getting involved with the baby.

## Grandparents

One of our culture's most enduring and romantic myths about the family is that there existed an idyllic time in the past when grandmothers and grandfathers were almost as intimate a part of the infant's day-to-day life as his parents. You see this notion celebrated in some television programs, including *The Waltons,* and in any one of a dozen Norman Rockwell paintings. But if you were to search through the demographic and social trends of the last 150 years, you would find that the only epoch that even remotely qualifies as a Golden Age of Grandparenting is—surprise—our own. One reason why is the medical gains, which in advanced nations have lengthened the life spans of both sexes to well past seventy. Thus, as one recent report notes, "The opportunity for a meaningful period of overlap in the lives of grandparents and grandchildren is a twentieth century phenomenon." A second reason why is the greater mobility, which allows today's grandparents to take advantage of this generational overlap in a way that even their predecessors of forty years ago couldn't.

Because of this new generational togetherness, recently we have begun to take a closer look at the grandparent's place in the fit, and out of this work have emerged some important and surprising findings. A case in point is a recent study by psychologist Barbara Myers of Virginia Commonwealth University. The subject of Dr. Myers's study was the role that traditionally has been associated with grandmothers and, according to one recent estimate, 10 percent still play—that of full-time surrogate care giver. And while Dr. Myers's findings have a special relevance for families where a grandmother fills this role, they also have implications for every family where a grandparent is called on to serve as a baby-sitter or as a helpmate in the parenting process.

The reason? Dr. Myers's data indicates that *on important issues of child rearing, such as discipline and skills training,*

*not only do grandmothers and their adult daughters often dis-
agree, usually they also are unaware that they disagree.* The
root of the confusion, Dr. Myers found, lies in the very different
memories mothers and adult daughters have of the daughter's
upbringing. While for both generations these memories serve
as standards and benchmarks which influence each woman's
interactive behavior toward the family's newest member, because their recollections are also different, their interactive
styles are too. Grandmothers, for example, tend to remember
themselves as putting little emphasis on teaching and instructional tasks, so they tend to assume a free-flowing play style
with their grandchildren. While their daughters, remembering
such tasks as an important part of their mothers' styles, tend
to duplicate this teaching orientation in their maternal behavior.

The point of this finding isn't that any one style—that of
mothers or grandmothers—is better, but rather that sharply
contrasting styles in two care givers (and this is as true for
baby nurses or other surrogates as for a grandmother) can
confuse and upset a baby. This is why even if your mother
isn't a surrogate, but simply spends a great deal of time with
the baby, it is a good idea for the two of you to compare
notes on your childhood so that on issues of discipline and
scheduling you can present a united front.

Also a good idea to discuss are any childhood memories
that remain a source of conflict and resentment. An honest
and frank discussion will make it easier for the two of you
to work together, and will allow your mother to make her
contributions to the fit secure in the knowledge that she has
your full support. This is important, because a grandparent
can play three very special roles in the life of an infant or
toddler:

1) *Playmate*
Though they may sometimes be quicker to correct a child
than a mother or father is, grandparents also wear their
authority more lightly, and this produces a uniquely engaging—and uniquely grandparental—style of play. Recent
studies suggest, for instance, that a grandmother or grand-

father usually is more willing to let a baby take the lead in exchanges. And because they are less concerned with teaching and less pressed for time, their play has an open-ended, unstructured quality which the young find particularly fetching. Infants can't speak, of course, but if they could I think most of them would agree with this assessment of grandparental companionship made recently by a precocious nine-year-old named Patsy Gray. "Everyone should have a grandparent, especially if they don't have a television set," declared Patsy, "because grandparents are the only people who have time."

2) *Family Historian*
Obviously, this isn't a role a grandparent can begin to play until a child reaches three or so. Nonetheless, it is a role that can illuminate a youngster's understanding in a uniquely important way. As a source of knowledge about values, ethnic heritage, and family traditions, a grandparent can help a child begin to place himself in the context of the world at large. The special knowledge of a parent a grandparent has also can lead to a deeper understanding of Mom or Dad, and so serve as a conduit for a better parent-child relationship.

3) *Buffer and Negotiator*
Again, this isn't a role a grandparent usually assumes until the child reaches toddlerhood, but it, too, is an important one. As the member of the family with a unique combination of wisdom, experience, and objectivity, a grandparent can act as a mediator when parent-child conflicts over minor misdeeds threaten to get out of hand. Or as another bright youngster, a ten-year-old patient of mine, explained to me recently after her grandmother had stepped in to mediate a dispute between her and her mother, "I think grandparents are the wisest, most understanding people in the world."

## Infant Peers
Do babies really interact with one another?
There are two reasons why it didn't even occur to us to

ask this question until about ten or twelve years ago. The first is that, as Dr. Anneliese Korner of Stanford University noted not long ago, "For 99 percent of human history infant-infant encounters were non-existent." The other reason it wasn't raised—even during the remaining 1 percent of human history in which they have existed—is that for most of that time, thinking about development had been dominated by Freud. And in his view, the primacy of the mother-infant tie left no room in the baby's psyche for other meaningful relationships.

Only as videotape studies began challenging this view by showing how other major figures in his social network—such as father, surrogate care giver, and grandparents—influence the child's growth, did curiosity arise about the effect of the peers the baby was meeting with increasing frequency at day-care center and in play groups. Investigators wondered—did these encounters also influence development in some way?

The field of infant-infant relations is so new, answers to this question necessarily must be tentative. But, yes, videotape studies suggest that babies, even young ones, are not only capable of forming what looks very much like a friendship (of sorts, admittedly), but that infants can benefit from these ties in two ways:

1) *Mutual Engagement*
In the simplest sense this means doing something together. And as we already have seen, it is an important building block of such social skills as cooperation and empathy. In your exchanges, you foster it through such activities as mutual gazing and vocalizing. Somewhat to our surprise, the video camera shows that peer encounters also encourage mutual engagement, though as you might imagine, in a less felicitous form than you do.

An example is a marvelously sweet (and funny) film we recently made of two six-month-olds. They are sitting on the floor and between them is a box, the lid of which one infant keeps opening (by pressing a lever attached to the box) and the other just as resolutely keeps closing. Hard as it may be to believe, the Sisyphean struggle these two are engaged in is teaching each an important lesson: the ability to influence another person. ("Ah ha, I know how to make you shut the lid on the box: I'll open it!")

## 2) *Socially Directed Behaviors*

One of the most striking things about the tape I just described is that not once do its two stars ever glance, point a finger, or smile at each other. These are three examples of socially directed behaviors and their development is important because they give the baby a tool, beyond sheer brute force, with which to influence the environment, and, equally important, they also allow him to engage in increasingly more complex and sustained forms of play.

While five-, six-, seven-, and eight-month-olds can share a single episode of mutual play—such as opening and shutting a box—they can't go beyond it because they don't yet understand how to influence their playmates. These isolated episodes are important because it is in them that an understanding of how to use winks and nods to influence others is fostered. This means that because of their earlier encounter, the next time the two six-month-olds in our film are placed together, they will be that much more likely to be able to use their socially directed behaviors in order to shift the focus of their mutual play from the box to a nearby block.

At the center, when one of our mothers or fathers asks about the advisability of placing their baby in a play group, we tell them about the advantages of infant contact which I've just described. But we also add a caution—and it is one you and other parents who are involved in the play groups, which are such an important part of the new sociology of infancy, should be aware of. In order for a baby to benefit from regular encounters with peers, three things are necessary:

## 1) *The play group must be small.*

Four infants constitute an absolute maximum, and research suggests that the ideal number of members is really two. This comes across very clearly in a study by Dr. L. Vandall of Boston University. Over the several months when Dr. Vandall followed a six-member and a two-member play group, he found that a number of significant differences had emerged between the two groups. One of the most important centered on the nature of the members' socially directed behaviors. While the two babies in the smaller group displayed an increasing sophistication in their use of these behaviors, no change was evident in their use by infants in the six-member group. Another important difference between the members of the two groups was the amount of time they spent interacting. This is an important index of social-skill growth. And by that criterion the babies in the small group could be said to have had highly developed skills, since they spent more and more of their time together involved in exchanges. The interactional rate among members of the large group, on the other hand, remained constant over the course of the study.

2) *Try to build the play group out of friends.*
What we at the center have long known from personal observation—that babies do, indeed, make friends—was recently documented by investigators at Rutgers University. Among the "pals" in the study group, the investigators found a very high percentage of the same touching and feeling behaviors we adults use to display our affection toward one another, while the baby "strangers," also like adults, displayed a standoffish approach toward one another. In terms of forming a play group, what this data means is that the more familiar the members already are with one another (through, say, their parents' visits to each other's homes), the richer and more immediate their emotional, and even cognitive, connections will be.

This isn't to say that a good play group can't also be formed out of infants who are strangers to one another. But be prepared: The first three or four of the groups' meetings will be characterized largely by what textbooks discreetly refer to as negative effect.

3) *Make sure that there are enough toys to go around.*
As the videotape I mentioned earlier suggests, objects have a way of serving as a connecting point for young infants

who might otherwise simply bump into one another and then, like ships passing in the night, crawl off in opposite directions. As the tape also suggests, however, the presence of just *one* toy (or two if there are three infants) is almost always an incitement to riot. Every member should have at least one toy he can call his own, even if he never looks at it, and if a toy is particularly popular, you should have several copies available. This is called the just-in-case strategy and it can help to avoid much needless anguish—both yours and the baby's. Also a good idea is to make sure the toys they get are big. This won't matter if the infants are three or four months old, but if they are eight or nine months, new research suggests it will matter a great deal. Indeed, within limits I think you will even notice a correlation—the bigger the play groups' toys, the smoother the group gets along. And while that's nice for them, it's even nicer for you.

# Coda

**I**n the clinical sense, the end point of a good fit is attachment. But whenever I'm asked to explain the result of such a fit, I try to illustrate the human dimension of that rather remote-sounding term by describing a scene I witnessed one May evening several years ago. Passing the playroom on my way out the door, I heard a man singing what I've always thought to be one of our loveliest and most haunting lullabys:

*Lavender's blue, dilly dilly, lavender's green;*
*When I am king, dilly dilly, you shall be queen.*

As it reached upward toward the high notes, the man's voice quivered, strained, and several times nearly broke, but the baby in his lap followed the uncertain progress of the father's voice as if he were watching an eagle soar into the sun.

The connections one human heart makes with one another are shaped by forces that are largely still beyond our understanding. But if this book can be said to represent a wish, it is that it helps to foster an *environment* for the growth of a connection between you and your baby as deep and rich as the one I saw alight in that infant's eyes.

# Bibliography

Adamson, L. B., and Bakeman, R. 1984. "Mothers' Communicative Acts: Changes During Infancy," *Infant Behavior and Development,* 7 (4): 467–478.

Ainslie, R. C., and Anderson, C. W. 1984. "Maternal Perceptions of Their Infants' Daycare," *Infant Mental Health Journal,* 5 (2): 91–106.

Als, H. 1982. "Toward a Synactive Theory of Development: Promise for the Assessment and Support of Infant Individuality," *Infant Mental Health Journal,* 3 (4): 229–243.

Antonucci, A. T. and Levitt, M. J. 1984. "Early Prediction of Attachment Security: A Multivariate Approach," *Infant Behavior and Development,* 7 (1): 1–18.

Brazelton, T., Koslowski, B., and Main, M. 1974. "The Origins of Reciprocity: The Early Mother-Infant Interaction." In M. Lewis and L. Rosenblum, eds. *The Effect of the Infant on His Caregiver.* New York: John Wiley & Son.

Bretherton, I. 1984. "Social Referencing and the Interfacing of Minds: A Commentary on the Views of Feinman and Campos," *Journal of Developmental Psychology,* 30 (4): 419–427.

Brody, J. "Influential Theory on 'Bonding' at Birth Is Now Questioned," *New York Times,* March 29, 1983, p. C1.

Bruner, J. S. 1977. "Early Social Interaction and Language Acquisition." In H. R. Schaffer, ed. *Studies in Mother-Infant Interaction,* pp. 271–289. New York: Academic Press.

Bruner, J. S. 1981. "Intention in the Structure of Action and Interaction." In L. P. Lipsitt and C. K. Rovee-Collier, eds. *Advances in Infancy Research,* Vol. I, pp. 41–56. Norwood, N.J.: Ablex Publishing.

Bruner, J. S., and Sherwood, V. 1983. "Thought, Language, and Interaction in Infancy." In J. D. Call, E. Galenson, and R. L. Tyson, ed. *Frontiers of Infant Psychiatry,* pp. 38–51. New York: Basic Books.

Butterfield, P. M., and Miller, L. 1984. "Read Your Baby: A Follow-up Intervention Program for Parents with NICU Infants," *Infant Mental Health,* 5 (2): 107–116.

Campos, J. 1976. "Heart Rate: A Sensitive Tool for the Study of Emotional Development in the Infant." In L. Lipsitt, ed. *Developmental Psychobiology,* pp. 1–31. Hillsdale, N.J.: Lawrence Erlbaum Associates.

Cicchetti, D., and Pogge-Hesse, P. 1981. "The Relation Between Emotion and Cognition in Infant Development." In M. Lamb and L. Sherrod, eds. *Infant Social Cognition,* pp. 205–240. Hillsdale, N.J.: Lawrence Erlbaum Associates.

Cochran, M., and Brassard, J. 1979. "Child Development and Personal Social Networks," *Child Development,* 50, 601–616.

Cohen, S. E. 1982. "Maternal Employment and Mother-Child." In J. Belsky, ed. *In the Beginning,* pp. 233–242. New York: Columbia University Press.

Collins, G. "Experts Debate Impact of Daycare on Children and on Society," *New York Times,* September 4, 1984, p. B11.

Condon, W. S. 1977. "A Primary Phase in the Organization of Infant Responding Behaviour." In H. R. Schaffer, ed. *Studies in Mother-Infant Interaction,* pp. 153–176. New York: Academic Press.

Crawley, S. B., and Sherrod, K. B. 1984. "Parent-Infant Play During the First Year of Life," *Infant Behavior and Development,* 7 (1): 65–75.

Crnic, K. A., Ragozin, R. A., Greenberg, M. T., Robinson, N. M., and Basham, R. B. 1983. "Social Interaction and Developmental Competence of Preterm and Full-term Infants During the First Year of Life," *Child Development,* 54, 1199–1210.

Crnic, K. A., Greenberg, M. T., Robinson, M. N., and Ragozin, A. S. 1984. "Maternal Stress and Social Support: Effects on the Mother-Infant Relationship from Birth to Eighteen Months," *American Journal of Orthopsychiatry,* 54 (2): 224–235.

deVries, M. W., and Sameroff, A. J. 1984. "Culture and Temperament: Influences on Infant Temperament in Three East African Societies," *American Journal of Orthopsychiatry,* 54 (1): 83–96.

Diana, M. S. 1984. "Contrasting Examples of Mother-Father-Infant Research, *Infant Mental Health Journal,* 5 (1): 56–57.

Donovan, W. L., and Leavitt, L. A. 1985. "Physiologic Assessment of Mother-Infant Attachment," *Journal of Child Psychiatry,* 24 (1): 65–70.

Dunn, J. B., and Richards, M.P.M. 1977. "Observations on the Developing Relationship Between Mother and Baby in the Neonatal Period." In H. R. Schaffer, ed. *Studies in Mother-Infant Interaction,* pp. 427–455. New York: Academic Press.

Earls, F., and Yogman, M. 1979. "The Father-Infant Relationship." In J. G. Howells, ed. *Modern Perspectives in the Psychiatry of Infancy,* pp. 213–239. New York: Brunner Mazel.

Eibl-Eibesfeldt, I. 1983. "Patterns of Parent-Child Interaction in a Cross-Cultural Perspective." In A. Oliverio and M. Zappella, eds. *The Behavior of Human Infants,* pp. 177–217. New York: Plenum Press.

Emde, R. M., and Scorce, J. F. 1983. "The Rewards of Infancy: Emotional Availability and Maternal Referencing." In J. D. Call, E. Galenson, and R. L. Tyson, eds. *Frontiers in Infant Psychiatry,* pp. 17–30. New York: Basic Books.

Fagan, J. F., and Singer, L. T. 1983. "Infant Recognition Memory as a Measure of Intelligence." In L. P. Lipsitt and C. K. Rovee-Collier, eds. *Advances in Infancy Research,* Vol. II, pp. 31–78. Norwood, N.J.: Ablex Publishing.

Fagan, J. F., and Singer, L. T. 1981. "Intervention During Infancy: General Considerations." In S. Friedman and M. Sigman, eds. *Preterm Birth and Psychological Development,* pp. 417–425. New York: Academic Press.

Feinman, S. 1982. "Social Referencing in Infancy," *Journal of Developmental Psychology,* 28 (4): 445–470.

Feiring, C., and Lewis, M. 1984. "Changing Characteristics of the U.S. Family: Implications for Family Networks, Relationships, and Child." In M. Lewis, ed. *Beyond the Dyad,* pp. 59–90. New York: Plenum Press.

Field, T. 1981. "Infant Arousal, Attention, and Affect During Early Interactions." In L. P. Lipsitt and C. K. Rovee-Collier, eds. *Advances in Infancy Research,* Vol. I, pp. 58–100. Norwood, N.J.: Ablex Publishing.

Field, T., Cohyen, D., Garcia, R., and Greenberg, R. 1984. "Mother-Stranger Face Discrimination by the Newborn," *Infant Behavior and Development,* 7 (1): 19–25.

Fox, N. A., and Gelles, M. G. 1984. "Face-to-Face Interaction in Term and Preterm Infants," *Infant Mental Health,* 5 (4): 192–205.

Freedman, D. 1976. "Infancy, Biology and Culture." In L. Lipsitt, ed. *Developmental Psychobiology,* pp. 35–54. Hillsdale, N.J.: Lawrence Erlbaum Associates.

Frye, D. 1981. "Developmental Changes in Strategies of Social Interaction." In M. Lamb and L. Sherrod, eds. *Infant Social Cognition,* pp. 315–329. Hillsdale, N.J.: Lawrence Erlbaum Associates.

Furman, E. P. 1982. "Some Thoughts on the Father-Child Relationship." In M. H. Klaus and M. O. Robertson, eds. *Birth, Interaction and Attachment,* Pediatric Round Table 6, pp. 75–81. Piscataway, N.J.: Johnson & Johnson Baby Products.

Gekoski, M. J., and Fagan, J. W. 1984. "Noncontingent Stimulation, Stimulus Familiarization, and Subsequent Learning in Young Infants," *Child Development,* 55 (6): 2226–2233.

Gekoski, M. J., Fagan, J. W., and Pearlman, M. A. 1984. "Early Learning and Memory in the Preterm Infant," *Infant Behavior and Development,* 7 (3): 267–276.

Haviland, J. M., Malatesta, C. Z., Lelwica, M. L. 1984. "Emotional Communication in Early Infancy," *Infant Mental Health Journal,* 5 (3): 135–147.

Hoffman-Wilde, S., and Rothbart, M. "A Longitudinal Investigation of Social Referencing in Infancy." Eugene Ore.: Department of Psychology, University of Oregon.

Howes, C., and Rebenstein, J. 1981. "Toddler Peer Behavior in Two Types of Daycare," *Infant Behavior and Development,* 4:387–393.

Kagan, J. 1982. *Psychological Research on the Human Infant: An Evaluative Summary.* New York: William T. Grant Foundation.

Kaye, K. 1983. *The Mental and Social Life of Babies.* Chicago: University of Chicago Press.

Kennell, J. H., and Klaus, M. H. 1983. "Early Events: Later Effects on the Infant." In J. D. Call, E. Galenson, and R. L. Tyson, eds. *Frontiers of Infant Psychiatry,* pp. 7–16. New York: Basic Books.

Klinnert, M. D. 1984. "The Regulation of Infant Behavior by Maternal Facial Expression," *Infant Behavior and Development,* 7 (4): 447–465.

Kriks, J. 1984. "Infant 'Talk.' " Paper presented at Fourth Biennial International Conference on Infant Studies, New York.

Lamb, M. E. 1981. "Developing Trust and Perceived Effectance in Infancy." In L. P. Lipsitt and C. K. Rovee-Collier, eds. *Advances in Infancy Research,* Vol. I, pp. 101–127. Norwood, N.J.: Ablex Publishing.

Lamb, M. E. 1981. "The Development of Father-Infant Relationships." In M. E. Lamb, ed. *The Role of the Father in Child Development,* 2nd ed., pp. 459–488. New York: John Wiley & Son.

Lamb, M. E. 1982. "Parent-Infant Interaction, Attachment and Socioemotional Development in Infancy." In R. N. Emde and R. J. Harmon, eds. *The Development of Attachment and Affiliative Systems,* pp. 195–211. New York: Plenum Press.

Lester, B. 1984. "A Biosocial Model of Infant Crying." In L. P. Lipsitt and C. K. Rovee-Collier, eds. *Advances in Infancy Research,* Vol. III, pp. 167–204. Norwood, N.J.: Ablex Publishing.

Lester, B. 1984. "Infant Crying and the Development of Communication." In N. Fox and R. Davidson, eds. *The Psychobiology of Affective Development,* pp. 231–258. Hillsdale, N.J.: Lawrence Erlbaum Associates.

Lester, B. M., and Zeskind, P. S. 1982. "A Biobehavioral Perspective on Crying in Early Infancy." In H. F. Fitzgerald, B. M. Lester, and M. W. Yogman, eds. *Theory and Research in Behavioral Pediatrics,* Vol. I. New York: Plenum Press.

Lewis, M., and Feiring, C. 1981. "Direct and Indirect Interactions in Social Relationships." In L. P. Lipsitt and C. K. Rovee-Collier, eds. *Advances in Infancy Research,* Vol. I, pp. 131–161. Norwood, N.J.: Ablex Publishing.

Lewis, M., Feiring, C., and Kotsonis, M. 1984. "The Social Network of the Young Child: A Developmental Perspective." In M. Lewis, ed. *Beyond the Dyad,* pp. 129–160. New York: Plenum Press.

Lewis, M., Feiring, C., and Weinraub, M. 1981. "The Father as a Member of the Child's Social Network." In M. E. Lamb, ed. *The Role of the Father in Child Development,* 2nd ed., pp. 259–294. New York: John Wiley & Son.

Lewis, M., and Michalson, L. 1983. *Children's Emotions and Moods.* New York: Plenum Press.

McBride, S., and Hock, E. 1984. "Relationship of Maternal Behavior and Anxiety Associated with Mother-Infant Separations." In Poster Session, Fourth Biennial International Conference on Infant Studies, New York.

MacLellan, C. B., and Miller, C. L. 1984. "Maternal Speech and the Development of Infant Babbling." Paper presented to the Fourth Biennial International Conference on Infant Studies, New York.

Malatesta, C. Z., and Izard, C. E. 1984. "The Ontogenesis of Human Social Signals: From Biological Imperative to Symbol Utilization." In N. A. Fox and R. Davidson, eds. *The Psychobiology of Affective Development,* pp. 161–198. Hillsdale, N.J.: Lawrence Erlbaum Associates.

Masur, E. F., and Ritz, E. G. 1984. "Patterns of Gestural, Vocal, and Verbal Imitation Performance in Infancy," *Journal of Developmental Psychology,* 30 (4): 369–392.

Meltzoff, A., and Moore, M. 1983. "The Origins of Imitation in Infancy: Paradigm, Phenomena and Theories." In L. Lipsitt, ed. *Advances in Infancy Research,* Vol. II, pp. 266–311. Norwood, N.J.: Ablex Publishing.

Messer, D. J., and Vietze, P. M. 1984. "Timing and Transitions in Mother-Infant Gaze," *Infant Behavior and Development,* 7 (2): 167–181.

Myers, G. J. 1984. "Child-Rearing Across the Generations: Grand-mother, Mothers, and Toddlers." Paper presented at Fourth Biennial International Conference on Infant Studies, New York.

Papousek, H., and Papousek, M. 1983. "Interactional Failures: Their Origins and Significance in Infant Psychiatry." In J. D. Call, E. Galenson, and R. L. Tyson, eds. *Frontiers of Infant Psychiatry,* pp. 31–37. New York: Basic Books.

Papousek, H., and Papousek, M. 1977. "Mothering and the Cognitive Head-Start: Psychobiological Considerations." In H. R. Schaffer, ed. *Studies in Mother-Infant Interaction,* pp. 63–85. New York: Academic Press.

Papousek, H., and Papousek, M. 1981. "Musical Elements in the Infant's Vocalization: Their Significance for Communication, Cognition, and Creativity." In L. P. Lipsitt and C. K. Rovee-Collier, eds. *Advances in Infancy Research,* Vol. I, pp. 164–224. Norwood, N.J.: Ablex Publishing.

Paret, I. 1983. "Night Waking and Its Relation to Mother-Infant Interaction in Nine-Month-Old Infants." In J. D. Call, E. Galenson, and R. L. Tyson, eds. *Frontiers of Infant Psychiatry,* pp. 171–177. New York: Basic Books.

Parke, R. D. 1982. "The Father's Role in Family Development." In M. H. Klaus and M. O. Robertson, eds. *Birth, Interaction and Attachment,* Pediatric Round Table 6, pp. 66–74. Piscataway, N.J.: Johnson & Johnson Baby Products.

Petrillo, M., and Sanger, S. (In press). *Emotional Care of Hospitalized Children,* 3rd ed. Philadelphia: J. B. Lippincott Company.

Proctor, A. 1984. "Book Review: *Pathological Cry, Stridor and Cough in Infants: A Clinical Acoustics Study,*" *Infant Mental Health,* 5 (4): 245–247.

Reznick, R. S., and Kagan, J. 1983. "Category Detection in Infancy." In L. P. Lipsitt and C. K. Rovee-Collier, eds. *Advances in Infancy Research,* Vol. II, pp. 80–111. Norwood, N.J.: Ablex Publishing.

Richter, R., and Boger, R. 1983. "The Influence of Selected Variables on Maternal Perceptions of Their Infants at One Month," *Infant Mental Health,* 4 (4): 321–335.

Rovee-Collier, C. K., and Fagen, J. W. 1981. "The Retrieval of Memory in Early Infancy." In L. P. Lipsitt and C. K. Rovee-

Collier, eds. *Advances in Infancy Research,* Vol. I, pp. 226–254. Norwood, N.J.: Ablex Publishing.

St. James-Roberts, I., and Wolke, D. 1984. "Comparison of Mothers' with Trained-Observers' Reports of Neonatal Behavioral Style," *Infant Behavior and Development,* 7 (3): 299–310.

Sander, L. 1983. "Polarity, Paradox, and the Organizing Process in Development." In J. D. Call, E. Galenson, and R. L. Tyson, eds. *Frontiers of Infant Psychiatry,* pp. 333–346. New York: Basic Books.

Sander, L. 1983. "A Twenty-five-Year Follow-up of the Pavenstedt Longitudinal Research Project, Its Relation to Early Intervention." In J. D. Call, E. Galenson, and R. L. Tyson, eds. *Frontiers of Infant Psychiatry,* pp. 225–234. New York: Basic Books.

Schwartz, M. 1984. "The Role of Sound for Space and Object Perception in the Congenitally Blind Infant." In L. P. Lipsitt and C. K. Rovee-Collier, eds. *Advances in Infancy Research,* Vol. III, pp. 23–56. Norwood, N.J.: Ablex Publishing.

Siegel, E. 1982. "A Critical Examination of Studies of Parent-Infant Bonding." In M. H. Klaus and M. O. Robertson, eds. *Birth, Interaction and Attachment,* Pediatric Round Table 6, pp. 51–60. Piscataway, N.J.: Johnson & Johnson Baby Products.

Spelke, E., and Cortelyou, A. 1981. "Perceptual Aspects of Social Knowing: Looking and Listening in Infancy." In M. Lamb and L. Sherrod, eds. *Infant Social Cognition,* pp. 61–81. Hillsdale, N.J.: Lawrence Erlbaum Associates.

Sroufe, L., and Wunsch, J. 1972. "The Development of Laughter in the First Year of Life," *Child Development,* 43, 1326–1344.

Stern, D. 1984. "The Levy Lecture: Infant's Intuition of Affect and Affective Rapport," *The Association for Psychoanalytic Medicine Bulletin,* 23 (3) 129–132.

Stern, D. 1982. "Mothers and Infants: The Early Transmission of Affect." In M. H. Klaus and M. O. Robertson, eds. *Birth, Interaction and Attachment,* Pediatric Round Table 6, pp. 43–50. Piscataway, N. J.: Johnson & Johnson Baby Products.

Stevenson, M., and Lamb, M. 1981. "The Effects of Social Experience and Social Style on Cognitive Competence and Performance." In

M. Lamb and L. Sherrod, eds. *Infant Social Cognition,* pp. 395–412. Hillsdale, N.J.: Lawrence Erlbaum Associates.

Stevenson, M., and Roach, M. 1984. "Fathers' and Mothers' Interactions with Their One-Year-Olds: Analyses of Behavioral Frequencies and Contingencies." Paper presented at the International Conference on Infant Studies, New York.

Sullivan, J., and Horowitz, F. 1983. "Infant Intermodal Perception and Maternal Multimodal Stimulation: Implications for Language Development." In L. P. Lipsitt and C. K. Rovee-Collier, eds. *Advances in Infancy Research,* Vol. II, pp. 184–232. Norwood, N.J.: Ablex Publishing.

Suomi, S. 1981. "The Perception of Contingency and Social Development." In M. Lamb and L. Sherrod, eds. *Infant Social Cognition,* pp. 177–201. Hillsdale, N.J.: Lawrence Erlbaum Associates.

Thelen, E., Fisher, D. M., and Ridley-Johnson, R. 1984. "The Relationship Between Physical Growth and a Newborn Reflex," *Infant Behavior and Development,* 7 (4): 479–493.

Trevarthen, C. 1977. "Descriptive Analyses of Infant Communicative Behaviour." In H. R. Schaffer, ed. *Studies in Mother-Infant Interaction,* pp. 227–270. New York: Academic Press.

Trevarthen, C. 1983. "Interpersonal Abilities of Infants as Generators for Transmission of Language and Culture." In A. Oliverio and M. Zappella, eds. *The Behavior of Human Infants,* pp. 147–176. New York: Plenum Press.

Tronick, E., Als, H., and Adamson, L. 1978. "Structure of Early Face to Face Communicative Interactions." In M. Bullowa, ed. *Before Speech: The Beginning of Human Communication.* Cambridge, England: Cambridge University Press.

Von Bargen, D. M. 1983. "Infant Heart Rate: A Review of Research and Methodology," *Journal of Developmental Psychology,* 29 (2): 115–149.

Weber, S., and Sackiem, H. 1984. "The Development of Functional Brain Asymmetry in the Regulation of Emotion." In N. Fox and R. Davidson, eds. *The Psychobiology of Affective Development,* pp. 325–345. Hillsdale, N.J.: Lawrence Erlbaum Associates.

Whiten, A. "Assessing the Effects of Perinatal Events on the Success of the Mother-Infant Relationship." In H. R. Schaffer, ed. *Studies in Mother-Infant Interaction,* pp. 403–425. New York: Academic Press.

Wong, J., and Miller, C. 1984. "Parental Perceptions of Infant Vocal Development." Paper presented to the Fourth Biennial International Conference on Infant Studies, New York.

Yarrow, L. J. 1979. "Development of the Child's Personality in the First Five Years." In J. G. Howells, ed. *Modern Perspectives in the Psychiatry of Infancy,* pp. 1–24. New York: Brunner Mazel.

Zelazo, P. R. 1981. "An Information Processing Approach to Infant Cognitive Assessment." In *Developmental Disabilities in Preschool Children,* pp. 229–255. Spectrum Publishers, Inc.

Zelazo, P. R., Brody, L. R., and Chaika, H. 1984. "Neonatal Habituation and Dishabituation of Head Turning to Rattle Sounds," *Infant Behavior and Development,* 7 (3): 311–321.

# Index